AF680071

ULTIMATE AI BLUEPRINT

AI Secrets for Marketing & Growth For Businesses

Jason J. Fleagle

Ultimate AI Blueprint: AI Secrets for Marketing & Growth For Businesses

This book is provided for informational and educational purposes only. The author and publisher make no representations or warranties with respect to the accuracy, applicability, or completeness of the contents of this book. The strategies, examples, tools, prompts, workflows, and recommendations described herein may not be suitable for every situation. You are responsible for your own decisions, actions, and results.
No Professional Advice. Nothing in this book constitutes legal, financial, tax, medical, or professional advice. You should consult qualified professionals for advice specific to your circumstances.
Technology & Third-Party Services Disclaimer. References to third-party products, services, companies, trademarks, or platforms are for identification and informational purposes only and do not imply endorsement. Product features, pricing, and policies may change without notice. All trademarks are the property of their respective owners.
AI Output Disclaimer. Artificial intelligence tools may produce inaccurate or incomplete outputs. Always verify critical information before relying on it for business, legal, financial, or other high-stakes decisions.
First edition: March 2026
Published by: Reachify

ISBN: 979-8-218-90299-5
Printed in USA

CONTENTS

Foreword v
About the Author vii
Prologue ix

1 **Introduction to the AI Revolution** 1
2 **AI for Content Marketing and Customer Engagement** 52
3 **AI for Social Media Marketing** 98
4 **AI for Email Marketing** 191
5 **AI for Paid Advertising** 221
6 **AI for Search Engine Optimization (SEO)** 244
7 **AI for Competitive Analysis** 265
8 **AI for Customer Understanding** 291
9 **AI for Marketing Automation** 326
10 **The Future of AI in Marketing** 351

FOREWORD

Artificial intelligence has entered a phase where visibility has outpaced understanding. What was once experimental is now embedded in real workflows, real organizations, and real decisions. At this stage, AI does not function as an independent actor. It functions as infrastructure, amplifying the judgment, values, and discipline of the people who design and deploy it.

Jason's work stands out because it is grounded in discernment, integrity, and care. He approaches AI not as a shortcut or a substitute for thinking, but as infrastructure—something that must be designed around the most capable decision-makers in an organization. His perspective reflects a deep respect for responsibility: responsibility to teams, to families, to institutions, and to society at large.

What Jason has written is a *measured, responsible, and human-centered articulation of AI adoption,* especially for business and marketing contexts. In fact, the book does several things *right* that many AI "playbooks" fail to do.

This distinction matters.

AI belongs inside human decision frameworks. It must be governed by capable people, clear authority, and ethical responsibility. When those conditions are present, AI becomes a powerful tool for clarity and scale. When they are absent, it becomes a multiplier of weak judgment and unowned outcomes. The technology itself is neutral. The people are not.

Ultimate AI Blueprint is grounded in this reality. Rather than presenting AI as a replacement for leadership or discernment, it frames AI as an operational system that must be designed around human capability. The work is practical, measured, and deliberately restrained.

It emphasizes verification, accountability, and governance, not automation for its own sake.

A central theme throughout the book is that **tools do not create good outcomes, people do**. AI systems inherit the intent, ethics, and maturity of the teams that use them. This is why culture readiness matters as much as technical readiness. Many teams are eager to adopt AI but are not yet structurally or culturally prepared. In those environments, AI can feel threatening rather than supportive. Discernment becomes critical.

Jason's approach reflects a long-term view. His frameworks prioritize value mapping, operational integration, and responsible oversight. AI is treated as decision support not decision authority. This posture aligns with a deeper responsibility to teams, families, organizations, and society as a whole. It assumes that the people closest to the work must remain accountable for the outcomes.

Ultimate AI Blueprint intent is explicit: to help organizations use AI **for good**, in service of human judgment, ethical leadership, and sustainable progress. The systems we build now will shape how AI serves us in the future. This work argues for stewardship over speed, responsibility over hype, and capability over novelty.

AI should work for us—not the other way around.

Dr. Christopher Skinner

Founder & Principal Architect, Stealth Dog Labs
Global Expert in Data Science

Jason J. Fleagle is an AI architect and an AI-driven growth consultant. As a hands-on practitioner, Jason helps organizations move beyond the hype and deploy production-ready AI systems that deliver measurable revenue, efficiency, and competitive advantage.

With a background in generating over $60 million in revenue for clients and his own companies, Jason uniquely bridges the gap between technical AI implementation and executive-level business strategy. He has led AI workshops and strategy sessions for some of the world's largest companies, including Verizon, Cisco Systems, and NTT Data, as well as numerous universities and high-growth startups.

Jason's work is centered on his proprietary Humanize DataTM Framework, a methodology designed to take AI initiatives from pilot to production by focusing on value, data readiness, operational integration, and governance. He is a respected voice in the AI community, known for his ability to speak "AI" to technical teams and "P&L" to the C-suite in the same conversation.

As the author of the AI Pathfinder newsletter and a sought-after consultant, Jason's mission is to demystify artificial intelligence and empower businesses to use it as a force for sustainable growth and human-centric value.

Prologue

My Journey from Agency Grind to AI Architect

For years, I lived in the trenches of digital marketing. I ran the agencies, managed the multi-million dollar ad spends, and obsessed over conversion rates. My world was a complex machine of PPC campaigns, SEO tactics, and intricate funnels. We were successful, generating over $60 million in revenue for clients and my own companies. But I saw a recurring, frustrating pattern: we were constantly hitting a ceiling of human scale.

There were never enough hours in the day. My teams were burning out trying to manually optimize campaigns, write endless content variations, and respond to every lead. We were data-rich but insight-poor, drowning in analytics dashboards that told us what happened yesterday but couldn't give us the leverage to change what would happen tomorrow.

Then came the AI explosion. At first, I saw it through the same lens as everyone else: a cool new toy for writing blog posts or generating funny images. But as I dug deeper, I realized I was looking at it all wrong. AI wasn't just another tool to add to the marketing stack, it was a new operating system for business itself. I got involved in AI and machine learning working with engineers at Facebook and Google in the San Franscisco bay area repurposing their exciting research about generative pre-trained transformers (GPTs), Computer Vision, generative adversarial networks (GANs), and so much more. I fell in love with AI and machine learning.

In recent years I started to watch as company after company made the same mistakes. They'd get excited about a cool AI demo, spend six months and a hundred thousand dollars on a "pilot program," and then watch it die a slow death in what I call "pilot purgatory." The tech was amazing, but it never made it into the hands of the people who needed it. It never moved the revenue needle. It was a solution in search of a problem.

The frustration was immense. I saw the incredible potential of AI being wasted on flashy demos and theoretical whitepapers, while real businesses were still struggling with the same old problems. I knew there had to be a better way.

That's why I wrote this book. I stepped away from the traditional agency model and became an AI architect, working with everyone from Fortune 500 companies like Cisco, AWS, NTT Data, and more enterprises to even more agile, high-growth startups. I got my hands dirty building the systems, writing the prompts, and deploying the AI agents that actually work in the real world, with all its messy data, office politics, and legacy systems. And at this point I've had the opportunity to help create over 200 AI applications and over 500 AI integrations, tools, and frameworks.

This book is the culmination of that journey. It's not a theoretical guide to what AI can do. It's a practitioner's blueprint for what AI is doing, right now, to drive measurable results and growth. It contains the frameworks, strategies, and hard-won lessons I use to help organizations turn AI from a buzzword into their most valuable asset.

I've also included many copy/paste AI prompts that you can use throughout each section of the book so you can 10x your AI performance.

You don't need a PhD in data science or a team of developers to make AI work for you. You need a blueprint. **This is it.**

| 1 |

Introduction to the AI Revolution

Welcome to the world of Artificial Intelligence, or AI as it's more commonly known! If you're a business owner, an entrepreneur, or just someone curious about how technology is shaping our future, you've come to the right place. You might hear "AI" and picture scenes from science fiction movies – robots taking over the world or super-intelligent computers making decisions for us. While some of that is still firmly in the realm of fiction, the reality of AI today is both incredibly exciting and, more importantly for you, immensely practical. AI is no longer a futuristic dream; it's a powerful tool that businesses, big and small, are using right now to grow, innovate, and connect with their customers in ways never before possible. This book, "The Ultimate AI Blueprint: Grow Your Business with Simple AI Secrets," is designed to demystify AI and show you, in simple terms, how you can harness its power to achieve your business goals. We're going to cut through the jargon and the hype to give you a clear, actionable blueprint.

In this first chapter, we'll lay the groundwork. We'll explore what AI actually is, moving beyond the movie portrayals to understand its core concepts. We'll look at how AI is already beginning to transform the business landscape, particularly in marketing and customer engagement. And finally, we'll get a bird's-eye view of the key AI technologies that are making all of this possible. Think of this chapter as your friendly introduction, your first step into a larger world of opportunity. By the end of it, you'll have a solid understanding of AI fundamentals and be ready to dive into the specific strategies and secrets that can help your business thrive in this new AI-powered era. So, let's begin our journey and uncover how AI can become your business's new best friend.

1.1 What is AI? Unpacking the Buzzword

Alright, let's tackle the big question first: What exactly *is* Artificial Intelligence? You hear the term everywhere – on the news, in business articles, maybe even from your tech-savvy nephew. But what does it really mean in plain English, especially for someone who isn't a computer scientist?

At its heart, Artificial Intelligence refers to the ability of computers or machines to perform tasks that typically require human intelligence. Think about the things your brain does every day: learning from experience, solving problems, understanding language, recognizing faces in a crowd, making decisions. AI is all about building machines that can do these kinds of things, or at least simulate them very effectively.

Imagine you're teaching a child a new skill, like identifying different animals. You show them pictures, tell them the names, and over time, they learn to recognize a cat, a dog, or a bird. AI systems learn in a somewhat similar way, but instead of a few pictures, they often process vast amounts of data – thousands, millions, or even billions of examples – to learn patterns and make intelligent connections. So, an AI might look at a million pictures of cats to learn what a cat looks like, far more than any human child would ever need!

It's important to understand that AI isn't a single thing; it's more like a broad field of study, an umbrella term that covers many different techniques and approaches. The common thread is the goal of creating intelligence in machines. These machines don't "think" in the same way humans do, with emotions and consciousness (at least, not yet!). Instead, they use complex algorithms – which are like detailed sets of instructions or recipes – and mathematical models to process information and produce an output that seems intelligent.

Two Main Flavors of AI: Narrow vs. General

To get a clearer picture, it helps to know that AI is generally talked about in two main categories: Narrow AI and General AI. Understanding this distinction is key to cutting through the hype and seeing AI for what it is today and what it might become tomorrow.

- **Narrow AI (or Weak AI): The Specialist**

This is the type of AI that we see and use every single day. Narrow AI is designed and trained for one particular task or a very limited set of tasks. It's like a highly skilled specialist who is brilliant at their one job but wouldn't know what to do in a completely different situation. Think of it as a master chess-playing computer – it can beat the world's best human players at chess, but you couldn't ask it for advice on your marketing strategy or to write a poem.

Examples of Narrow AI are all around us:

- **Virtual Assistants:** When you ask Siri, Alexa, or Google Assistant to set a timer, play a song, or tell you the weather, you're using Narrow AI. They are very good at understanding your voice commands and performing specific actions, but their abilities are confined to what they've been programmed and trained to do.
- **Recommendation Engines:** Ever wonder how Netflix knows what movies you might like, or how Amazon suggests products you might be interested in? That's Narrow AI at work. These systems analyze your past behavior (what you've watched, bought, or clicked on) and the behavior of millions of other users to make surprisingly accurate recommendations. They are specialized in *recommending.*

- **Spam Filters in Your Email:** Your email service uses Narrow AI to look at incoming messages and decide if they're legitimate emails or unwanted spam. It learns from patterns in spam messages to get better at this one specific job.
- **Chatbots on Websites:** Many businesses use chatbots to answer common customer questions or guide users through a website. These are Narrow AI systems trained to understand and respond to queries related to a specific business or product line.
- **Self-Driving Cars (in their current state):** While incredibly complex, the AI in today's self-driving cars is still considered Narrow AI. It's focused on the multifaceted task of driving – perceiving the environment, making decisions about speed and direction, and navigating. It's not designed to, say, hold a philosophical conversation.

The power of Narrow AI lies in its focus. Because it's dedicated to a specific task, it can often perform that task much faster, more accurately, and at a larger scale than a human could. This is where the real business value of AI lies today.

- **General AI (or Strong AI): The All-Rounder (Still a Dream)**

General AI, sometimes called Artificial General Intelligence (AGI), is the stuff of science fiction, at least for now. And it's coming faster than you think. This refers to an AI that would have the intellectual capability of a human being – the ability to learn, reason, plan, solve problems, think abstractly, comprehend complex ideas, and learn from experience across a wide range of different tasks, just like a person can. A General AI wouldn't just be good at one thing; it could, in theory, learn to do almost anything a human can do, and potentially even more.

Imagine an AI that could not only play chess but also write a novel, compose a symphony, make a scientific discovery, and then discuss these achievements with you in a deeply meaningful way. That's the vision of General AI.

It's crucial to understand that **General AI does not currently exist.** While researchers are working towards it, creating AGI is an incredibly complex challenge, and we are likely many years, if not decades, away from achieving it. So, when you hear about AI breakthroughs today, they are almost certainly advancements in Narrow AI.

For business owners, this distinction is vital. You don't need to wait for some far-off General AI to benefit from this technology. The Narrow AI tools and techniques available right now offer incredible opportunities to make your business smarter, more efficient, and more customer-focused. That's what this book is all about – unlocking those practical, real-world AI secrets.

Key Capabilities of AI: The Building Blocks

So, we know AI tries to mimic human intelligence, and Narrow AI is the specialist we work with today. But what are the actual *capabilities* that make these AI systems useful? Let's break down some of the core building blocks, again in simple terms:

1. Machine Learning (ML): The Engine of Modern AI - Expanded

Machine Learning, or ML, is a term you'll encounter frequently in any discussion about AI, and for good reason. It's not just a component of AI; in many ways, it's the driving force behind most of the AI advancements and applications we see today. If AI is the car, then Machine Learning is often its powerful, adaptable engine.

- **What it is:** At its core, Machine Learning is a subfield of Artificial Intelligence where computer systems are given the ability to "learn" from data without being explicitly programmed for every single task. Think about traditional programming: a developer writes precise, step-by-step instructions (an algorithm) telling the computer exactly what to do to achieve a specific outcome. If the situation changes slightly, the program might fail unless the developer updates the instructions.

Machine Learning flips this on its head. Instead of providing exhaustive instructions, developers provide the ML system with vast amounts of data relevant to a task and an algorithm that allows the system to explore that data, identify patterns, make connections, and essentially teach itself how to perform the task. The more data the system processes, and the more feedback it gets on its performance, the better it becomes at the task over time. It's like an apprentice who learns by observing, doing, and getting corrected, eventually becoming a master.

For instance, to build an ML model that identifies pictures of cats, you wouldn't write code describing pointy ears, whiskers, and furry tails. Instead, you'd feed it thousands, or even millions, of images, some labeled "cat" and some labeled "not a cat." The ML algorithm would then analyze these images, identifying common features and patterns associated with cats. Over time, it learns to recognize these patterns so well that it can accurately identify cats in new images it has never seen before.

- **The Fuel for ML: Data, Data, and More Data** It cannot be stressed enough: data is the lifeblood of Machine Learning. ML algorithms are hungry for data. The quality, quantity, and relevance of the data used to "train" an ML model will directly impact its performance and accuracy. This data can come in many forms:

    - **Structured Data:** This is data that's neatly organized, typically in rows and columns like in a spreadsheet or a database. Examples include customer purchase histories, website traffic numbers, sales figures, or inventory levels.

  - **Unstructured Data:** This is data that doesn't have a predefined format, making it more challenging for traditional computers to process but often rich in insights. Examples include text from emails and social media posts, images, videos, audio recordings, and customer reviews.
  - **Semi-structured Data:** This data has some organizational properties but doesn't fit neatly into a traditional database. Examples include JSON or XML files often used in web applications.

Modern ML techniques, especially Deep Learning (which we'll touch on), are increasingly adept at extracting value from unstructured data, opening up a wealth of new possibilities for businesses.

- **Simple Analogy:** Let's go back to our strawberry-picking analogy. Initially, someone tells you, "Ripe strawberries are red." This is a simple, explicit rule. But as you pick more strawberries (gather more data), you start to learn nuances. You notice that some red strawberries are still hard and sour (misclassifications, or errors in your initial model). You observe that the *sweetest* ones have a particular deep red hue, a slight give when gently squeezed (firmness), and a distinct aroma. You also learn that tiny bruises or slightly misshapen berries don't necessarily mean they aren't delicious. You're not just following one rule anymore; your brain has built a complex internal model based on multiple features and experiences.

Machine Learning algorithms work in a conceptually similar way. They analyze many different features (like color, size, shape, texture in images, or words and phrases in text) and learn the complex relationships between these features and the desired outcome (e.g., "is a cat," "is a ripe strawberry," "is a fraudulent transaction"). The algorithm adjusts its internal

2. Natural Language Processing (NLP): Understanding Human Language

Natural Language Processing, or NLP, is another cornerstone of modern Artificial Intelligence that you'll find woven into many of the AI tools and applications we'll discuss. If Machine Learning is often the engine, then NLP is frequently the way that engine communicates with and understands the human world, specifically through our most natural form of communication: language.

- **What it is:** NLP is a specialized branch of AI focused on enabling computers to understand, interpret, manipulate, and generate human language – whether it's text you type into a search bar, words spoken to a virtual assistant, customer reviews on a website, or the vast ocean of articles and documents available online. The "natural" in Natural Language Processing refers to human language as it's naturally spoken and written, with all its complexities, ambiguities, slang, and even misspellings, as opposed to the structured, precise languages that computers traditionally use (like programming languages).

  The ultimate goal of NLP is to bridge the communication gap between humans and machines, allowing computers to process and make sense of our language in a way that's meaningful and useful. It's about teaching computers not just to read words, but to understand the intent, context, and sentiment behind them.

- **Simple Analogy:** Imagine you're talking to a friend. When they speak, you don't just hear a string of sounds; your brain instantly processes those sounds into words, understands the grammar connecting them, grasps the meaning of the individual words and the sentence as a whole, and even picks up on their tone of voice or the underlying emotion. If they say, "This coffee is wicked!" you understand from context (and perhaps their Boston accent) that "wicked" means "very good," not evil.

NLP tries to equip computers with a similar, albeit more rudimentary, set of skills. It involves breaking down language into smaller components, analyzing the relationships between these components, and then using that analysis to perform a specific task, like answering a question, translating text, or summarizing a document. It's like giving the computer a highly advanced grammar and vocabulary lesson, combined with a course in understanding context and intent.

- **Core Tasks and Components of NLP (The Toolkit Within the Toolkit):** NLP is not a single technique but a collection of methods and tasks. Here are a few key ones, explained simply:
    - **Tokenization:** This is often the very first step. It means breaking down a piece of text into smaller units, called tokens. These tokens are usually words or sometimes sub-word units. For example, the sentence "AI is transforming business" would be tokenized into: ["AI", "is", "transforming", "business"]. This makes the text easier for the computer to process.
    - **Part-of-Speech (POS) Tagging:** After tokenization, the computer tries to identify the grammatical role of each word – is it a noun, verb, adjective, adverb, etc.? So, for our example, it might tag it as: ["AI (Noun)", "is (Verb)", "transforming (Verb/Adjective)", "business (Noun)"]. This helps the computer understand the grammatical structure of the sentence.

- **Named Entity Recognition (NER):** This task involves identifying and categorizing key pieces of information in text, such as names of people, organizations, locations, dates, monetary values, and more. For instance, in the sentence "Jason Fleagle, CEO of Catalyst, will visit New York on May 15th to discuss a $1 million AI project," NER would identify "Jason Fleagle" as a Person, "Catalyst" as an Organization, "New York" as a Location, "May 15th" as a Date, and "$1 million" as a Monetary Value. This is incredibly useful for extracting structured information from unstructured text.
    - *Business Example:* A company could use NER to scan news articles or social media mentions to quickly find all mentions of their brand, their competitors, or key industry figures.
- **Sentiment Analysis:** This is about determining the emotional tone or attitude expressed in a piece of text. Is it positive, negative, or neutral? For example, analyzing a customer review like "The product is amazing, but the customer service was slow" would reveal mixed sentiment – positive about the product, negative about the service.
    - *Business Example:* Businesses use sentiment analysis extensively to understand customer opinions about their products, services, or brand by analyzing social media comments, reviews, and survey responses. This helps them identify areas for improvement or gauge public reaction to a new marketing campaign.
- **Language Translation:** This is one of the most well-known applications of NLP. Modern machine translation tools (like Google Translate) use sophisticated NLP and ML models to translate text or speech from one language to another with increasing accuracy.

        - *Business Example:* Companies looking to expand globally can use machine translation to make their website content and marketing materials accessible in multiple languages, though human review is often still recommended for critical content.
    - **Topic Modeling:** When you have a large collection of documents (like thousands of customer support tickets or a library of research papers), topic modeling algorithms can automatically discover the main underlying topics or themes present in the text without you having to read everything.
        - *Business Example:* A company could use topic modeling to analyze customer feedback and identify the most common issues or feature requests, helping them prioritize product development efforts.
    - **Question Answering:** These systems are designed to understand questions posed in natural language and find or generate relevant answers from a given body of text or a knowledge base. Chatbots and virtual assistants heavily rely on this capability.
        - *Business Example:* A website chatbot can answer frequently asked questions about product features, pricing, or shipping, providing instant support to customers.
    - **Text Summarization:** NLP can also be used to automatically create a short, coherent summary of a longer document, highlighting the most important information.
        - *Business Example:* A busy executive could use a text summarization tool to quickly get the gist of long reports or articles, saving valuable time.
- **NLP and Machine Learning: A Powerful Partnership** It's important to note that many modern NLP techniques rely heavily on Machine Learning. ML algorithms, especially Deep

Learning models, are trained on massive amounts of text data to learn the patterns, nuances, and structures of human language. This allows NLP systems to achieve much higher accuracy and handle a wider range of linguistic variations than older, rule-based approaches.

- **Why NLP Matters for Your Business (The "So What?"):** Understanding and leveraging NLP can open up numerous avenues for business growth and efficiency:

    - **Enhanced Customer Interaction:** Powering intelligent chatbots, analyzing customer feedback at scale, and personalizing communications.
    - **Improved Information Access:** Quickly extracting insights from large volumes of text, whether it's internal documents, market research, or online conversations.
    - **Automation of Language-Based Tasks:** Automating aspects of content creation, translation, or summarization.
    - **Better Decision Making:** Gaining a deeper understanding of customer sentiment, market trends, and competitor activities by analyzing textual data.

As a business owner, you don't need to become an NLP expert, but recognizing its potential can help you identify opportunities to use AI tools that incorporate these powerful language-understanding capabilities. From improving your customer service with a smarter chatbot to gaining deeper insights from customer reviews, NLP is a key ingredient in many of the "simple AI secrets" we'll be exploring to help you grow your business.

- **Challenges and Considerations (Keeping it Real):** While NLP is incredibly powerful, it's not magic. Human language is complex, ambiguous, and constantly evolving. Sarcasm, irony, cultural nuances, and slang can still be challenging for NLP systems. The accuracy of NLP tools can also depend heavily on the quality and quantity of data they were trained on and the specific domain they are applied to. Therefore, while NLP can automate and assist in many ways, human oversight and critical thinking remain important, especially for sensitive applications or when the cost of an error is high. For example, while an AI might draft an email, a human should always review it before it's sent to ensure it aligns with the brand's voice and the specific context of the communication.

By understanding these fundamental aspects of Natural Language Processing, you're better equipped to appreciate how AI can interpret and interact with the most human of all data: our words. This capability is transforming how businesses connect with customers, understand markets, and unlock the value hidden within their textual information.

3. Computer Vision: Seeing and Interpreting the Visual World

Following our exploration of how AI processes language (NLP), let's turn our attention to another fascinating and increasingly vital AI capability: Computer Vision. Just as NLP enables computers to understand text and speech, Computer Vision empowers them to "see" and interpret information from images and videos. In a world saturated with visual content – from product photos and social media feeds to security camera footage and medical scans – the ability for AI to make sense of this visual data is transforming industries, including marketing and business operations.

- **What it is:** Computer Vision is a field of Artificial Intelligence that trains computers to capture, process, analyze, and understand visual information from the digital world much like human vision does. However, it's not just about replicating human sight; it's about enabling machines to perform visual tasks with speed, scale, and endurance that humans cannot match. This involves a complex interplay of image acquisition (getting the image into the system), image processing (enhancing or manipulating the image), and image analysis (extracting meaningful information).

The core challenge in Computer Vision is that while humans interpret visual scenes effortlessly and almost instantaneously, for a computer, an image is initially just a grid of pixels – tiny dots of color and brightness. Computer Vision algorithms, often powered by sophisticated Machine Learning models (especially Deep Learning neural networks), learn to detect patterns, shapes, textures, colors, and spatial relationships within these pixels to identify objects, understand scenes, and extract useful data.

- **Simple Analogy:** Think about looking at a photograph of a busy street. Your brain instantly recognizes cars, pedestrians, buildings, traffic lights, and perhaps even reads signs or notices the expressions on people's faces. You understand the spatial relationships – which objects are in front, which are behind, which are moving, and in what direction. You can infer the context – it's a city street, likely during the daytime.

Computer Vision aims to give machines a similar level of understanding. It's like teaching a computer to be an incredibly observant detective for visual information. It learns to distinguish a car from a bicycle, a cat from a dog, or a happy face from a sad one by analyzing countless examples. It can also go beyond simple recognition to perform tasks like tracking moving objects in a video, measuring distances, or identifying subtle defects in a manufactured product that might be invisible to the naked eye.

- **Key Tasks and Applications in Computer Vision (The Visual Toolkit):** Computer Vision encompasses a wide array of tasks. Here are some of the most relevant for businesses:

    - **Image Classification:** This is one of the most fundamental tasks. Given an image, the AI system assigns it a label from a predefined set of categories. For example, classifying an image as containing a "cat," a "dog," or a "car."
        - *Business Example:* An e-commerce platform could use image classification to automatically categorize product images uploaded by sellers, ensuring they are placed in the correct sections of the website.
    - **Object Detection:** This goes a step further than classification. Instead of just saying what's in an image, object detection identifies multiple objects within an image and draws bounding boxes around them, pinpointing their location. For example, in a street scene, it might detect and locate several cars, pedestrians, and traffic signs.

        - *Business Example:* In retail, object detection can be used for automated checkout systems (identifying products a customer is taking) or for inventory management by analyzing images of shelves to see which items are running low.
    - **Object Tracking:** This involves following a specific object (or multiple objects) as it moves through a sequence of video frames.
        - *Business Example:* Logistics companies might use object tracking to monitor packages moving through a warehouse via security cameras. Marketers could analyze how customers move through

a physical store (anonymously and with consent) to optimize store layout.

- **Image Segmentation:** This is an even more detailed task where the AI system partitions an image into multiple segments or regions, often by assigning a label to every single pixel. This allows for a very precise understanding of what's in the image and where. For example, it could separate the foreground from the background, or identify all the pixels that belong to a specific person in a group photo.
  - *Business Example:* In medical imaging, segmentation can help identify tumors or other anomalies. In marketing, it could be used to automatically remove the background from product photos or to analyze the visual composition of marketing materials.
- **Facial Recognition:** This technology identifies or verifies a person from a digital image or a video frame. It works by comparing selected facial features from the image to faces within a database.
  - *Business Example:* While controversial and requiring careful ethical consideration and consent, facial recognition has applications in security (e.g., unlocking a smartphone) or, potentially, in retail for personalized customer experiences (e.g., recognizing a loyal customer when they enter a store, with their permission).
- **Optical Character Recognition (OCR):** OCR technology converts images of typed, handwritten, or printed text into machine-encoded text. This means the computer can then process, search, and edit the text that was originally in an image format.
  - *Business Example:* Businesses use OCR to digitize paper documents like invoices, contracts, or

receipts, making them searchable and easier to manage. Marketers might use it to extract text from images in social media posts for analysis.

- **Content-Based Image Retrieval (CBIR) / Visual Search:** This allows users to search for images using an existing image as a query, rather than keywords. The system finds images that are visually similar to the query image.
    - *Business Example:* E-commerce sites are increasingly using visual search to allow customers to upload a photo of an item they like (e.g., a piece of clothing seen on the street) and find similar products in their inventory. This enhances product discovery and user experience.
- **Image Generation and Manipulation:** Advanced AI models, particularly Generative Adversarial Networks (GANs) and Diffusion Models, can now generate highly realistic new images from text descriptions or modify existing images in sophisticated ways (e.g., changing an object's color, adding elements, or altering artistic style).
    - *Business Example:* Marketers can use these tools to create unique visual content for campaigns, generate product mockups, or create variations of existing images without needing extensive graphic design resources, though authenticity and ethical use are key considerations.

- **The Role of Deep Learning in Computer Vision:** Much like in NLP, Deep Learning (a subset of Machine Learning using neural networks with many layers) has been the driving force behind the most significant breakthroughs in Computer Vision in recent years. Convolutional Neural Networks (CNNs) are a type of deep learning model particularly well-suited for processing visual data, and they form the backbone of many state-of-the-art computer vision systems.

- **Why Computer Vision Matters for Your Business (The Visual Advantage):** The ability to extract insights and automate tasks based on visual data offers numerous benefits:

    - **Enhanced Customer Experience:** Through visual search, personalized visual content, or even augmented reality applications that overlay digital information onto the real world (e.g., trying on virtual clothes).
    - **Improved Operational Efficiency:** Automating tasks like quality control in manufacturing, inventory management, or document processing.
    - **Better Safety and Security:** Through applications like surveillance monitoring or defect detection.
    - **Deeper Market Insights:** Analyzing visual trends on social media, understanding how customers interact with products visually, or assessing the effectiveness of visual branding.
    - **New Product and Service Opportunities:** Creating entirely new offerings based on visual data analysis or generation

- **Challenges and Ethical Considerations (Seeing Clearly):** Computer Vision, while powerful, also comes with its challenges and important ethical considerations:

    - **Data Requirements:** Training accurate computer vision models often requires very large, high-quality, and well-labeled datasets, which can be expensive and time-consuming to acquire.
    - **Bias in Data:** If the training data is biased (e.g., if facial recognition systems are trained predominantly on

images of one demographic group), the AI system can inherit and even amplify these biases, leading to unfair or inaccurate outcomes.

- **Privacy Concerns:** Technologies like facial recognition or the analysis of public video feeds raise significant privacy concerns that businesses must address responsibly and transparently, adhering to regulations and ethical best practices.
- **Robustness and Adversarial Attacks:** Computer vision systems can sometimes be fooled by subtle manipulations of images (adversarial attacks) that are imperceptible to humans, or they may not perform well in unfamiliar environments or under poor lighting conditions.

As a business owner, it's crucial to be aware of these limitations and ethical implications when considering or implementing computer vision solutions. The focus should always be on using these technologies responsibly and for the benefit of both the business and its customers.

By understanding the capabilities and applications of Computer Vision, you can start to see how your business might leverage the power of AI to interpret and act upon the rich visual information that surrounds us. From making your products more discoverable through visual search to understanding customer behavior in new ways, the "eyes" of AI offer a new lens through which to view and grow your business.

4. Predictive Analytics: Forecasting the Future (Based on the Past)

Predictive Analytics is a powerful application of AI, particularly Machine Learning, that allows businesses to move beyond simply understanding what happened in the past to making educated, data-driven forecasts about what is likely to happen in the future. It's about harnessing historical and current data to identify trends, patterns, and probabilities, thereby enabling more proactive and strategic decision-making. For business owners, this capability can be a significant game-changer, offering insights that can optimize operations, enhance customer experiences, and drive growth.

- **What it is:** Predictive Analytics encompasses a variety of statistical techniques, modeling, data mining, and machine learning algorithms that analyze current and historical facts to make predictions about unknown future events. It's not a crystal ball that offers infallible prophecies, but rather a sophisticated tool that calculates the likelihood of various outcomes. The core idea is that by understanding the relationships and patterns hidden within past data, we can project those patterns forward.

  The process typically involves several key steps:

1. **Defining the Objective:** What specific future outcome do you want to predict? (e.g., Which customers are likely to churn? What will sales be next quarter? Which marketing campaign will yield the highest ROI?)
2. **Data Collection:** Gathering relevant historical data from various sources (CRM systems, sales records, website analytics, social media, market data, etc.). The quality and completeness of this data are crucial.
3. **Data Preparation (Data Preprocessing):** Cleaning the data (handling missing values, correcting errors), transforming it into a suitable format, and selecting the most relevant features (variables) for the model.
4. **Model Building:** Selecting an appropriate predictive modeling technique (e.g., regression analysis, decision trees, neural networks) and training the model using the prepared historical data. This is where the AI "learns" the patterns.

5. **Model Evaluation (Validation):** Testing the model's accuracy and reliability using a separate set of data (validation or test data) that it hasn't seen before. This helps ensure the model generalizes well to new, unseen data and isn't just "memorizing" the training data.
6. **Model Deployment:** If the model performs well, it is deployed into the business's operational systems to make real-time or batch predictions.
7. **Model Monitoring and Maintenance:** Continuously monitoring the model's performance over time and retraining or updating it as new data becomes available or as underlying patterns change.

- **Simple Analogy:** Let's expand on the weather analogy. A meteorologist doesn't just look at today's clouds to predict tomorrow's rain. They analyze vast amounts of historical weather data (temperature, pressure, humidity, wind patterns, satellite imagery from past years for similar dates and conditions) using complex computer models (which are essentially predictive analytics models). These models identify patterns that have historically led to rain in specific circumstances. So, when current conditions match those historical rain-predicting patterns, the model forecasts a high probability of rain.

Similarly, in business, if you notice that customers who haven't purchased anything in 90 days, have stopped opening your emails, and have visited your "cancel subscription" page are highly likely to churn (based on past data of customers who did churn), you're using predictive analytics principles. AI automates and scales this process, analyzing hundreds or even thousands of variables simultaneously to make much more nuanced and accurate predictions.

- **Key Applications in Business and Marketing (Where the Magic Happens):** The applications of predictive analytics are vast and span across numerous business functions:
    - **Customer Relationship Management (CRM):**
        - **Churn Prediction:** Identifying customers at high risk of leaving your business. This allows you to proactively intervene with retention offers, personalized support, or special incentives before they actually depart. *Example:* A subscription-based software company uses predictive analytics to flag accounts showing decreased usage and engagement, then triggers a targeted email campaign offering a discount or a new feature tutorial to re-engage them.
        - **Customer Lifetime Value (CLV) Prediction:** Forecasting the total revenue a business can reasonably expect from a single customer account throughout their relationship. This helps businesses segment customers based on their potential value and tailor marketing spend and service levels accordingly. *Example:* An e-commerce retailer might invest more in acquiring and retaining high-CLV customers.
        - **Lead Scoring:** Prioritizing sales leads by assigning a score based on their likelihood to convert into paying customers. This helps sales teams focus their efforts on the most promising prospects. *Example:* A B2B company scores leads based on their website activity, email engagement, company size, and industry, allowing sales reps to contact "hot" leads first.
    - **Marketing Optimization:**

    - **Campaign Targeting:** Predicting which customers are most likely to respond positively to a specific marketing campaign or offer, leading to more effective ad spend and higher conversion rates. *Example:* A fashion retailer uses predictive analytics to identify customers who have previously bought similar styles or brands and targets them with ads for a new clothing line.
    - **Product Recommendations:** Suggesting products or services that a customer is likely to be interested in based on their past purchases, browsing history, and the behavior of similar customers. *Example:* Streaming services like Netflix or e-commerce giants like Amazon excel at this.
    - **Content Personalization:** Predicting what type of content (articles, videos, offers) will be most engaging for individual website visitors or email subscribers.

- **Sales Forecasting:** Predicting future sales volumes, revenue, and trends based on historical sales data, seasonality, market conditions, and marketing activities. This is crucial for inventory management, resource planning, and financial budgeting.

- **Risk Management:**
    - **Fraud Detection:** Identifying potentially fraudulent transactions in real-time by spotting unusual patterns or deviations from normal behavior. *Example:* Credit card companies use predictive models to flag suspicious purchases.
    - **Credit Scoring:** Assessing the creditworthiness of loan applicants to predict the likelihood of default.

- **Operations and Supply Chain:**
    - **Demand Forecasting:** Predicting future demand for products to optimize inventory levels, reduce stockouts, and minimize holding costs.
    - **Predictive Maintenance:** Forecasting when machinery or equipment is likely to fail, allowing businesses to perform maintenance proactively and avoid costly downtime. *Example:* Airlines use predictive maintenance for jet engines.

- **The Interplay with Machine Learning:** Predictive analytics heavily relies on Machine Learning algorithms to build its models. Techniques like linear regression, logistic regression, decision trees, random forests, gradient boosting machines, support vector machines, and neural networks are all commonly used in predictive modeling. The choice of algorithm often depends on the nature of the data and the specific problem being addressed.

- **Why Predictive Analytics Matters for Your Business (The Foresight Advantage):** The ability to anticipate future trends and behaviors provides a significant competitive edge:

    - **Improved Decision-Making:** Moving from reactive to proactive strategies based on data-driven forecasts.
    - **Increased Efficiency:** Optimizing resource allocation, reducing waste, and streamlining operations.
    - **Enhanced Customer Satisfaction:** By anticipating customer needs and personalizing experiences.
    - **Higher Profitability:** Through better targeting, reduced churn, optimized pricing, and more effective risk management.
    - **Competitive Advantage:** Staying ahead of market changes and competitor moves.

- **Challenges and Considerations (Looking Before You Leap):**
    - **Data Quality and Quantity:** Predictive models are only as good as the data they are trained on. Inaccurate, incomplete, or biased data will lead to flawed predictions.
    - **Complexity:** Developing and deploying robust predictive models can be complex and may require specialized skills.
    - **Correlation vs. Causation:** Predictive models can identify correlations between variables (e.g., customers who buy product A also tend to buy product B), but they don't necessarily explain the underlying cause. It's important not to misinterpret correlation as causation.
    - **Changing Environments:** The patterns of the past may not always hold true in the future, especially in rapidly changing markets. Models need to be regularly monitored and updated.
    - **Ethical Implications:** Predictions, especially about individuals, can have ethical consequences if not handled responsibly (e.g., potential for bias in loan applications or hiring). Transparency and fairness are paramount.

Predictive Analytics, fueled by AI and Machine Learning, offers businesses a powerful lens into the future. By understanding its principles and potential applications, you can start to identify how forecasting future outcomes can help you make smarter, more informed decisions that drive growth and success. It's about transforming data from a historical record into a strategic asset for future planning.

5. Adaptability and Learning: Getting Smarter Over Time

One of the most remarkable and valuable characteristics of many AI systems, particularly those built upon Machine Learning, is their inherent capacity for adaptability and continuous learning. Unlike traditional software programs that operate based on fixed, pre-programmed rules and remain static unless manually updated by developers, AI systems can evolve, refine their performance, and essentially get "smarter" over time as they are exposed to new data, new scenarios, and feedback on their actions.

- **What it is:** Adaptability in AI refers to the system's ability to adjust its internal parameters, models, or behaviors in response to changes in its input data or its environment. Learning, in this context, is the process through which this adaptation occurs. The AI system analyzes new information, compares its outputs or decisions against desired outcomes or feedback signals, and modifies its internal workings to improve future performance. This iterative process of learning and adapting is what allows AI to tackle complex, dynamic problems where the rules are not always clearly defined or may change over time.

This is not to say that all AI systems learn continuously and autonomously without any human intervention. The degree and nature of learning can vary significantly:

  - **Offline Learning (Batch Learning):** The AI model is trained on a fixed dataset, and then deployed. It doesn't learn from new data in real-time once deployed. To update it, the entire model needs to be retrained with a new, expanded dataset.
  - **Online Learning (Incremental Learning):** The AI model can learn from new data as it arrives, updating its parameters incrementally without needing to be retrained from scratch. This allows the model to adapt more quickly to changing patterns.
  - **Reinforcement Learning:** This is a specific type of learning where the AI agent learns by interacting with an environment. It takes actions, receives feedback in the form of rewards or penalties, and learns a policy (a strat-

egy) to maximize its cumulative reward over time. This is akin to how humans and animals learn through trial and error.

- **Simple Analogy:** Consider learning to ride a bike. When you first learn, you're wobbly and might fall (negative feedback). . When you first learn, you're wobbly and might fall (negative feedback). Your brain processes this feedback along with sensory input (balance, speed, terrain) and makes tiny adjustments to your muscle movements and posture (adapting your internal model of how to ride). Each successful pedal stroke or maintained balance is positive feedback, reinforcing those actions. Over time, with more practice (more data and feedback), your riding becomes smoother, more confident, and almost automatic. You can even adapt to different types of bikes or different terrains.

An AI-powered spam filter works on a similar principle. Initially, it's trained on a large dataset of emails labeled as "spam" or "not spam." When a new email arrives, it makes a prediction. If the user marks an email it classified as "not spam" as "spam" (feedback), the system can learn from this correction and adjust its internal criteria to better identify similar spam messages in the future. The more feedback it receives, the more accurate its spam detection becomes.

Another example is an AI playing a video game. Through reinforcement learning, it might initially make random moves. If a move leads to a higher score (reward), it learns to favor that move in similar situations. If a move leads to losing a life (penalty), it learns to avoid it. After playing thousands or millions of games, it can develop super-human skills by continuously learning and adapting its strategy.

- **Mechanisms of Learning and Adaptation in AI:** The core mechanism behind this learning is often the adjustment of "weights" or "parameters" within the AI model. In a neural network, for example, these weights determine the strength of connections between artificial neurons. During training, an algorithm (like backpropagation) calculates how much each weight contributed to an error in prediction and adjusts the weights slightly to reduce that error in the future. This process is repeated many times with many data examples.

  Feedback can come in various forms:

  - **Explicit Feedback:** Users directly telling the system it made a mistake (e.g., correcting a misclassified email, downvoting a bad recommendation).
  - **Implicit Feedback:** The system inferring feedback from user behavior (e.g., if a user clicks on a recommended product, it's a positive signal; if they ignore it, it might be a negative signal).
  - **Rewards/Penalties:** In reinforcement learning, these are predefined signals from the environment that guide the learning process.
- **Why Adaptability and Learning Matter for Your Business (The Evolution Advantage):** The ability of AI systems to learn and adapt offers profound benefits for businesses operating in dynamic environments:

  - **Sustained Performance:** As market conditions, customer preferences, and data patterns change, adaptive AI systems can maintain or even improve their performance, unlike static rule-based systems that would quickly become outdated.
  - **Personalization at Scale:** Learning systems can continuously refine their understanding of individual cus-

tomer preferences, leading to increasingly personalized experiences, recommendations, and communications over time.

- **Increased Efficiency and Accuracy:** As AI models learn from more data and feedback, they often become more accurate in their predictions and more efficient in their operations.
- **Discovery of New Insights:** By constantly analyzing new data, AI systems can uncover emerging trends, new customer segments, or unexpected correlations that humans might miss. This can lead to new business opportunities or strategies.
- **Automation of Complex Tasks:** AI systems that can learn and adapt are better suited to automate tasks that involve variability and uncertainty, as they can adjust their approach based on new information.

- **Challenges and Considerations (Navigating the Learning Curve):**

  - **Data Drift and Concept Drift:** If the underlying data patterns change significantly over time (data drift) or the meaning of what you're trying to predict changes (concept drift), a model trained on old data may become inaccurate. Online learning and continuous monitoring are crucial to address this.
  - **Feedback Loops:** Poorly designed feedback mechanisms can lead to undesirable outcomes. For example, if a recommendation system only shows users what they've liked in the past, it might create a "filter bubble" and prevent them from discovering new things. Or, if a system learns from biased user feedback, it can perpetuate or even amplify those biases.

- **Stability vs. Plasticity:** There's often a trade-off between a model's ability to learn new things quickly (plasticity) and its ability to retain past knowledge without being overly influenced by noisy or irrelevant new data (stability). This is known as the stability-plasticity dilemma.
- **Explainability (The Black Box Problem):** As AI models, especially deep learning networks, become more complex and learn from vast amounts of data, it can become difficult to understand *why* they make certain decisions. This lack of transparency can be a concern, especially in critical applications.
- **Resource Intensive:** Continuously training and updating AI models can be computationally expensive and require significant data infrastructure.

Despite these challenges, the capacity for adaptability and learning is a defining feature of advanced AI and a key reason for its transformative potential. For businesses, this means investing in AI solutions that are not just intelligent at a single point in time, but can grow and evolve alongside your business, becoming more valuable assets over time. It's about building systems that are not just programmed, but are capable of learning their way to better performance.

Understanding these core capabilities – Machine Learning, NLP, Computer Vision, Predictive Analytics, and Adaptability – is the first step to seeing how AI can be practically applied in your business. You don't need to be an expert in how these technologies work under the hood, but knowing *what they can do* will help you identify opportunities where AI can provide real value. In the next sections, we'll start connecting these capabilities to the world of marketing and business growth.

1.2 How AI is Transforming Marketing: A Sneak Peek into the Future (That's Already Here!)

Having established a foundational understanding of Artificial Intelligence and its core operational capabilities, our focus now shifts to a domain where AI's impact is not just profound but also rapidly accelerating: the world of marketing. For many business owners, the term "AI" might still conjure images of highly technical, back-end operations. However, the reality is that AI is increasingly becoming a customer-facing and strategy-shaping force, particularly in how businesses connect with their audiences, understand their needs, and deliver value. If you've ever felt overwhelmed by the sheer volume of marketing tasks, the challenge of truly personalizing customer interactions, or the difficulty in measuring the real impact of your campaigns, then AI offers not just solutions, but a fundamental transformation in approach.

Think of AI in marketing not as a replacement for human ingenuity and creativity – the heart of great marketing – but as an incredibly powerful amplifier and enabler. It's like equipping your marketing team with a suite of intelligent tools that can analyze data at speeds and scales far beyond human capacity, automate repetitive tasks with precision, and uncover insights that might otherwise remain hidden. This augmentation allows marketers to focus more on strategic thinking, creative development, and building genuine customer relationships, while AI handles the heavy lifting in data analysis, personalization, and optimization.

Let's delve deeper into the specific ways AI is revolutionizing the marketing landscape. While we will explore these areas in much greater detail with actionable strategies in subsequent chapters, this expanded overview will provide a clearer picture of the transformative potential that is already being realized by businesses, both large and small.

1. Supercharged Content Creation: From Blank Page to Engaging Narratives

- **The Traditional Challenge:** Content creation is the cornerstone of modern marketing. However, consistently producing high-quality, engaging, and relevant content – be it blog posts, articles, social media updates, email copy, video scripts, or product descriptions – is a significant undertaking. It demands time, creativity, and often, specialized writing skills. Marketers frequently face challenges like writer's block, the pressure to maintain a high publishing velocity, and the need to tailor content for different platforms and audience segments.

- **The AI-Powered Transformation:** AI, particularly through Natural Language Generation (NLG) and other machine learning models, is dramatically changing the content creation workflow.
    - **Idea Generation and Research:** AI tools can analyze trending topics within your industry, sift through competitor content, identify keywords your audience is searching for, and even suggest compelling angles or headlines for your next piece. This research phase, which can be very time-consuming manually, is significantly accelerated.
    - **Drafting and Outlining:** NLG tools can generate initial drafts of articles, blog posts, or product descriptions based on a set of keywords, a brief outline, or even existing data (like product specifications). While these drafts almost always require human editing and refinement to ensure accuracy, brand voice, and originality, they provide a substantial head start. For example, an e-commerce business with thousands of products can use AI to generate initial product descriptions, which can then be polished by human copywriters. This is a massive efficiency gain.
    - **Content Repurposing and Variation:** AI can help repurpose existing content into different formats (e.g., turning a long blog post into a series of social media up-

dates or a video script). It can also generate multiple variations of ad copy, email subject lines, or calls to action, allowing marketers to A/B test and identify what resonates best with their audience.

- **Grammar, Style, and Tone Checking:** Beyond basic spell-checking, AI-powered writing assistants can provide sophisticated feedback on grammar, clarity, conciseness, style, and even the emotional tone of your content, helping to ensure it aligns with your brand and objectives.
- **Personalized Content Snippets:** AI can dynamically insert personalized elements into content at scale, going beyond simple name tokenization to include relevant product recommendations, location-specific information, or references to past interactions.

Business Impact: The result is a more efficient content creation process, the ability to produce a higher volume of targeted content, and the freeing up of marketers' time to focus on higher-value tasks like strategy, in-depth storytelling, and creative direction. It's about augmenting human creativity, not replacing it.

2. Deeper Customer Understanding: Knowing Your Audience with Unprecedented Clarity

- **The Traditional Challenge:** Understanding customers – their needs, preferences, pain points, and behaviors – is fundamental to effective marketing. Traditionally, businesses have relied on methods like surveys, focus groups, website analytics, and sales data. While valuable, these methods can be slow, expensive, and often provide only a partial or aggregated view of the customer.

- **The AI-Powered Transformation:** AI, particularly Machine Learning and Natural Language Processing, allows businesses to analyze vast and diverse datasets about their customers with incredible speed and granularity.
    - **Unified Customer View (360-Degree Profile):** AI can help consolidate customer data from disparate sources – CRM systems, website interactions, mobile app usage, social media activity, email engagement, purchase history, customer service logs, third-party data – to create a comprehensive, unified profile for each customer.
    - **Advanced Segmentation:** Moving beyond broad demographic segments (age, gender, location), AI can identify micro-segments of customers based on subtle behavioral patterns, psychographics, purchase intent, or predicted lifetime value. This allows for highly targeted and relevant marketing messages. For example, an online retailer might identify a segment of "eco-conscious millennial shoppers interested in sustainable fashion" based on their browsing history, social media engagement, and past purchases.
    - **Sentiment Analysis at Scale:** NLP techniques can analyze thousands or millions of customer reviews, social media comments, survey responses, and support chat logs to gauge overall sentiment (positive, negative, neutral) towards a brand, product, or service. It can also identify emerging themes, common complaints, or areas of delight, providing actionable feedback for product development and marketing strategy.
    - **Predictive Behavioral Insights:** AI models can predict future customer behavior, such as which customers are likely to make a purchase, which are at risk of churning (leaving the business), or what products they might

be interested in next. This allows businesses to be proactive rather than reactive.

- **Understanding the Customer Journey:** AI can map out and analyze complex customer journeys across multiple touchpoints, identifying friction points, drop-off rates, and opportunities for optimization.

Business Impact: This deeper understanding enables businesses to create truly customer-centric marketing strategies, deliver highly personalized experiences, improve customer retention, and identify new market opportunities. It's about moving from assumptions to data-driven empathy.

3. Hyper-Precise Ad Targeting: Reaching the Right Person, at the Right Time, with the Right Message

- **The Traditional Challenge:** Advertising, whether digital or traditional, often involves a degree of wastage – showing ads to people who have little to no interest in the product or service. While digital advertising platforms offer targeting options, optimizing campaigns for maximum ROI can be complex and time-consuming.

- **The AI-Powered Transformation:** AI algorithms are revolutionizing ad targeting by enabling unprecedented levels of precision and automation.

  - **Predictive Audience Targeting:** AI models analyze vast datasets (including user demographics, online behavior, purchase history, contextual information, and lookalike audiences) to predict which specific individuals are most likely to convert for a particular ad campaign. This allows advertisers to focus their budget on the highest-potential audiences.

- **Real-Time Bidding (RTB) Optimization:** In programmatic advertising, AI algorithms can make millions of bidding decisions in milliseconds, automatically adjusting bids for ad impressions based on the predicted value of showing an ad to a specific user in a specific context. This maximizes the efficiency of ad spend.
- **Dynamic Creative Optimization (DCO):** AI can automatically assemble and serve different variations of an ad (e.g., different headlines, images, calls to action, offers) to different individuals based on their profile and real-time context, optimizing for the combination most likely to drive engagement. For example, an ad for a travel destination might show images of beaches to someone who has previously searched for beach vacations, and images of mountains to someone interested in hiking.
- **Cross-Channel Attribution and Optimization:** AI can help marketers understand how different advertising channels and touchpoints contribute to conversions, moving beyond simplistic last-click attribution models. This allows for more effective allocation of budget across channels.
- **Fraud Detection in Advertising:** AI can identify and filter out fraudulent ad impressions or clicks generated by bots, ensuring that advertising budgets are spent on reaching real human audiences.

Business Impact: Hyper-precise targeting leads to higher conversion rates, lower customer acquisition costs, improved return on ad spend (ROAS), and a better experience for users who see more relevant ads.

4. Smarter Campaign Management: Automating and Optimizing Marketing Workflows

- **The Traditional Challenge:** Managing marketing campaigns, especially multi-channel campaigns with complex customer journeys, involves many repetitive tasks, manual adjustments, and often, a lot of guesswork in terms of timing and sequencing of messages.

- **The AI-Powered Transformation:** AI is bringing a new level of intelligence and automation to campaign management.

    - **Intelligent Marketing Automation:** AI enhances traditional marketing automation platforms by adding predictive capabilities. For example, AI can determine the optimal time to send an email to an individual subscriber for maximum open rates, predict which content is most likely to nurture a lead at a specific stage of the sales funnel, or dynamically adjust the sequence of messages in an automated workflow based on a user's real-time engagement.
    - **Predictive Lead Scoring:** AI models can analyze various attributes and behaviors of leads (e.g., website activity, email clicks, firmographic data, social media engagement) to assign a score indicating their likelihood to convert. This allows sales and marketing teams to prioritize their efforts on the most promising leads, improving efficiency and conversion rates.
    - **Automated A/B Testing and Optimization:** AI can automate the process of A/B testing different elements of a campaign (e.g., email subject lines, landing page layouts, ad creatives) and automatically allocate more budget or traffic to the winning variations, continuously optimizing campaign performance.
    - **Budget Allocation and Pacing:** AI can help marketers optimize the allocation of their campaign budgets across different channels and activities based on pre-

dicted performance and ROI. It can also help with budget pacing to ensure campaigns stay on track throughout their duration.

Business Impact: Smarter campaign management leads to increased operational efficiency, better lead nurturing, higher conversion rates, and a more agile marketing function that can adapt quickly to changing market dynamics.

5. Chatbots & Virtual Assistants: 24/7 Intelligent Customer Engagement

- **The Traditional Challenge:** Providing timely and effective customer support can be a significant operational cost. Customers increasingly expect instant answers and support, regardless of business hours. Human agents can only handle a limited number of queries simultaneously.

- **The AI-Powered Transformation:** AI-powered chatbots and virtual assistants are revolutionizing customer service and engagement.

    - **Instantaneous Response:** Chatbots can provide immediate answers to frequently asked questions (FAQs), guide users to relevant information on a website, or help with simple tasks like order tracking or appointment booking, 24/7.
    - **Scalability:** Chatbots can handle a virtually unlimited number of conversations simultaneously, a feat impossible for human agents. This is particularly valuable during peak demand periods.
    - **Natural Language Understanding:** Modern chatbots, powered by NLP and ML, are becoming increasingly sophisticated in their ability to understand user intent, even with informal language, typos, or complex

queries. They can hold more natural, human-like conversations.

- **Personalization:** Chatbots can access customer data (with permission) to provide personalized responses and recommendations. For example, a banking chatbot might provide a customer with their account balance or recent transactions.
- **Lead Qualification and Routing:** Chatbots can ask qualifying questions to website visitors and, based on their responses, route them to the appropriate sales team or human agent for more complex issues.
- **Proactive Engagement:** Some chatbots can be programmed to proactively engage website visitors who seem to be struggling or who meet certain criteria, offering assistance before the user even asks.

Business Impact: AI chatbots improve customer satisfaction through instant support, reduce customer service costs, free up human agents to handle more complex and high-value interactions, and can even contribute to lead generation and sales.

6. Next-Level Marketing Analytics: From Data Overload to Actionable Intelligence

- **The Traditional Challenge:** Marketers are often drowning in data from various sources (website analytics, social media platforms, email marketing tools, CRM systems, ad platforms). Manually sifting through this data to extract meaningful insights, identify trends, and measure campaign effectiveness can be an overwhelming and error-prone task.

- **The AI-Powered Transformation:** AI, particularly Machine Learning, is transforming marketing analytics by enabling faster, deeper, and more predictive insights.

- **Automated Data Integration and Processing:** AI can help consolidate and process large volumes of data from disparate marketing channels, creating a unified view of performance.
- **Advanced Pattern Recognition:** AI algorithms can identify complex patterns, correlations, and anomalies in marketing data that might be invisible to human analysts. For example, it might uncover an unexpected relationship between website traffic from a particular source and a high conversion rate for a specific product.
- **Predictive Forecasting:** As discussed under Predictive Analytics, AI can forecast key marketing metrics like website traffic, conversion rates, sales, or customer churn, helping marketers set realistic goals and anticipate future performance.
- **Marketing Mix Modeling and Attribution:** AI can provide more sophisticated models for understanding how different marketing channels and touchpoints contribute to conversions (attribution), allowing for better optimization of the overall marketing mix. This moves beyond simplistic "last-click" attribution to provide a more holistic view of what's driving results.
- **Automated Reporting and Dashboards:** AI can automate the generation of insightful marketing reports and interactive dashboards, highlighting key performance indicators (KPIs), trends, and areas that require attention. This frees up marketers from manual report creation and allows them to focus on strategic interpretation and action.

Business Impact: AI-powered analytics transforms data from a passive resource into an active driver of marketing strategy, enabling more informed decision-making, continuous optimization, and ultimately, a greater return on marketing investment.

In essence, AI is not just adding a few new tricks to the marketer's toolkit; it's fundamentally reshaping the marketing function. By automating routine tasks, providing deeper customer insights, enabling hyper-personalization at scale, and optimizing campaigns with unprecedented precision, AI is empowering businesses to build stronger customer relationships and achieve their growth objectives more effectively. The "future" of AI in marketing is, in many respects, already here, and the businesses that embrace these capabilities will be best positioned to thrive in the evolving digital landscape. The subsequent chapters of this book will equip you with the practical knowledge and "simple AI secrets" to do just that.

1.3 Why This Matters to YOU (The Business Owner/Entrepreneur): Setting the Stage for Simple AI Secrets

So, we've journeyed through the what, why, and how of Artificial Intelligence, exploring its core capabilities like Machine Learning, Natural Language Processing, and Computer Vision. We've also taken a peek at the incredible ways AI is already revolutionizing the marketing landscape, from supercharging content creation to understanding customers with unprecedented clarity. At this point, especially if you're a small business owner or an entrepreneur juggling a million tasks, you might be thinking: "This all sounds fascinating, and maybe a bit overwhelming, but what does it *really* mean for *me* and *my* business? I don't have a massive tech department or a Silicon Valley budget!"

That's a perfectly valid question, and it's precisely why this book, "The Ultimate AI Blueprint: Grow Your Business with Simple AI Secrets," was written. The good news – no, the *great* news – is that AI is no longer the exclusive playground of giant corporations. The power of AI is becoming increasingly accessible, affordable, and, most importantly, *actionable* for businesses of all sizes, including yours. You don't need to be a data scientist or a coding wizard to start reaping the benefits.

This section is all about connecting the dots between the broader AI revolution and your day-to-day business reality. It's about shifting your perspective from seeing AI as a complex, distant technology to recognizing it as a set of practical tools and strategies – "simple AI secrets" – that can give you a genuine competitive edge, help you work smarter, not just harder, and ultimately fuel your business growth.

* * *

Bridging the Gap: AI Isn't Just for the Big Players Anymore

For a long time, the narrative around AI was dominated by stories of tech behemoths investing billions in research and development. This created a perception that AI was out of reach for the average business owner. However, the landscape has changed dramatically, and here's why this matters to you:

1. **Democratization of AI Tools:** Many AI-powered tools and platforms are now available as user-friendly software-as-a-service (SaaS) solutions. These often come with intuitive interfaces, require no coding, and are offered on affordable subscription models. Think about AI-powered email marketing tools, social media management platforms with AI features, AI writing assistants, or customer service chatbots that you can set up in an afternoon. The barrier to entry has been significantly lowered.

2. **The Power of Cloud Computing:** Cloud platforms (like Amazon Web Services, Google Cloud, Microsoft Azure) provide access to immense computing power and sophisticated AI services on a pay-as-you-go basis. This means you don't need to invest in expensive hardware or infrastructure to leverage advanced AI capabilities. Many of the AI tools you'll use are built on these cloud foundations, making them scalable and cost-effective. But there are more cost-effective on-premises AI hard-

ware solutions that can become cheaper over time especially when there's AI workloads being done 24/7.

3. **Focus on Practical Applications, Not Just Theory:** While the underlying technology of AI can be complex, the focus for business owners should be on its practical applications. You don't need to understand the intricate mathematics of a neural network to use an AI tool that helps you write better email subject lines or analyze customer feedback. You just need to understand what the tool can *do* for your business and how to use it effectively.

4. **Leveling the Playing Field:** AI can help smaller businesses compete more effectively with larger organizations. By automating tasks, gaining deeper customer insights, and personalizing marketing efforts, small businesses can achieve a level of sophistication and efficiency that was previously only possible for companies with much larger resources. AI can be your secret weapon to punch above your weight.

Why YOU, the Entrepreneur, Should Care Deeply About AI:

As a business owner or entrepreneur, your time is precious, your resources are often constrained, and your passion is what drives you. AI isn't just another tech trend to keep an eye on; it's a fundamental shift that can directly impact your ability to succeed and grow. Here's a more personal take on why this matters:

- **Reclaim Your Time and Boost Efficiency:** Many of the tasks that consume your valuable time – repetitive administrative work, sifting through data, manually posting on social media, answering the same customer questions over and over – can be significantly streamlined or automated with AI. Imagine what you could do with even a few extra hours each week.

You could focus more on strategy, innovation, building relationships, or even just achieving a better work-life balance.

- **Understand Your Customers Like Never Before:** You know your customers are the lifeblood of your business. AI can help you move beyond gut feelings and basic analytics to truly understand their needs, preferences, pain points, and behaviors. This deeper empathy, powered by data, allows you to create products, services, and marketing messages that resonate far more effectively, leading to increased loyalty and sales.

- **Make Smarter, Data-Driven Decisions:** Instead of relying solely on intuition or past experiences (which are valuable, but not always scalable or foolproof), AI provides you with data-driven insights to inform your decisions. Whether it's deciding which marketing channels to invest in, which products to promote, or how to price your offerings, AI can help you make choices with greater confidence and a higher probability of success.

- **Personalize at Scale (Without Losing the Human Touch):** Customers today expect personalized experiences. They want to feel understood and valued, not like just another number. AI enables you to deliver personalized marketing messages, product recommendations, and customer service interactions at a scale that would be impossible to achieve manually. And the beauty is, when done right, this AI-driven personalization can actually *enhance* the human touch by making your interactions more relevant and timely.

- **Stay Competitive in a Changing World:** Your competitors, whether big or small, are likely starting to explore or already using AI. Ignoring this technological shift is not a sustainable strategy. Embracing AI, even in small, incremental ways, can help you stay competitive, adapt to changing market dynamics, and even leapfrog businesses that are slower to adopt.

- **Unlock New Opportunities for Growth:** AI can help you identify new customer segments, uncover unmet needs in the market, or even spark ideas for new products or services. By analyzing data in novel ways, AI can reveal opportunities that you might not have seen otherwise.

- **Do More with Less:** This is often the mantra for small businesses. AI is a powerful force multiplier. It allows you to achieve more significant results with your existing resources, whether that's a small marketing budget, a lean team, or limited time.

Setting the Stage for Simple AI Secrets: This Book is Your Blueprint

This book is not about turning you into an AI programmer. It's about empowering you, the business owner, with the knowledge and practical strategies – the "simple AI secrets" – to effectively leverage readily available AI tools and techniques for tangible business growth. We will break down complex concepts into easy-to-understand language, provide real-world examples, and offer actionable steps you can start implementing right away.

Throughout the upcoming chapters, we will explore:

- **Specific AI tools and platforms** that are accessible and relevant for small to medium-sized businesses.
- **Actionable strategies** for using AI in key areas like marketing, sales, customer service, and operations.
- **How to identify the right AI solutions** for your specific business needs and goals.

- **Practical tips for implementing AI** without needing a dedicated tech team.
- **How to measure the impact of AI** on your business and continuously optimize your approach.
- **Ethical considerations** and how to use AI responsibly.

Think of this book as your friendly guide and blueprint. We're not just going to talk about what AI *can* do; we're going to show you *how* you can make it work for *your* business. The "secrets" are not about some hidden, complex algorithms, but about understanding the strategic application of these powerful new capabilities in a way that is simple, effective, and drives real results.

The AI revolution is here, and it's not just for the tech giants. It's for you, the agile entrepreneur, the dedicated business owner, the innovator looking for a smarter way to grow. By the end of this book, you'll have a clear understanding of how to harness these simple AI secrets to build a more efficient, more customer-focused, and ultimately, a more successful business. The future is intelligent, and with the right blueprint, your business can be too. Let's unlock that potential together.

My Approach: The Humanize Data™ Framework

Throughout this book, we will explore dozens of AI tools and tactics. But a list of tools is not a strategy. To successfully integrate AI into your business, you need a repeatable system—a framework that ensures your efforts are focused, measurable, and aligned with your core business goals. This is why I developed the Humanize DataTM Framework.

After implementing over 50 production AI use cases, I've seen firsthand why most initiatives fail. They get stuck in endless pilots, they lack clear ROI, or they are rejected by the very teams they are meant to help. The Humanize DataTM Framework is my four-pillar approach designed to prevent these failures and ensure AI projects land, stick, and scale effectively.

This is the exact system I use with every client, from startups to the Fortune 500. Consider it the master blueprint that underpins all the strategies in this book.

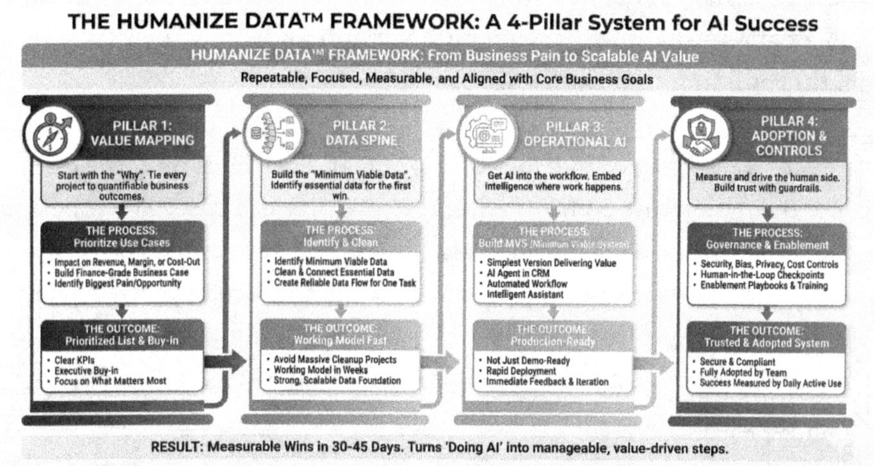

Pillar 1: Value Mapping

This is where it all begins. Before we write a single line of code or choose a single tool, we must tie every potential AI project to a clear, quantifiable business outcome. We don't ask, "What can we do with AI?" We ask, "Where is the biggest pain or opportunity in our business, and can AI solve it 10x better?"

- The Process: We prioritize use cases that directly impact revenue, margin, or cost-out. We build a finance-grade business case before we build a technical one.
- The Outcome: A prioritized list of AI projects with clear KPIs and executive buy-in, ensuring we are always working on what matters most.

Pillar 2: Data Spine

AI is fueled by data, but the myth is that you need perfect, massive datasets to start. This is wrong. The key is to identify the minimum viable data needed to ship your first version and get your first win. I call this building the "Data Spine."

- The Process: We identify, clean, and connect only the essential data required for the highest-priority use case. We focus on creating a clean, reliable data flow for one specific task.
- The Outcome: We avoid boiling the ocean with massive data cleanup projects. We get to a working model in weeks, not years, by starting small and building a strong, scalable data foundation.

Pillar 3: Operational AI

This pillar is about getting AI out of the slide deck and into the workflow. An AI model that isn't used by your team or your customers has zero value. The goal is to embed AI intelligence where work already happens.

- The Process: We build a Minimum Viable System (MVS)—the simplest possible version of the AI solution that delivers value. This could be an AI-powered agent in your CRM, an automated workflow in your contact center, or an intelligent assistant in your marketing platform.
- The Outcome: We focus on production-ready, not demo-ready. This ensures rapid deployment and immediate feedback, allowing us to iterate based on real-world usage.

Pillar 4: Adoption & Controls

An AI system without guardrails is a liability. From day one, we must build in the necessary controls for security, bias, privacy, and cost. But controls are useless without adoption. This pillar is about measuring and driving the human side of AI.

- The Process: We implement governance from the start, including data access rules, audit logs, and human-in-the-loop checkpoints. Simultaneously, we create enablement playbooks, training programs, and feedback loops to ensure teams embrace the new technology.
- The Outcome: A secure, compliant, and fully adopted AI system that your team trusts and your customers love. We measure success not by deployment, but by daily active use.

By following this framework, most of the organizations I work with see their first measurable win in 30-45 days. It turns the overwhelming prospect of "doing AI" into a series of manageable, value-driven steps. As you read through the coming chapters, think about how each strategy fits into this four-pillar system.

AI Prompts: Chapter 1

How to Use These Prompts

Each prompt below is designed to be copied directly into your favorite AI tool (ChatGPT, Claude, Grok, or Gemini). Simply:

1.Copy the entire prompt (including the bracketed placeholders)

2. Replace the [bracketed sections] with your specific information

3.Paste into your AI tool and hit enter

4.Refine the output by asking follow-up questions or requesting revisions

These are battle-tested prompts I use with organizations around the world. They're designed to give you professional-quality outputs that you can use immediately in your business.

Prompt 1.1: AI Opportunity Assessment for Your Business

I own a [type of business] that serves [target audience] with [main products/services]. Our current annual revenue is approximately [revenue range] and we have [number] employees.

I want to identify the top 3 AI opportunities that could have the biggest impact on our business in the next 90 days.

For each opportunity, please provide:

1. The specific business problem it solves
2. The AI technology or tool that could address it
3. The estimated time and cost to implement
4. The expected ROI or business impact
5. The first 3 steps to get started

Focus on practical, achievable wins rather than complex or expensive solutions.

Prompt 1.2: Create Your AI Adoption Roadmap

I'm ready to create a 90-day AI adoption roadmap for my [type of business]. Here's our current situation:

- Main business challenges: [list 2-3 biggest pain points]
- Current marketing channels: [e.g., email, social media, paid ads, SEO]
- Team size and technical capability: [describe your team]
- Monthly marketing budget: [budget range]
- Primary business goal: [e.g., increase leads, reduce costs, improve customer retention]

Create a week-by-week 90-day implementation plan that includes:

- Specific AI tools to implement and when
- What to measure for success
- Resource requirements (time, budget, people)
- Quick wins we can achieve in the first 30 days

- How to get team buy-in and adoption

Make this actionable and realistic for a business with limited technical resources.

Prompt 1.3: AI vs. Traditional Approach Cost-Benefit Analysis

I'm considering implementing AI for [specific business process, e.g., "content creation" or "customer service"].

Current approach:

- Time spent per week: [hours]
- People involved: [number and roles]
- Current costs: [monthly cost]
- Current results/output: [describe current performance]

Help me create a cost-benefit analysis comparing my current approach to an AI-powered approach. Include:

1. Estimated time savings with AI
2. Potential cost savings or costs to implement
3. Expected improvement in quality or output
4. Recommended AI tools for this use case (with pricing)
5. Payback period calculation
6. Risks or downsides to consider

Be realistic and conservative in your estimates.

For prompts and bonus resources, visit **thejasonfleagle.com/blueprint-resources**. You can copy and paste the prompts from there—no retyping needed.

| 2 |

AI for Content Marketing and Customer Engagement

Section 2.1: Using AI to Generate Content Ideas

Welcome to the exciting world of using Artificial Intelligence, or AI, to supercharge your content marketing! If you've ever stared at a blank page wondering what to write about next, or felt like you're just guessing what your audience wants to read, then this section is for you. One of the biggest headaches for any business owner, especially when you're juggling a million other tasks, is consistently coming up with fresh, relevant, and engaging content ideas. It's easy to fall into a rut, recycle old topics, or simply run out of inspiration. This is often called "content idea fatigue," and it's a real challenge when you're trying to attract new customers and keep your current ones interested.

But what if you had a super-smart assistant who could sift through mountains of information, understand what people are searching for, see what your competitors are doing successfully, and even listen in on what your customers are talking about? That's essentially what AI can do for your content idea generation. Think of AI not as a magical black box, but as an incredibly powerful research partner. It can analyze data at a scale and speed that humans simply can't match, uncovering hidden opportunities and insights that can lead to content that truly hits the mark.

In this section, we're going to explore some simple AI secrets that can transform how you find content ideas. We'll look at how AI can help you with:

- **AI-Driven Keyword Research:** Going beyond just basic keywords to understand what your audience is *really* asking.
- **Competitor Content Analysis with AI:** Learning from what's working (and not working) for others in your field.
- **AI for Customer Insight Mining:** Tuning into the voice of your customer to discover their true needs and wants.
- **AI-Powered Trend Spotting:** Catching the wave of emerging topics before they become yesterday's news.
- **Analyzing Your Own Content Performance with AI:** Learning from your own successes and identifying areas for improvement.

Let's dive in and see how these AI techniques can make finding great content ideas a whole lot easier and more effective for your business.

AI-Driven Keyword Research: Uncovering What Your Audience Truly Seeks

Most business owners are familiar with keywords – those words and phrases people type into search engines like Google when they're looking for information, products, or services. Basic keyword research might involve brainstorming terms related to your business and seeing how often they're searched. However, AI takes keyword research to a whole new level. It's like moving from a simple map to a sophisticated GPS that not only shows you the roads but also traffic conditions, points of interest, and the best routes based on real-time data.

So, how does AI make keyword research smarter? AI tools don't just look at individual keywords; they analyze the *intent* behind the search. Are people looking to learn something (informational intent), buy something (transactional intent), find a specific website (navigational intent), or compare options (commercial investigation)? Understanding this intent is crucial for creating content that actually meets the searcher's needs.

Furthermore, AI excels at identifying **long-tail keywords.** These are longer, more specific phrases that people use when they're closer to making a decision or have a very particular question. While popular, short keywords (like "flowers") are highly competitive, long-tail keywords (like "best drought-resistant flowering plants for beginner gardeners in Phoenix Arizona") often have less competition and attract a more targeted, motivated audience. AI algorithms can sift through vast amounts of search data to unearth these valuable long-tail opportunities that you might never think of on your own.

AI also helps in understanding **semantic relationships** between keywords. This means it looks at how different words and concepts are related. For example, if you sell coffee, AI can identify related topics like "cold brew techniques," "sustainable coffee beans," "best grinders for French press," or "health benefits of coffee." This allows you to create a cluster of related content that positions you as an expert and helps search engines understand the breadth of your topic.

Another powerful aspect is AI's ability to analyze **question-based queries.** Many people type full questions into search engines (e.g., "How do I stop my roses from getting black spot?"). AI tools can identify these questions, providing you with ready-made content ideas that directly address your audience's problems.

Finally, some AI tools can even help **predict keyword trends,** showing you which topics are gaining popularity and which are fading. This allows you to be proactive and create content that will be in demand.

Simple Example in Action:

Imagine you run a local bakery. A basic keyword approach might focus on "cakes" or "bakery near me." An AI-driven approach could uncover long-tail keywords like:

- "custom birthday cakes for kids allergy-friendly [your city]"
- "where to buy fresh sourdough bread [your neighborhood]"
- "easy vegan cupcake recipes for beginners"

See the difference? The AI-identified keywords are much more specific and reveal distinct customer needs. Creating content around these (e.g., a blog post titled "Our Top 5 Allergy-Friendly Kids' Birthday Cake Designs" or "A Beginner's Guide to Baking Vegan Cupcakes") is far more likely to attract the right audience and lead to a sale or inquiry than a generic post about "cakes."

The key takeaway here is that AI-driven keyword research provides deeper insights. It's not just about finding words people search for, but understanding the *context, intent,* and *specific needs* behind those searches. This allows you to create content that is not only discoverable but also incredibly relevant and valuable to your potential customers.

Competitor Content Analysis with AI: Learning from the Landscape

Knowing what your competitors are up to is a fundamental part of any business strategy, and content marketing is no exception. Manually tracking every piece of content your competitors publish, figuring out what's resonating with their audience, and identifying gaps you could fill can be an overwhelming and time-consuming task. This is another area where AI can provide a significant advantage, acting like a tireless scout that constantly monitors the competitive landscape for you.

AI tools designed for competitor content analysis can automatically discover and analyze the content being published by others in your niche. They don't just tell you *what* your competitors are publishing, but can also provide insights into *how well* that content is performing. This includes metrics like social media shares, backlinks (other websites linking to their content, which is a good sign for search engines), and sometimes even estimated organic traffic for specific pieces.

Here's how AI helps you learn from your competitors to spark your own content ideas:

- **Identifying Top-Performing Content:** AI can quickly show you which articles, blog posts, videos, or social media updates from your competitors are getting the most engagement (likes, shares, comments) or ranking well in search results. This gives you a clear idea of what topics and formats are currently popular with your shared target audience. You're not looking to copy them, but to understand the themes and approaches that work.

- **Discovering Content Gaps:** By analyzing the breadth of your competitors' content, AI can help you spot areas they *aren't* covering, or topics they've only touched upon superficially. These gaps represent prime opportunities for you to create comprehensive, authoritative content that fills a void in the market. For example, if your competitors have lots of content on "choosing a coffee machine" but very little on "maintaining your coffee machine," AI can help highlight this gap.

- **Understanding Successful Formats:** Is video content king in your niche? Are long-form blog posts outperforming shorter ones? Do infographics get a lot of shares? AI can analyze the types of content your competitors are using and which formats are driving the best results. This can inform your own decisions about where to invest your content creation efforts.

- **Analyzing Headlines and Angles:** AI can break down the characteristics of successful headlines and content angles used by competitors. Are they using numbers, asking questions, or creating a sense of urgency? Understanding these patterns can help you craft more compelling titles for your own content.

- **Monitoring New Content:** AI tools can alert you when competitors publish new content on specific topics, allowing you to stay informed and react quickly if necessary. Perhaps they've covered a new trend you should also address, or launched a new product you need to be aware of.

Simple Example in Action:

Let's say you own a small, independent bookstore. An AI competitor analysis tool might reveal that a larger chain bookstore in your city has a blog, and their most shared posts are author interviews and articles about local literary events. However, the AI also notes they have very little content aimed at parents looking for children's books or resources for starting a book club.

This insight is gold! You could then decide to create content like:

- "Top 10 Read-Aloud Books for Toddlers This Season"
- "How to Start a Neighborhood Book Club: A Simple Guide"
- Interviews with local children's book authors (a niche the competitor isn't fully exploring).

By using AI to understand the competitive content landscape, you're not just guessing. You're making data-informed decisions about where to focus your content efforts to stand out, provide unique value, and attract your ideal customers. It's about finding your unique voice and angle by understanding what's already out there.

AI for Customer Insight Mining: Listening to the Voice of Your Customer

Understanding your customers – their needs, wants, pain points, and preferences – is the cornerstone of any successful business. Traditionally, businesses have gathered customer insights through surveys, focus groups, or direct feedback. While valuable, these methods can be time-consuming, expensive, and may only capture a snapshot of customer sentiment. AI offers a powerful way to continuously and deeply understand the "voice of the customer" by analyzing the vast amounts of unstructured data they generate every day.

Think about all the places your customers and potential customers are talking: social media comments, online reviews (on your site or third-party sites like Yelp or Google Reviews), support chat logs, emails, forum discussions, and more. Manually sifting through all this text to find meaningful patterns is nearly impossible for a small business owner. This is where AI, particularly techniques like **Natural Language Processing (NLP)** and **sentiment analysis**, comes into play.

Here's how AI helps you mine customer insights for content ideas:

- **Identifying Pain Points and Frustrations:** AI can scan through customer feedback to pinpoint common problems or frustrations they are experiencing with your products, services, or even with the industry in general. Content that addresses these pain points directly can be incredibly valuable and attract an engaged audience. For example, if AI analysis of support tickets for your software company reveals many users struggle with a particular feature, you could create a detailed tutorial blog post or video on how to use that feature effectively.

- **Discovering Frequently Asked Questions (FAQs):** AI can identify questions that customers repeatedly ask across different channels. Instead of answering them one by one, you can create comprehensive content (like an FAQ page, a series of blog posts, or explainer videos) that addresses these common queries. This not only saves you time but also positions you as a helpful expert.

- **Uncovering Desired Features or Services:** Customers often mention what they wish a product or service could do. AI can pick up on these suggestions for new features, improvements, or even entirely new service offerings. While not all suggestions are feasible, they can spark ideas for content that explores these possibilities or explains why current solutions are designed the way they are.

- **Understanding Customer Language and Terminology:** How do your customers actually talk about your products or industry? Are they using the same jargon you use, or do they have their own terms? AI can analyze customer conversations to help you understand their language, which you can then incorporate into your content to make it more relatable and easier to find via search.

- **Gauging Sentiment Around Topics or Your Brand:** Sentiment analysis AI can determine the emotional tone (positive, negative, neutral) expressed in customer text. This can help you understand how customers feel about your brand, specific products, or general topics in your industry. If you see a lot of negative sentiment around a particular issue, you could create content that addresses the concerns and offers solutions. Conversely, positive sentiment can highlight what you're doing well and what topics your audience enjoys.

Simple Example in Action:

Imagine you run an online store selling eco-friendly cleaning products. By using AI to analyze product reviews and social media comments, you might discover:

- **Pain Point:** Many customers mention confusion about how to properly dilute concentrated cleaning solutions.
- **FAQ:** A common question is, "Are your packaging materials recyclable?"
- **Desired Feature:** Several customers express a wish for a subscription service for their favorite products.

- **Sentiment:** Positive sentiment around your new lavender-scented all-purpose cleaner, but some neutral or slightly negative comments about the spray bottle nozzle on another product.

These AI-driven insights could lead to content ideas like:

- A blog post with a clear dilution guide and video: "Get it Right Every Time: How to Perfectly Dilute Your Eco-Concentrates."
- A dedicated page on your website: "Our Commitment to Sustainable Packaging (And How to Recycle Everything!)."
- An article exploring the benefits of a subscription model: "Never Run Out Again! The Perks of a Cleaning Subscription."
- A social media post highlighting the popular lavender cleaner and subtly addressing feedback by mentioning you're looking into improved spray bottle designs.

By using AI to listen to the voice of your customer, you move beyond assumptions and tap into a rich source of content ideas that are directly relevant to their needs and concerns. This not only helps you create more effective content but also shows your customers that you are listening and value their input.

AI-Powered Trend Spotting: Riding the Wave of What's Next

In today's fast-paced digital world, trends can emerge and fade with lightning speed. Being able to identify and capitalize on relevant trends early can give your business a significant edge, making your content timely, highly shareable, and positioning you as an innovator. However, manually keeping a finger on the pulse of everything happening online – across news sites, social media platforms, industry forums, and search engines – is a monumental task. This is where AI-powered trend spotting tools become invaluable, acting as your early warning system for what's gaining traction.

AI algorithms are designed to process and analyze massive datasets in real-time. They can monitor millions of online sources, looking for patterns, shifts in conversation volume, and the emergence of new keywords or topics that indicate a growing trend. Unlike humans, who might only notice a trend once it's already well-established, AI can often detect the faint signals of an emerging trend much earlier.

Here's how AI helps you spot trends for content ideas:

- **Monitoring Broad Social and Search Data:** AI tools can scan social media conversations (like Twitter, TikTok, Instagram, Facebook), search engine queries (like Google Trends), news articles, and blog posts globally or within specific regions or industries. They look for spikes in mentions, changes in search volume, or the rapid adoption of new hashtags or phrases.

- **Identifying Niche-Specific Trends:** Beyond general pop culture trends, AI can be tailored to monitor trends specifically relevant to your industry or niche. This ensures you're not just chasing viral cat videos (unless you sell cat products!) but are focusing on developments that matter to your target audience.

- **Predicting Trend Longevity:** Some advanced AI tools attempt to predict whether a trend is a fleeting fad or something with more staying power. This can help you decide whether to create quick, reactive content or invest in more evergreen pieces related to a longer-term shift.

- **Understanding the Context of a Trend:** AI doesn't just tell you *what* is trending; it can also help you understand *why* it's trending by analyzing the surrounding conversations, key influencers discussing it, and the sentiment associated with it. This context is crucial for creating content that genuinely resonates and isn't just a superficial attempt to jump on a bandwagon.

- **Providing Early Mover Advantage:** By getting early insights into emerging trends, AI allows you to be one of the first in your space to create content around that topic. This can lead to significant organic traffic, social shares, and brand recognition as a thought leader.

Simple Example in Action:

Imagine you own a small business that sells sustainable home goods. An AI trend-spotting tool might flag a growing online conversation and search interest around "zero-waste kitchen swaps" or "DIY natural cleaning recipes" long before these become mainstream topics covered by major publications.

Armed with this early information, you could quickly create content such as:

- A blog post: "5 Easy Zero-Waste Swaps for a Greener Kitchen Today."
- A series of short videos demonstrating DIY natural cleaning recipes using ingredients you sell.
- A social media campaign highlighting your products that align with the zero-waste trend.

By creating relevant content early, you capture the attention of an audience actively seeking information on that emerging trend. This not only drives traffic but also positions your brand as forward-thinking and in tune with evolving consumer values.

Using AI for trend spotting isn't about blindly following every new fad. It's about using data-driven insights to identify relevant, emerging opportunities where your business can provide valuable information or solutions, thereby capturing audience interest before your competitors do.

Analyzing Your Own Content Performance with AI: Learning from Your Successes (and Failures!)

While looking outwards at keywords, competitors, customers, and trends is crucial for generating new content ideas, it's equally important to look inwards at how your *own* existing content is performing. Your website analytics, blog engagement metrics, and social media insights are a goldmine of information. AI can help you dig through this data more effectively to understand what's resonating with your audience, what's falling flat, and where your content gaps lie.

Many businesses collect a lot of data but struggle to extract actionable insights from it. AI-powered analytics tools, or even the AI-driven features within platforms like Google Analytics, can help you make sense of the numbers and turn them into concrete content ideas.

Here's how AI helps you analyze your own content performance for idea generation:

- **Identifying Your Top-Performing Content:** AI can quickly identify which of your blog posts, articles, videos, or social media updates are getting the most views, engagement (likes, shares, comments), time on page, or conversions. This tells you what topics, formats, and styles your audience loves. You can then create more content similar to your winners or delve deeper into those successful topics.
    - **Example:** If AI analytics show that your blog post titled "A Beginner's Guide to Container Gardening" is consistently your most popular piece, you could create follow-up content like "Advanced Container Gardening Techniques," "Best Plants for Small Balcony Gardens," or a video series on container gardening.
- **Pinpointing Underperforming Content:** Conversely, AI can highlight content that isn't getting much traction. This doesn't always mean the topic is bad; perhaps the content needs to be updated, better optimized for SEO, promoted differently,

or presented in a new format. Understanding what isn't working can be just as valuable as knowing what is.

  - **Example:** If an old article on "Spring Planting Dates for [Your Region]" is no longer getting traffic, AI can flag it. You could then update it with the current year's dates and new tips, or repurpose the core information into a shareable infographic.

- **Discovering Content Gaps on Your Own Site:** By analyzing the topics you've covered and how users navigate your site, AI can help identify gaps in your content. Are there logical follow-up topics to your popular posts that you haven't written about? Are users searching your site for terms you don't have content for?

  - **Example:** If users frequently land on your "Rose Care Basics" article and then search your site for "natural pest control for roses" (and find nothing), AI can highlight this as a content gap, prompting you to write an article on that specific topic.

- **Understanding User Behavior and Journeys:** AI can provide deeper insights into how users interact with your content. Which articles lead to the most newsletter sign-ups? Where do users typically drop off on a long page? Which calls-to-action are most effective? This behavioral data can inform both new content ideas and optimizations for existing content.
- **Optimizing for Search Intent:** AI can analyze which search queries are leading users to your existing content and whether that content truly satisfies their intent. If users land on a page and quickly leave (high bounce rate), it might indicate a mismatch between what they searched for and what your content delivered. This can spark ideas for creating new, more targeted content or revising the existing piece.

Simple Example in Action:

Suppose you run a small accounting firm and have a blog. AI analysis of your website data might reveal:

- **Top Performer:** An article titled "Understanding Tax Deductions for Freelancers" gets consistent high traffic and long read times.
- **Underperformer:** A very technical article on a niche corporate tax law gets almost no views.
- **Content Gap:** Many users who read the freelancer tax article also visit your "Services" page but don't convert. Your site search shows queries like "bookkeeping for freelancers."

These AI-driven insights could lead to content ideas like:

- Expanding the freelancer topic: "Quarterly Estimated Tax Guide for Freelancers," "Best Accounting Software for Solopreneurs."
- Simplifying or repurposing the technical tax law article for a broader audience if relevant, or deciding to focus less on such niche topics.
- Creating a new service page or a detailed blog post specifically about "Affordable Bookkeeping Services for Freelancers," directly addressing the identified need and search query.

By regularly using AI to analyze your own content performance, you create a powerful feedback loop. You learn directly from your audience's behavior what works best, allowing you to refine your content strategy, fill gaps, and double down on topics and formats that drive results. This data-driven approach to ideation is far more effective than relying on guesswork alone.

AI as Your Content Idea Powerhouse

Coming up with a steady stream of compelling content ideas is a common hurdle for businesses of all sizes. As we've seen in this section, Artificial Intelligence offers a suite of powerful tools and techniques to transform this challenge into an opportunity. By leveraging AI, you can move beyond guesswork and tap into data-driven insights to uncover what your audience truly wants and needs.

We've explored several "simple AI secrets" for idea generation:

- **AI-Driven Keyword Research** helps you understand search intent, discover valuable long-tail keywords, and identify question-based queries, leading to highly relevant content topics.
- **Competitor Content Analysis with AI** allows you to learn from what's working in your niche, spot content gaps, and understand successful formats and angles your competitors are using.
- **AI for Customer Insight Mining** tunes you into the voice of your customer by analyzing reviews, social media, and support interactions to uncover pain points, FAQs, and desired features that can inspire content.
- **AI-Powered Trend Spotting** gives you an early advantage by identifying emerging topics and conversations relevant to your industry before they become saturated.
- **Analyzing Your Own Content Performance with AI** creates a vital feedback loop, helping you identify your most successful content, find underperforming pieces to improve, and discover gaps in your existing content library.

By integrating these AI-powered strategies into your content planning process, you're not just finding ideas; you're finding the *right* ideas – those that are more likely to attract your target audience, engage them deeply, and ultimately contribute to your business growth. Think of AI as your tireless research assistant, your insightful analyst, and your forward-looking trend forecaster, all rolled into one, helping you build a content strategy that is both strategic and effective.

Section 2.2: Leveraging AI for Content Creation

The idea of Artificial Intelligence actually *writing* content can bring about a mix of excitement and perhaps a little apprehension. Can a machine truly be creative? Will AI-generated content sound robotic or generic? Will it replace human writers altogether? These are all valid questions. For business owners, the key is to understand AI not as a magical content-creating genie or a threat to human creativity, but as an incredibly powerful **assistant and collaborator** in the content creation process.

When we talk about "simple AI secrets" for content creation, we're focusing on how AI can help you overcome common hurdles like writer's block, speed up tedious tasks, and even enhance the quality of your writing. It's about working smarter, not necessarily replacing the human touch that gives your brand its unique voice and personality. AI can handle some of the heavy lifting, freeing you and your team to focus on strategy, creativity, and adding those unique insights that only a human expert can provide.

In this section, we'll explore practical ways AI can be integrated into your content creation workflow, from generating initial drafts to refining your final pieces. We'll look at:

- **Natural Language Generation (NLG) for First Drafts:** Getting a head start on your writing.
- **AI for Intelligent Research and Fact-Gathering:** Quickly building a foundation of knowledge.
- **AI-Powered Writing Assistants:** Going beyond basic spell check to improve your writing style and clarity.
- **AI for Content Repurposing:** Making your existing content work harder for you.

- **Maintaining Authenticity and Brand Voice:** Ensuring your AI-assisted content still sounds like *you.*
- **Ethical Considerations:** Using AI responsibly in content creation.

Let's uncover how AI can become an indispensable partner in your content creation efforts.

AI in the Content Creation Workflow: Your Digital Writing Partner

Integrating AI into your content creation workflow doesn't mean handing over the reins entirely. Instead, it's about strategically using AI tools at different stages to enhance efficiency and output. Here's how AI can assist:

Natural Language Generation (NLG) for First Drafts: Overcoming the Blank Page

One of the most talked-about applications of AI in content creation is **Natural Language Generation (NLG)**. Simply put, NLG is a type of AI that can generate human-like text based on data inputs and prompts you provide. If you've ever struggled with the dreaded blank page, wondering how to even start an article or a product description, NLG can be a game-changer.

How it Works (Simply Put): You give the AI a topic, some keywords, perhaps an outline or a few key points you want to cover, and specify the desired tone or style. The AI then processes this information and generates a piece of text – a first draft – based on its training data and the instructions you gave it.

Common Uses for NLG in First Drafts:

- **Blog Posts:** Generating an initial structure and some foundational paragraphs for an article.
- **Product Descriptions:** Creating basic descriptions for e-commerce products, especially if you have a large inventory.

- **Social Media Updates:** Drafting short posts or captions for different platforms.
- **Email Snippets:** Generating introductory lines or calls to action for marketing emails.
- **Ad Copy Variations:** Quickly creating multiple versions of ad headlines and body text for A/B testing.

The Crucial Role of Human Oversight: This is perhaps the most important "secret" when using AI for draft generation: **AI-generated content should almost always be treated as a starting point, not the finished product.** While AI can produce surprisingly coherent and grammatically correct text, it lacks true understanding, personal experience, and your unique brand voice. Human editing and refinement are essential to:

- **Ensure Factual Accuracy:** AI can sometimes generate incorrect or outdated information (often called "hallucinations"). Always fact-check.
- **Inject Brand Voice and Personality:** AI drafts can be generic. You need to infuse your brand's unique tone, style, and perspective.
- **Add Original Insights and Expertise:** AI synthesizes existing information; it doesn't have your specific experiences or novel ideas. Add your unique value.
- **Improve Flow and Readability:** While often good, AI drafts might need tweaking for better transitions and overall coherence for your specific audience.
- **Check for Originality:** Ensure the content isn't too similar to existing online material to avoid plagiarism concerns, even if unintentional by the AI.

Simple Example in Action:

Imagine you own an e-commerce store selling handmade soaps. You have 50 new soap varieties to add to your website, and writing unique descriptions for each is daunting. You could use an AI NLG tool by providing it with the key ingredients, scent profile, and main benefits of each soap (e.g., "Lavender and Oatmeal Soap, calming scent, gently exfoliates, good for sensitive skin").

The AI might generate a basic description like: "This Lavender and Oatmeal Soap features a calming lavender scent. It gently exfoliates the skin and is suitable for sensitive skin types. Made with natural ingredients."

This is a decent start, but it's generic. A human copywriter (perhaps you!) would then take this AI-generated draft and enhance it:

"Indulge your senses and soothe your skin with our artisan-crafted Lavender and Oatmeal Dream Soap. Breathe in the tranquil aroma of pure lavender essential oil, renowned for its calming properties, as finely ground oatmeal gently buffs away dullness, revealing a softer, smoother you. Specially formulated for even the most sensitive skin, this bar is a pure, natural escape in your daily routine."

See how the human touch adds evocative language, emotional appeal, and a more distinct brand voice? AI provided the factual scaffold, saving time on the initial, repetitive part of the task, while the human provided the artistry and connection.

Using NLG for first drafts is about leveraging AI for speed and scale in the initial stages, allowing you to focus your valuable human creativity on refinement and adding that irreplaceable personal touch.

AI for Intelligent Research and Fact-Gathering: Building a Solid Foundation Quickly

Creating high-quality, informative content often requires significant research. Whether you're writing a blog post about industry trends, a whitepaper on a complex topic, or even a detailed product guide, you need accurate facts, statistics, and supporting information. Traditionally, this research process can be incredibly time-consuming, involving sifting through numerous articles, studies, and websites. AI can dramatically speed up this foundational stage by acting as an intelligent research assistant.

How AI Streamlines Research:

AI tools designed for research can rapidly scan and process vast amounts of information from the internet or specific databases. They can help you by:

- **Quickly Gathering Information:** Instead of manually opening dozens of tabs and reading through lengthy documents, you can ask an AI research tool to find information on a specific topic. It can pull relevant snippets, articles, and data points from a wide array of sources much faster than a human could.
- **Summarizing Long Documents:** Faced with a 20-page research paper or a lengthy industry report? AI can provide concise summaries, highlighting the key findings and main arguments. This allows you to quickly assess whether a source is relevant and worth a deeper dive, saving you hours of reading time.
- **Synthesizing Information from Multiple Sources:** Some AI tools can take information from several different sources and synthesize it into a coherent overview. This can be particularly helpful when you need to understand different perspectives on a topic or gather a broad range of supporting evidence.
- **Identifying Key Statistics and Data Points:** If you need specific data to back up your claims (e.g., market size, growth rates, survey results), AI can help locate these statistics more efficiently. You still need to verify the source and its credibility, but AI can point you in the right direction much faster.
- **Finding Relevant Sources and Citations:** AI can help identify seminal papers, influential authors, or recent studies related to your topic, which can be crucial for creating authoritative content.

The Human Role in AI-Assisted Research:

While AI is a powerful research accelerator, human judgment remains critical. Here's why:

- **Source Vetting:** AI can pull information from anywhere. It's your responsibility to evaluate the credibility, authority, and potential bias of the sources AI presents. Always prioritize reputable sources.
- **Fact-Checking:** As mentioned before, AI can make mistakes or present outdated information. Double-check any facts, statistics, or critical pieces of information before including them in your content.
- **Contextual Understanding and Nuance:** AI might provide facts, but it may not fully grasp the nuances or the broader context of the information. Human analysis is needed to interpret the data correctly and apply it meaningfully to your specific content goals.
- **Original Analysis and Interpretation:** AI can gather facts; it can't (yet) provide deep, original analysis or connect disparate pieces of information in a novel way that reflects your unique expertise. That's where your human insight shines.

Simple Example in Action:

Let's say you're writing an article for your renewable energy company's blog about the recent growth in residential solar panel installations in your state. Instead of spending hours manually searching for government reports, industry analyses, and news articles, you could use an AI research tool.

You might prompt it with: "Find recent statistics and key drivers for residential solar panel adoption in [Your State] over the last two years."

The AI could quickly return:

- Links to relevant sections of reports from the Department of Energy or local energy authorities.
- Summaries of news articles discussing new state incentives for solar.
- Key data points on the percentage increase in solar installations and average system costs.

This gives you a solid foundation of facts and figures in minutes rather than hours. You would then verify these sources, dig deeper into the most promising ones, and use this information to write your well-researched, data-backed article, adding your company's perspective and local expertise.

Using AI for intelligent research and fact-gathering isn't about replacing critical thinking; it's about augmenting your research capabilities. It allows you to cover more ground, gather information more efficiently, and spend less time on the tedious aspects of research, freeing you up to focus on crafting compelling and insightful content.

AI-Powered Writing Assistants: Your Real-Time Editor and Coach

Beyond just generating initial drafts or helping with research, AI has also given rise to sophisticated writing assistant tools that act like a real-time editor and writing coach, sitting right beside you as you type. These tools go far beyond the basic spell check and grammar correction you might be used to in word processors. They leverage AI, particularly Natural Language Processing (NLP), to provide nuanced feedback on various aspects of your writing, helping you to refine your message, improve clarity, and ensure your tone is appropriate for your audience.

Think of these AI writing assistants as a second pair of eyes that can catch subtle errors, suggest better word choices, and help you communicate more effectively. They are designed to enhance human writing, not replace it, by providing data-driven suggestions to improve quality and impact.

What Can AI Writing Assistants Do?

- **Advanced Grammar and Punctuation Correction:** They catch complex grammatical errors, incorrect punctuation usage, and stylistic inconsistencies that basic checkers might miss.
- **Style and Tone Suggestions:** This is where AI assistants truly shine. They can analyze the tone of your writing (e.g., formal, informal, confident, empathetic, analytical) and suggest adjustments to better match your intended audience or purpose. Some tools can even be set to a specific target audience (like "8th-grade reading level" or "expert audience").
- **Clarity and Conciseness:** AI can identify wordy sentences, jargon that might confuse your readers, passive voice usage that weakens your message, and overly complex sentence structures. They offer suggestions for making your writing clearer, more direct, and easier to understand.
- **Vocabulary Enhancement:** These tools can suggest alternative word choices to avoid repetition, enhance impact, or use more precise language. They might offer synonyms or rephrase sentences for better effect.
- **Readability Scores:** Many AI writing assistants provide readability scores (e.g., Flesch-Kincaid Grade Level, Gunning Fog Index) to help you gauge how easy your content is to understand. This is particularly useful if youRe_aiming for a specific reading level, like the 8th-grade level weRe_targeting for this book.
- **Consistency Checks:** They can help ensure consistency in terminology, hyphenation, capitalization, and other stylistic elements throughout a document, which is especially helpful for longer pieces or when multiple people are contributing to content.
- **Plagiarism Detection (in some tools):** Some advanced writing assistants also include plagiarism checkers to ensure

your content is original and properly attributes any sourced material.

- **SEO Suggestions (in some tools):** Certain AI writing tools focused on web content can also offer basic SEO feedback, such as keyword density or suggestions for improving headlines for search engines, though dedicated SEO tools are usually more comprehensive for this.

How to Use AI Writing Assistants Effectively:

- **Integrate into Your Workflow:** Use them as you write or as a final review step before publishing. Many tools offer browser extensions or integrate directly with popular writing platforms.
- **Don't Accept Every Suggestion Blindly:** AI suggestions are just that – suggestions. Use your judgment. Sometimes the AI might misunderstand the nuance of what youRe_trying to say, or its suggestion might alter your intended meaning or unique voice. You are the ultimate authority.
- **Focus on Learning:** Pay attention to the types of suggestions the AI makes. Over time, this can help you become a better writer by making you more aware of your common mistakes or areas for improvement.
- **Customize Settings (if available):** If the tool allows, customize its settings to align with your specific style guide, audience, or writing goals.

Simple Example in Action:

Imagine youVe_written the following sentence for a blog post aimed at busy entrepreneurs: "It is imperative for organizational stakeholders to proactively conceptualize and implement multifaceted strategic initiatives to enhance market penetration."

An AI writing assistant might flag this sentence and offer suggestions like:

- **Clarity/Conciseness:** "This sentence is very wordy and uses complex language. Consider simplifying."
- **Alternative Phrasing:** "To grow your business, you need to plan and act on smart strategies to reach more customers."
- **Tone:** "The original tone is very formal. For busy entrepreneurs, a more direct and conversational tone might be better."

By using the AI assistant's feedback, you can transform a clunky, jargon-filled sentence into something much clearer, more accessible, and more impactful for your target audience.

AI-powered writing assistants are a fantastic example of AI augmenting human capabilities. They help polish your writing, catch errors you might have missed, and ensure your message is delivered with clarity and impact, ultimately making your content more effective.

AI for Content Repurposing: Making Your Best Content Work Harder

Creating high-quality content takes time and effort. So, once you have a great piece of content – a comprehensive blog post, an insightful whitepaper, or a popular webinar – it makes sense to get as much mileage out of it as possible. This is where content repurposing comes in: transforming existing content into new formats to reach a wider audience, reinforce your message, and cater to different learning or consumption preferences. AI can be a fantastic assistant in this process, helping you efficiently identify repurposing opportunities and even automate parts of the transformation.

Why Repurpose Content?

- **Reach New Audiences:** People consume content in different ways. Some prefer reading long articles, others prefer watching videos, listening to podcasts, or scanning quick social media updates. Repurposing allows you to present the same core message in various formats to connect with these different segments.

- **Reinforce Your Message:** Seeing or hearing information in multiple formats can help reinforce learning and recall.
- **Improve SEO:** Having your core ideas presented in different formats across various platforms can improve your online visibility and search engine rankings for related keywords.
- **Save Time and Resources:** It's often quicker and more cost-effective to repurpose existing, proven content than to create something entirely new from scratch every single time.

How AI Helps with Content Repurposing:

- **Summarization for Different Formats:** AI can quickly summarize long-form content (like a blog post or ebook chapter) into key takeaways. These summaries can then be used as:
    - Social media posts (e.g., a Twitter thread, a LinkedIn update, an Instagram carousel).
    - Bullet points for an email newsletter.
    - Talking points for a short video or podcast segment.
- **Extracting Key Quotes and Snippets:** AI can identify impactful quotes or concise snippets from your existing content that can be used as standalone social media graphics, pull quotes in articles, or soundbites.
- **Generating Outlines or Scripts from Existing Content:** AI can analyze a blog post or article and generate an outline for a video script or a podcast episode based on its main sections and key points. This gives you a structured starting point for creating audio-visual content.
- **Transforming Text to Other Formats (with human oversight):**

  - **Text-to-Speech:** AI can convert written articles into audio files, creating instant podcast episodes or audio versions of your blog posts.
  - **Text-to-Video (Basic):** Some AI tools can take text and create simple videos by matching it with stock footage or animations and adding voiceover. These often require significant human refinement but can be a starting point.
  - **Creating Presentation Slides:** AI can help extract key points from a document to create an initial draft of a PowerPoint or Google Slides presentation.
- **Identifying Repurposing Opportunities:** Some AI analytics tools can highlight your most popular existing content pieces, which are often the best candidates for repurposing since you already know the topic resonates with your audience.

Simple Example in Action:

Let's say you wrote a successful, in-depth blog post titled "10 Essential Financial Tips for New Small Business Owners." It's 3,000 words long and has received great feedback.

Using AI, you could repurpose this one piece of content in numerous ways:

1. **AI Summarization:** Generate a 300-word summary for your email newsletter and a series of 10 individual tweets, each highlighting one financial tip.
2. **AI Quote Extraction:** Identify 5 powerful quotes from the article to turn into shareable graphics for Instagram and Facebook.
3. **AI Script Outline:** Use AI to create an outline for a 10-minute YouTube video where you discuss the 10 tips in a more conversational format.
4. **AI Text-to-Speech:** Convert the original blog post into an audio file that people can listen to on the go.

5. **AI Presentation Draft:** Extract the 10 main tips and their brief explanations to create a first draft of a slide deck for a short webinar or workshop.

By leveraging AI for content repurposing, you significantly extend the life and reach of your best work. It allows you to efficiently create a diverse range of content assets from a single core piece, ensuring your valuable insights connect with more people in the formats they prefer, all while saving you considerable time and effort.

Section 2.3: Optimizing Content with AI

Creating great content is a huge step, but it's not the final one. If your brilliant blog post, insightful article, or engaging video doesn't reach the right audience or fails to achieve its intended goal (like generating leads or making sales), then a lot of your hard work might go unnoticed. This is where content optimization comes in – the process of refining your content to ensure it's discoverable, engaging, and effective. And once again, Artificial Intelligence can be your powerful, data-driven partner in this crucial stage.

Think of AI in content optimization as a meticulous editor and a savvy strategist rolled into one. It can analyze how your content is performing, compare it against benchmarks, and provide specific, actionable recommendations to improve its impact. For busy business owners, AI takes the guesswork out of optimization, helping you make informed decisions to maximize the return on your content investment.

In this section, we'll explore the "simple AI secrets" to optimizing your content for better results. We'll cover:

- **AI-Driven A/B Testing and Multivariate Testing:** Experimenting to find what works best.
- **AI for Content Personalization:** Tailoring content to individual user preferences.

- **AI-Powered SEO Optimization (Post-Creation):** Fine-tuning your content for search engines.
- **AI for Analyzing Content Performance and Engagement:** Understanding how users interact with your content.
- **Predictive Content Analytics:** Getting a glimpse into future content performance.
- **The Iterative Loop:** Embracing continuous improvement with AI.

Let's delve into how AI can help you polish your content until it shines and delivers the results you're looking for.

AI Techniques for Continuous Content Improvement

Content optimization isn't a one-time task; it's an ongoing process of learning and refinement. AI provides the tools to make this process more efficient and effective.

AI-Driven A/B Testing and Multivariate Testing: Finding the Winning Formula

A/B testing (also known as split testing) is a common marketing practice where you compare two versions of something (like a webpage headline, an email subject line, or a call-to-action button) to see which one performs better. Multivariate testing is similar but allows you to test multiple variations of multiple elements simultaneously. While incredibly valuable, manually setting up and analyzing these tests can be complex and time-consuming.

How AI Enhances A/B and Multivariate Testing:

- **Generating Variations:** AI can quickly generate multiple variations of headlines, calls-to-action, email copy, or even different layouts for you to test. This saves you the creative effort of coming up with all the test versions yourself.

- **Automated Test Management:** Some AI-powered platforms can manage the testing process, automatically distributing traffic between variations and collecting performance data.
- **Faster Analysis and Insights:** AI can analyze the results of these tests much faster than a human, identifying statistically significant winners and providing insights into why certain variations performed better. It can look at complex interactions between different elements in multivariate tests that would be hard for a human to decipher.
- **Dynamic Optimization:** Some advanced AI tools can even dynamically adjust content in real-time based on ongoing A/B test results, automatically favoring the version that is performing best for the majority of your audience, or even for specific audience segments.

Simple Example in Action:

Imagine you have a landing page for a new online course. You want to test which headline converts more visitors into sign-ups. Instead of manually creating two headlines and splitting your traffic, an AI tool could:

1. Help you generate five different headline options based on best practices and your course description.
2. Automatically show these different headlines to different visitors.
3. Track which headline leads to the most course registrations.
4. After a statistically significant period, declare the winning headline and perhaps even automatically set it as the default for all future visitors.

AI-driven A/B and multivariate testing allows you to experiment more broadly and efficiently, continuously fine-tuning your content and calls-to-action to achieve the best possible conversion rates. It takes the heavy lifting out of experimentation, so you can focus on implementing what works.

AI for Content Personalization: Tailoring Experiences for Individuals

In today's crowded digital landscape, generic content often gets ignored. Customers increasingly expect personalized experiences – content, offers, and recommendations that are relevant to their specific interests, needs, and past behavior. Delivering this level of personalization at scale can be a massive challenge for businesses, but AI offers powerful solutions to make it achievable.

Content personalization means dynamically tailoring elements of your content to individual users or specific audience segments. This goes beyond simply addressing someone by their first name in an email. It involves showing them the most relevant articles, product recommendations, or calls-to-action based on what AI has learned about them.

How AI Enables Content Personalization:

- **Analyzing User Data:** AI algorithms can analyze a wealth of user data, including:
  - **Behavioral Data:** Pages visited, content viewed, links clicked, time spent on site, purchase history, search queries used on your site.
  - **Demographic Data:** Age, location, gender (if ethically and legally collected and relevant).
  - **Contextual Data:** Time of day, device used, referral source.
- **Creating User Segments or Individual Profiles:** Based on this data, AI can group users into segments with similar characteristics or even build individual user profiles that capture their unique preferences and interests.

- **Predicting User Intent and Preferences:** AI can use machine learning models to predict what a user might be interested in next, what problem they are trying to solve, or what products they are most likely to purchase.
- **Dynamically Adjusting Content:** Based on these predictions and profiles, AI-powered systems can then automatically adjust the content a user sees. This could include:

    - **Personalized Article Recommendations:** Showing related articles or blog posts that align with the user's past reading history (think of how news sites or platforms like Medium suggest content).
    - **Personalized Product Recommendations:** Displaying products within a blog post or on a webpage that are relevant to the user's browsing or purchase history (common in e-commerce).
    - **Tailored Calls-to-Action (CTAs):** Showing different CTAs to different users based on where they are in the customer journey (e.g., a new visitor might see a CTA to download a free guide, while a returning customer might see a CTA for a product demo).
    - **Personalized On-Site Search Results:** Prioritizing search results on your website based on the user's past behavior or expressed interests.
    - **Dynamic Website Content:** Changing images, headlines, or even entire sections of a webpage to better match the visitor's profile.

Simple Example in Action:

Imagine you run a travel blog that covers various destinations and travel styles (e.g., budget backpacking, luxury resorts, adventure travel, family vacations).

- A user who has previously read several articles about "budget backpacking in Southeast Asia" and clicked on links for hostel bookings might, on their next visit, see a homepage featuring your latest posts on backpacking, recommendations for budget travel gear (if you have affiliate links), and a CTA for your "Ultimate Guide to Backpacking Southeast Asia."
- Another user who has primarily read articles about "luxury family resorts in the Caribbean" and searched for "all-inclusive family packages" would see a completely different set of featured articles, perhaps highlighting family-friendly luxury destinations, and a CTA for a consultation on planning a high-end family vacation.

AI-driven personalization makes your content feel more relevant and valuable to each individual user. This can lead to increased engagement, longer time on site, higher conversion rates, and greater customer loyalty. While highly sophisticated personalization might seem like something only large corporations can do, many marketing automation platforms and even some website content management systems are now incorporating AI-powered personalization features that are becoming more accessible to smaller businesses.

The key is to start with understanding your audience and collecting relevant data (always with a focus on privacy and consent), and then exploring how AI tools can help you deliver more tailored and meaningful content experiences.

AI-Powered SEO Optimization (Post-Creation): Fine-Tuning for Discoverability

Search Engine Optimization (SEO) is vital for ensuring your content gets found by people searching online. While some AI writing assistants offer basic SEO suggestions during content creation, dedicated AI-powered SEO tools provide more in-depth analysis and recommendations for optimizing your content *after* it has been drafted or even published. These tools help you fine-tune your content to improve its chances of ranking higher in search engine results pages (SERPs) for your target keywords.

How AI Helps with Post-Creation SEO Optimization:

- **On-Page SEO Analysis:** AI SEO tools can analyze your published content (or a draft) against the current top-ranking pages for your target keywords. They assess various on-page factors, such as:
    - **Keyword Usage:** Is your primary keyword used appropriately in the title, headings, body text, and meta description? Are you using relevant secondary keywords (LSI keywords – Latent Semantic Indexing keywords, which are terms semantically related to your main keyword)? AI can identify if you've overused (keyword stuffing) or underused important terms.
    - **Content Structure and Readability:** Is your content well-structured with clear headings (H1, H2, H3)? Is it easy to read and understand? AI can assess readability scores and suggest improvements.
    - **Meta Description and Title Tag Optimization:** Are your meta descriptions compelling and within the optimal length? Are your title tags optimized for clicks and keywords?
    - **Internal Linking:** Are you effectively linking to other relevant content on your own website? AI can suggest internal linking opportunities to help distribute link equity and guide users (and search engines) through your site.
    - **Image Optimization:** Are your images properly tagged with alt text that includes relevant keywords?
- **Content Gap Analysis (vs. Competitors):** AI can compare your content to top-ranking competitor pages for the same key-

words and identify specific topics, subtopics, or entities that they cover but you don't. This helps you understand what information search engines (and users) expect to see for that query, allowing you to enrich your content to make it more comprehensive.

- **Semantic Content Optimization:** Modern SEO is less about exact keyword matching and more about covering a topic comprehensively and semantically. AI tools can suggest related terms and concepts that you should include in your content to demonstrate its topical authority to search engines.
- **Technical SEO Insights (Sometimes):** While primarily focused on content, some AI SEO tools might also flag basic technical SEO issues on a page that could hinder its performance (e.g., slow loading speed, mobile-friendliness issues, though dedicated technical SEO tools are better for this).

Simple Example in Action:

Suppose you've written a blog post about "The Benefits of Drip Irrigation for Home Gardens." You've published it, but it's not ranking well.

You could use an AI SEO optimization tool, inputting your blog post URL and the target keyword "benefits of drip irrigation." The AI tool might analyze your content and compare it to the top 5 articles currently ranking for that keyword. It could then provide recommendations like:

- "Your article mentions water saving, but top competitors also discuss reduced weed growth and prevention of fungal diseases. Consider adding sections on these benefits."
- "The keyword 'drip irrigation system' appears 15 times. This might be considered keyword stuffing. Try to vary your language and use synonyms."
- "You have no internal links to your product page for drip irrigation kits. Add a relevant internal link."

- "Consider adding a section on 'how to install a simple drip irrigation system' as this is a common related query."
- "Your meta description is too short. Expand it to include more compelling reasons to click."

By implementing these AI-driven suggestions, you can significantly improve your content's relevance, comprehensiveness, and on-page SEO factors, increasing its likelihood of ranking higher in search results and attracting more organic traffic.

AI-powered SEO optimization tools provide actionable, data-backed recommendations that take much of the guesswork out of SEO. They help you understand what search engines are looking for and how to refine your content to meet those expectations, ultimately making your valuable content more discoverable.

AI for Analyzing Content Performance and Engagement: Understanding How Users Interact

Creating and optimizing content is only part of the equation; you also need to understand how your audience is actually interacting with it. Are they reading your articles to the end? Which sections are they skipping? What actions do they take after consuming your content? Traditional analytics can provide some of this data, but AI can help you dive deeper, uncovering more nuanced insights into user engagement and content performance.

How AI Enhances Content Performance Analysis:

- **Deeper Engagement Metrics:** Beyond basic metrics like page views and bounce rates, AI can help analyze more granular engagement signals. This includes:
  - **Scroll Depth:** How far down a page are users typically scrolling? This can indicate if your content is engag-

ing enough to keep them reading or if there are drop-off points.

- **Time on Page (with context):** AI can help differentiate between someone who genuinely spent 5 minutes reading an article versus someone who left the tab open and walked away. It might look at active engagement signals like mouse movements or clicks.
- **Heatmaps:** AI-powered heatmap tools visually represent where users are clicking, moving their mouse, and how far they scroll on a page. This can reveal which elements are attracting attention and which are being ignored.
- **Video Engagement:** For video content, AI can analyze watch time, drop-off points, re-watches of certain sections, and click-through rates on in-video calls-to-action.

- **Identifying High-Performing Content Segments:** AI can analyze which specific parts of your content (e.g., particular paragraphs in an article, specific scenes in a video) are most engaging or lead to the most conversions. This helps you understand what truly resonates with your audience.
- **Understanding User Journeys:** AI can help map out the typical paths users take through your website after consuming a particular piece of content. Do they navigate to related articles? Visit a product page? Sign up for your newsletter? Understanding these journeys can help you optimize your content funnels.
- **Attribution Analysis:** AI can assist in more accurately attributing conversions (like leads or sales) to specific pieces of content, especially when users interact with multiple touchpoints before converting. This helps you understand the true ROI of your content efforts.
- **Sentiment Analysis on Comments and Feedback:** AI can analyze the sentiment expressed in comments on your blog

posts or social media shares of your content, giving you a qualitative understanding of how your audience is reacting.

Simple Example in Action:

Let's say you have a long, comprehensive guide on your website about "Choosing the Right Project Management Software for Small Businesses." AI-powered analytics might reveal:

- **Scroll Depth Analysis:** Most users only scroll about 60% of the way through the article.
- **Heatmap Analysis:** The section comparing the top 3 software options gets a lot of clicks and mouse hovers, while an earlier section on the history of project management is largely ignored.
- **User Journey:** A significant number of users who read the comparison section then click through to your individual review of "Software A."
- **Video Engagement (if you have a summary video):** Viewers consistently drop off during a lengthy explanation of a complex feature in one of the software options.

These AI-driven insights could lead to optimization strategies like:

- Moving the popular software comparison section higher up in the article.
- Shortening or removing the less engaging history section.
- Adding a more prominent call-to-action within the comparison section to read the full review of "Software A."
- Editing the summary video to be more concise when explaining complex features, or adding timestamps so viewers can skip to sections of interest.

By using AI to gain a deeper understanding of content performance and user engagement, you can make data-informed decisions to refine your existing content, improve user experience, and create new content that is even more effective at capturing and retaining audience attention.

Predictive Content Analytics: Getting a Glimpse into the Future

While analyzing past performance is crucial, what if you could get an idea of how your content might perform *before* you even hit publish, or predict which of your existing pieces are likely to gain or lose traction in the near future? This is the realm of predictive content analytics, an emerging area where AI is beginning to offer some exciting capabilities.

Predictive analytics uses machine learning models, historical data, and current trend analysis to make forecasts about future outcomes. In the context of content, this could mean:

- **Forecasting Potential Performance:** Some AI tools attempt to predict the potential reach, engagement, or even conversion rate of a piece of content before it's published. They might analyze factors like the topic, headline strength, keyword competitiveness, readability, and current trends to give you a projected score or likelihood of success. This can help you prioritize which content pieces to focus on or identify areas for improvement pre-publication.

- **Identifying Content Decay:** AI can monitor your existing content library and predict which articles or pages are likely to see a decline in traffic or engagement soon. This could be due to seasonality, emerging competitor content, or shifts in search engine algorithms. This early warning allows you to proactively update or refresh that content before its performance significantly drops.

- **Suggesting Optimal Publishing Times:** Based on historical engagement data for your audience and broader trends, AI might predict the best days or times to publish certain types of content to maximize visibility and interaction.

Important Considerations for Predictive Analytics:

- **It's a Forecast, Not a Guarantee:** Predictions are based on probabilities and historical data; they are not crystal balls. Many factors can influence actual content performance.
- **Data Quality is Key:** The accuracy of predictive models heavily depends on the quality and quantity of the data they are trained on. If your historical data is sparse or messy, predictions might be less reliable.
- **Still an Evolving Field:** While promising, predictive content analytics is still a relatively new area, and the tools are continuously improving. It's often best used as one input among others in your decision-making process, rather than the sole driver.

Simple Example in Action:

Imagine you have three blog post drafts ready to be finalized and published. An AI tool with predictive capabilities might analyze each draft and provide a "potential engagement score." Draft A gets a high score, Draft B a medium score, and Draft C a low score. This doesn't mean you should discard Draft C, but it might prompt you to:

- Prioritize finalizing and publishing Draft A.
- Re-examine Draft C: Is the topic less relevant? Is the headline weak? Could it be improved based on the AI's feedback before investing more time in it?

Predictive content analytics offers a tantalizing glimpse into using AI to be more proactive and strategic in your content efforts, helping you allocate your resources more effectively and anticipate future needs.

The Iterative Loop: Create, Measure, Learn, Optimize with AI

The true power of using AI in content optimization lies in embracing an iterative loop: **Create -> Measure -> Learn -> Optimize.** This is a continuous cycle of improvement, and AI can play a role in each step.

1. **Create:** You create your content, perhaps with AI assistance for drafting or research (as discussed in Section 2.2).
2. **Measure:** You publish your content and use AI-powered analytics tools (as discussed in this section) to measure its performance and how users are engaging with it.
3. **Learn:** AI helps you extract meaningful insights from that performance data – what's working, what's not, why, and for whom.
4. **Optimize:** Based on these learnings, you use AI-driven suggestions (or your own informed decisions) to optimize existing content or to inform the creation of new, better content. And then the cycle begins again.

AI makes this iterative loop more efficient, more data-driven, and more scalable. It helps you move away from a "publish and pray" approach to a more strategic, responsive, and continuously improving content marketing operation.

AI as Your Content Optimization Strategist

Creating content is just the beginning; optimizing it is how you ensure it achieves its goals. In this section, we've explored how AI can act as your data-driven strategist, helping you refine your content for maximum discoverability, engagement, and effectiveness.

The "simple AI secrets" for content optimization include:

- **AI-Driven A/B and Multivariate Testing** to efficiently experiment with different content variations and identify what resonates best with your audience.
- **AI for Content Personalization** to tailor content experiences to individual users, making your messages more relevant and impactful.
- **AI-Powered SEO Optimization (Post-Creation)** to fine-tune your content for search engines by analyzing on-page factors, comparing against competitors, and ensuring topical comprehensiveness.
- **AI for Analyzing Content Performance and Engagement** to gain deeper insights into how users are interacting with your content, from scroll depth to heatmap analysis.
- **Predictive Content Analytics** to get a potential glimpse into future content performance or identify content decay, allowing for proactive adjustments.

By embracing the **iterative loop of create, measure, learn, and optimize** with AI as your partner, you transform your content from static pieces into dynamic assets that continuously adapt and improve. This data-informed approach to optimization is key to maximizing the ROI of your content marketing efforts and ensuring your valuable messages reach and resonate with the right people.

My Personal Take on AI for Content Marketing (From Jason's Desk):

When I first started using AI for content creation with a B2B SaaS client, we made a critical mistake: we let the AI write entire blog posts without enough human oversight. The content was grammatically perfect and SEO-optimized, but it was completely soulless. It missed the nuanced pain points and the specific language our ideal customer profile was using.

What Actually Happened: Engagement dropped by 30%. Our bounce rate went up. Readers could tell it was generic, even if they couldn't explain why. We had sacrificed authority for efficiency.

What I Learned: AI is a brilliant research assistant and a tireless first-draft writer, but it is not a replacement for your expertise. Its job is to handle the 80% of commodity work so you can focus on the 20% of unique insight that only you can provide.

What You Should Do: Always add a "human insight layer" to AI-generated content. Inject your personal stories, specific client examples, and contrarian perspectives. That's what makes content valuable and builds a brand people trust.

Learn from my mistakes and make sure you give AI tools or AI agents the right context it needs to write or create content in your tone, style, and voice that you need for your brand.

AI Prompts: Chapter 2

How to Use These Prompts

Each prompt below is designed to be copied directly into your favorite AI tool (ChatGPT, Claude, Grok, or Gemini). Simply:

1.Copy the entire prompt (including the bracketed placeholders)

2. Replace the [bracketed sections] with your specific information

3.Paste into your AI tool and hit enter

4.Refine the output by asking follow-up questions or requesting revisions

These are battle-tested prompts I use with organizations around the world. They're designed to give you professional-quality outputs that you can use immediately in your business.

Prompt 2.1: Generate a 30-Day Content Calendar

I need a 30-day content calendar for my [type of business] targeting [specific audience].

Our business:

- Industry: [your industry]
- Main value proposition: [what makes you unique]
- Target audience pain points: [list 3-5 main challenges your audience faces]
- Content channels: [blog, LinkedIn, email newsletter, etc.]
- Brand voice: [e.g., professional but approachable, witty and bold, empathetic and supportive]

Create a 30-day content calendar with:

- 4 blog post topics (with headlines and key points to cover)
- 12 social media post ideas (3 per week)
- 4 email newsletter topics
- 2 long-form content ideas (e.g., guides, case studies)

For each piece of content, include:

- The headline or hook
- The main points or outline
- The primary keyword or SEO focus
- The call-to-action
- Which audience pain point it addresses

Make sure the content builds on itself and tells a cohesive story over the 30 days.

Prompt 2.2: Transform One Piece of Content into 10 Formats

I have the following piece of content that I want to repurpose into multiple formats:

[Paste your original content here - could be a blog post, video transcript, podcast episode, or article]

Transform this into 10 different content pieces optimized for different channels:

1. A LinkedIn post (300 words max, engaging hook)
2. A Twitter/X thread (8-10 tweets)
3. An Instagram caption with 5 relevant hashtags
4. A 60-second video script
5. An email newsletter (subject line + 200-word body)

6. 3 quote graphics (pull the most impactful statements)
7. A one-page infographic outline (key stats and takeaways)
8. A podcast episode outline (5 main talking points)
9. A LinkedIn carousel post (5-7 slides with headlines)
10. A FAQ section (5 questions and answers)

Maintain the core message and brand voice, but optimize each format for its specific platform and audience behavior.

Prompt 2.3: Write High-Converting Blog Posts

Write a comprehensive blog post for my [type of business] on the topic: [your topic].

Target audience: [describe your ideal reader]

Main keyword: [primary SEO keyword]

Secondary keywords: [2-3 related keywords]

Goal of the post: [e.g., generate leads, educate, build authority, drive product sales]

Structure the blog post with:

- An attention-grabbing headline (provide 3 options)
- A compelling introduction that hooks the reader (100-150 words)
- 5-7 main sections with H2 subheadings
- Practical examples, statistics, or case studies in each section
- Actionable takeaways or tips
- A strong conclusion with a clear call-to-action
- Meta description for SEO (155 characters max)

Tone: [professional, conversational, authoritative, friendly - choose one]

Length: Approximately [1,500 / 2,000 / 2,500] words

Include natural keyword placement for SEO without keyword stuffing. Make it valuable and engaging for human readers first, search engines second.

Prompt 2.4: Create Customer Persona Research Summary

I need help creating a detailed customer persona for my [type of business].

What I know about my customers:

- Demographics: [age range, location, job titles, income level]
- What they buy from us: [products/services]
- Common questions they ask: [list 3-5 questions]
- Where we find them: [marketing channels that work]

Based on this information, create a comprehensive customer persona that includes:

1. **Persona Overview**: Name, age, job title, and background
2. **Goals and Aspirations**: What they're trying to achieve (professional and personal)
3. **Pain Points and Challenges**: The top 5 problems they face daily
4. **Buying Behavior**: How they research and make purchase decisions
5. **Content Preferences**: What type of content they consume and where
6. **Objections**: The top 3 reasons they might not buy from us
7. **Messaging That Resonates**: The exact language and phrases that speak to them
8. **A Day in Their Life**: A narrative description of their typical day and where our solution fits

Also provide 5 content topic ideas specifically designed to attract and engage this persona.

For prompts and bonus resources, visit **thejasonfleagle.com/blueprint-resources**. You can copy and paste the prompts from there—no retyping needed.

| 3 |

AI for Social Media Marketing

Introduction: Social Media Overwhelm? AI to the Rescue!

Ever feel like you're drowning in a sea of social media demands? You're not alone. For many small business owners and entrepreneurs, keeping up with the constant need for fresh content, engaging with followers across multiple platforms, and trying to figure out if any of it is actually working can feel like a full-time job in itself. It's a whirlwind of hashtags, algorithms, and the pressure to be constantly "on." You know social media is important, a place where your customers are hanging out, but how do you manage it all without losing your mind or your entire marketing budget? Many feel the pressure to be everywhere, all the time, leading to burnout and a sense that their efforts are scattered and ineffective. The digital landscape is noisy, and cutting through that noise to genuinely connect with your audience requires not just effort, but smart strategies.

What if I told you there's a secret weapon that can help you conquer this social media mountain? And no, it's not some super-expensive, overly complicated tech that requires a PhD to understand. It's Artificial Intelligence, or AI, and it's more accessible and user-friendly than you might think. Forget the sci-fi movie robots; think of AI as your super-smart, incredibly efficient virtual assistant, ready to help you work smarter, not harder, on your social media marketing. As we'll explore, tools like ChatGPT, which you might have heard about for anything from coding to telling jokes, are now powerful allies in crafting effective social media strategies. The aim isn't to replace your unique human touch, but to augment your capabilities, allowing you to achieve more with less stress.

In this chapter, we're going to pull back the curtain on some simple AI secrets that can transform your social media efforts from a time-draining chore into a powerful engine for business growth. You'll discover how AI, including versatile platforms like ChatGPT, can help you:

- **Create engaging content almost effortlessly:** Say goodbye to writer's block and hello to a stream of fresh ideas and compelling posts. We'll look at how AI can help generate social media posts that are more engaging and personalized, increasing the chances of them being shared and liked by followers, a key aspect covered in modern AI marketing courses.
- **Automate tedious tasks intelligently:** Imagine scheduling posts at the perfect times or handling common questions without lifting a finger, freeing you up for the stuff only you can do. This isn't just about saving time; it's about optimizing your output for maximum impact.
- **Gain deeper insights from your social data:** Move beyond just counting likes and followers to truly understanding what your audience wants and how your efforts are paying off. AI can help analyze patterns and sentiments that would be nearly impossible for a human to discern at scale.
- **Boost your follower growth and engagement:** Learn how to connect with more of the right people and build a thriving online community by leveraging AI to understand and cater to their preferences more effectively.

This chapter will draw upon practical applications and insights, similar to those found in comprehensive AI and ChatGPT courses designed for marketing professionals, to provide you with actionable strategies. The goal is to demystify AI for social media and show you how to integrate these powerful tools into your daily workflow seamlessly.

So, if you're ready to stop feeling overwhelmed by social media and start making it work for your business in a simpler, more effective way, you're in the right place. Let's dive into how AI can become your trusted partner in crafting a social media presence that not only looks great but also delivers real results, turning potential social media chaos into a well-oiled, growth-driving machine.

B. AI Tools for Intelligent Scheduling and Content Curation

Beyond simply queuing up posts you've already created, modern AI-powered social media tools bring a new level of intelligence to both scheduling your own content and discovering and curating relevant third-party content to share with your audience. This ensures your feed remains active, valuable, diverse, and optimized for engagement without requiring constant manual intervention. It's about creating a smart, semi-autonomous content pipeline.

Overview of AI-Powered Scheduling Platforms: Smart Timing and Efficient Workflows

Many social media management platforms now incorporate AI to enhance their scheduling capabilities, moving far beyond basic date-and-time selection. These platforms offer features designed to maximize your content"s impact and streamline your workflow, making your social media management more strategic and less reactive. When evaluating these tools, look for:

- **Best-Time-to-Post Suggestions:** As discussed earlier, AI analyzes your audience's activity patterns on each platform and your historical engagement data to recommend the optimal times to publish your content. This isn"t a generic best practice; it"s tailored to *your* specific audience. Tools like **SocialBee** are noted for suggesting the best times to post based on past performance. Many comprehensive platforms like **Sprout Social**, **Hootsuite**, and **Buffer** also offer similar AI-driven scheduling optimization, often showing you a heatmap of when your audience is most engaged.

- **Content Queues and Categories:** Organize your approved content into categories (e.g., "Blog Posts," "Industry News," "Behind-the-Scenes," "User-Generated Content," "Promotional Offers," "Educational Tips"). AI can then help you create a balanced posting schedule, ensuring a good mix of content types goes out regularly, preventing your feed from becoming too monotonous or overly promotional. **SmarterQueue** is a tool that emphasizes its intelligent content categorization and evergreen recycling features, allowing you to set rules for how often content from each category should be posted.
- **Bulk Scheduling with AI Optimization:** Upload multiple posts at once (e.g., from a spreadsheet or by connecting to a content library), and let the AI distribute them across your calendar at optimal times or according to predefined category schedules. This is a massive time-saver for campaigns or when you have a batch of content ready.
- **AI-Powered Performance Predictions:** Some advanced tools, like **FeedHive** (mentioned by Zapier), offer AI-powered performance predictions to help you tune your posts for maximum engagement *even before* they are scheduled. This might involve suggestions for improving copy, visuals, or hashtag choices based on what the AI predicts will perform well.
- **Content Recycling and Evergreen Posting:** Not all content has a short shelf life. AI can identify your top-performing past content (evergreen content like how-to guides, foundational industry insights, or popular case studies) and intelligently reschedule it to reach new audiences or remind existing followers, extending the lifespan of your best work. **FeedHive** is also highlighted for its AI-powered content recycling, ensuring your best pieces continue to deliver value.
- **Visual Calendar Interface:** A clear, drag-and-drop visual content calendar makes it easy to see your schedule at a glance,

identify gaps, and make adjustments as needed. Most leading schedulers like **SocialPilot**, **Buffer**, and **Sprout Social** offer this, often color-coded by platform or content category.

Practical Example: The Busy Bakery Owner

A local bakery owner wants to maintain an active presence on Instagram and Facebook but has limited time. She uses an AI-powered scheduler to:

1. Create content categories: "New Products," "Customer Spotlights (UGC)," "Baking Tips," "Holiday Specials," and "Behind the Scenes."
2. Bulk uploads photos and pre-written captions (perhaps drafted with an AI writing assistant) for the month into these categories.
3. Lets the AI tool determine the optimal posting times for Instagram (e.g., evenings and weekends when people are looking for treats) and Facebook (e.g., lunchtimes and early evenings).
4. Sets rules for the AI to post one "New Product" shot every Monday, a "Customer Spotlight" every Wednesday, a "Baking Tip" every Friday, and sprinkle "Behind the Scenes" content throughout the week, ensuring a varied feed.
5. The AI also identifies her most popular past posts (e.g., a video on frosting techniques) and automatically re-shares them every few months to capture new followers.

This system allows her to spend just a few hours a month on social media planning, while AI ensures a consistent and optimized posting schedule.

AI for Content Curation: Keeping Your Feed Fresh and Valuable

Sharing only your own content can sometimes feel overly promotional or repetitive. Curating and sharing high-quality, relevant content from other reputable sources within your industry (e.g., articles, studies, infographics, videos from non-competing thought leaders) can add significant value for your audience, position you as a knowledgeable resource and hub of information, and help fill gaps in your content calendar. However, finding truly great content to curate can be as time-consuming as creating it yourself. AI can make this process much more efficient.

AI-powered content curation tools work by:

- **Monitoring Sources:** Scanning blogs, news sites, industry publications, academic journals, and even social media for content relevant to keywords, topics, or specific sources you specify.
- **Filtering and Relevance Scoring:** Using AI (often NLP and machine learning) to assess the quality, credibility, and relevance of potential content to your audience and brand. Some tools can even analyze sentiment to avoid sharing negatively skewed articles unintentionally.
- **Suggesting Content:** Presenting you with a feed of suggested articles, blog posts, or videos to share, often with a summary or key takeaways highlighted by the AI.
- **Automated Sharing (with review):** Some tools can even automatically add approved curated content to your posting schedule, often allowing you to add your own commentary or introductory text.

Platforms like **Quuu** are specifically known for curated content automation, finding relevant third-party content (often hand-curated by humans initially, then categorized by AI) and integrating with schedulers like Buffer or Hootsuite. **ContentStudio**, mentioned by Zapier, is strong in content discovery and staying on top of content topics, which aids curation by suggesting articles, videos, and GIFs. **SocialPilot** is also often cited as a cost-effective tool with comprehensive content curation features, allowing you to find and schedule relevant content from various sources. **Sprinklr**, in its blog, mentions that its platform helps find and share relevant content faster using AI, by sifting through millions of articles to surface the most relevant ones for your brand.

Simple Secret: **Use AI content curation to become a trusted resource, not just a broadcaster. Set up AI to monitor key industry blogs, news sites, and thought leaders. Review the AI's suggestions daily or weekly, add your own insightful comment or question to the curated piece, and schedule it. This shows your audience you're engaged with your industry and dedicated to bringing them value beyond your own products or services.**

By using AI for intelligent scheduling of your own content and smart curation of external content, you ensure that your social media presence is not only consistent but also rich with a variety of valuable information, posted at times when your audience is most likely to see and engage with it. This strategic automation frees you to focus on creating high-impact original content and building deeper, more meaningful relationships with your followers.

C. Automating Engagement (Carefully!): The Human-AI Partnership

While AI can automate many aspects of social media posting and scheduling, automating direct engagement with your audience – the comments, messages, and conversations – requires a much more nuanced and careful approach. Genuine human connection is the cornerstone of strong community building on social media. People follow and interact with brands they feel a connection to, and overly robotic or impersonal automated responses can quickly erode trust and alienate your audience. However, AI can still play a valuable role in managing initial interactions, filtering communications, and providing quick answers to common questions, provided it's implemented thoughtfully and with clear human oversight. It's about creating a human-AI partnership where AI handles the volume and repetition, and humans handle the nuance and relationship-building.

AI Chatbots for Basic Social Media Interactions: Your First Line of Response

AI-powered chatbots can be integrated with your social media messaging platforms (like Facebook Messenger, Instagram DMs, or even X/Twitter DMs) to handle common, repetitive inquiries. This can be particularly useful for:

- **Answering Frequently Asked Questions (FAQs):** Chatbots can be trained on your business's FAQs (e.g., store hours, shipping policies, return procedures, basic product information, service areas) to provide instant answers to customers, 24/7, even outside of business hours. This immediate responsiveness can significantly improve customer satisfaction.
- **Initial Lead Qualification:** They can ask preliminary questions to gather information from potential leads (e.g., budget, timeline, specific needs) before passing them on to a human sales representative. This ensures that your sales team spends their time on more qualified prospects.
- **Directing Users to Resources:** Chatbots can guide users to relevant pages on your website, specific blog posts, help articles, video tutorials, or product pages, helping users find the information they need quickly without human intervention.
- **Taking Simple Orders or Bookings:** For some businesses, chatbots can be configured to handle basic transactions like booking an appointment or taking a simple order for a standardized product.

Platforms like **Chatfuel** are well-known for building AI chatbots for Facebook and Telegram, enabling businesses to provide instant replies and capture leads, as mentioned by Great Scott Social Media and Sprinklr. **Metricool** also notes that AI-driven chatbots can handle customer queries and recommend products. Many other platforms like **Tidio**, **ManyChat**, or even custom solutions using **Dialogflow** (from Google) or **Microsoft Bot Framework** allow for the creation of sophisticated chatbots. Your course notes also highlight "Generating content for chatbots" and "Generating customer service responses" as key uses for ChatGPT, which can be the engine behind some of these chatbot interactions.

When implementing chatbots, it"s crucial to:

- **Clearly Disclose It's a Bot:** Users should generally know when they are interacting with an AI to manage expectations. A simple "Hi, I'm [Brand Name]\"s automated assistant! I can help with X, Y, and Z. If you need more help, just type \"speak to a human\"."
- **Design Clear Escalation Paths:** Ensure there's an easy and obvious way for users to connect with a human if the bot can't help, if the query is complex, sensitive, or if the user simply prefers to speak to a person. Frustrating a user by trapping them in a bot loop is a sure way to lose them.
- **Train and Test Thoroughly:** Continuously train your chatbot with new information, common customer questions, and variations of how those questions are asked. Test its responses rigorously to ensure accuracy, a helpful tone, and that it aligns with your brand voice.
- **Focus on Simple, Repetitive Tasks:** Don't try to make chatbots handle nuanced, emotionally charged, or highly personalized conversations. Their strength lies in efficiency for straightforward interactions.
- **Monitor Interactions:** Regularly review chatbot conversations to identify areas for improvement, common pain points the bot can"t solve, and opportunities to update its knowledge base.

Simple Secret: **Use AI for quick answers to common questions and for guiding users, but always keep a human touch readily available for deeper engagement and complex issues. Think of chatbots as helpful receptionists or triage nurses who can han-**

dle the basics efficiently, freeing up your human team for more meaningful conversations and problem-solving that require empathy and critical thinking.

AI for Comment Moderation (Basic Filtering): Maintaining a Healthy Community

Managing comments on your social media posts can be overwhelming, especially if you have a large or very active audience, or if your content touches on sensitive topics. Unfortunately, not all comments are positive or constructive; spam, abusive language, hate speech, or irrelevant self-promotion can detract from the community experience you're trying to build and can even damage your brand reputation. AI can assist in the initial filtering and management of these comments.

AI-powered comment moderation tools use Natural Language Processing (NLP) and machine learning to:

- **Identify Spam:** Automatically detect and hide or flag comments that are clearly spammy (e.g., repetitive links to unrelated websites, generic promotional messages, strings of emojis or gibberish).
- **Filter Potentially Harmful Content:** Flag comments containing profanity, hate speech, bullying language, or personal attacks based on predefined keyword lists, learned patterns, or sentiment analysis. **Tribe.AI** discusses how AI-powered moderation helps maintain safe online communities by identifying harmful content.
- **Categorize Comments:** Some tools might categorize comments by sentiment (positive, negative, neutral) or topic, helping you prioritize which ones need an urgent human response (e.g., a very negative comment or a customer complaint) versus those that can be addressed later (e.g., a simple positive comment).

Tools like **Smart Moderation** (mentioned by CommentGuard) allow real-time comment monitoring with customizable AI algorithms. **Sprinklr** also provides a robust social media moderation suite, leveraging AI for large enterprises, as noted by Social Factor. **Utopia Analytics** offers AI content moderation software designed to protect platforms from toxic content. Many native social media platforms (like Facebook and Instagram) also have built-in moderation tools that use AI to filter certain types of comments, and you can often add your own keyword blocklists.

However, it is absolutely critical to emphasize the need for **human review and oversight** in comment moderation. AI is not perfect and can sometimes misinterpret context, sarcasm, cultural nuances, or slang. Relying solely on AI for comment deletion could lead to censoring legitimate (though perhaps critical) feedback, accidentally removing valuable user contributions, or failing to identify subtle forms of abuse. Instead, use AI as a first-pass filter and assistant:

- **Automate Hiding/Deleting of Obvious Spam:** For clear-cut spam with no redeeming value, automation can be very effective and save a lot of time.
- **Flag Potentially Problematic Comments for Human Review:** For anything ambiguous, potentially harmful, or negative, AI should flag it for a human moderator to make the final decision on whether to hide, delete, respond, or ignore.
- **Never Auto-Delete Based on Sentiment Alone:** Negative feedback, even if critical, can be valuable. It offers insights into customer dissatisfaction and opportunities to improve or publicly address concerns. Deleting it automatically can damage trust and make your brand appear as though it's hiding something.
- **Develop Clear Moderation Guidelines:** Your human moderators should have clear guidelines on how to handle different types of comments, ensuring consistency and fairness.

Practical Example: The Gaming Community Manager

A popular online gaming company uses AI to help moderate comments on its busy Facebook page and Discord server. The AI automatically filters out and deletes comments containing known spam links and racial slurs. It flags comments with excessive profanity or personal attacks for review by human community managers. This allows the human team to focus on responding to genuine player feedback, answering questions about game updates, and fostering positive interactions, rather than constantly battling spam and overt toxicity. They also use the AI to identify frequently asked questions in comments, which then informs their FAQ chatbot and future content creation.

Automating engagement with AI is about finding the right balance. Use AI to handle the high-volume, low-complexity interactions and to filter out the noise, but always ensure that genuine human interaction, empathy, and strategic oversight remain at the heart of your community management strategy. This approach allows you to be responsive and maintain a positive online environment efficiently, without sacrificing the authenticity that builds lasting relationships and brand loyalty.

A. Understanding Your Audience with AI – The Foundation of Engagement

Before you can create social media content that truly clicks, you need to know who you're talking to. Not just their basic age and location, but what they care about, what problems they face, what language they use, and how they feel about your brand and industry. This deep understanding is the bedrock of engagement. In the past, gathering this intelligence was a painstaking manual process, often relying on surveys, focus groups, or sifting through comments one by one. Today, AI offers powerful shortcuts to get inside your audience's head, providing insights that are both broad and deep, and doing so with remarkable speed.

AI-Powered Social Listening: Hearing What Your Audience *Really* Says

Imagine being a fly on the wall in every online conversation relevant to your business. That's essentially what AI-powered social listening tools allow you to do, but on a massive scale. These tools scan millions of social media posts, blogs, forums, news sites, and review platforms to pick up mentions of your brand, your competitors, specific keywords, or industry trends. But they don't just collect mentions; they use AI, particularly Natural Language Processing (NLP) and machine learning, to analyze the context and sentiment behind those mentions. This is a far cry from simple keyword tracking; it's about understanding the *meaning* and *emotion* behind the words.

This means you can quickly get a pulse on:

- **Trending Topics:** What are people in your niche buzzing about right now? AI can spot emerging trends, helping you create timely and relevant content. For example, if you run a local bakery, AI listening might pick up on a sudden surge in conversations about a new viral baking trend (like a specific type of croissant or cake), allowing you to quickly develop content or even a product to capitalize on that interest.
- **Audience Sentiment:** How do people feel about your brand, products, or a particular campaign? Is the sentiment positive, negative, or neutral? Some advanced tools can even detect nuanced emotions like joy, anger, or frustration. For example, Sprout Social highlights how their AI can analyze billions of data points in seconds, using their "Queries by AI Assist" to focus searches and their "Summarize by AI Assist" to quickly pull key information from lengthy text. They also emphasize their sentiment analysis model's ability to apply aspect-clustering to identify relevant details and calculate sentiment polarity using deep neural networks. This means you could see not just that people are talking about your new software up-

date, but whether they are excited about new features or frustrated by a bug.

- **Customer Pain Points:** What problems are your potential customers struggling with? Listening to their frustrations can reveal unmet needs and inspire content that offers solutions. If you sell project management software, AI listening might reveal that many users in your target audience are complaining about the difficulty of collaborating with remote team members. This insight could fuel blog posts, webinars, or social media content showcasing how your software solves that specific problem.
- **Language and Lingo:** How does your target audience actually talk? AI can help you pick up on the specific words, phrases, slang, and even emojis they use, enabling you to communicate in a more authentic and relatable way. This is crucial for crafting copy that doesn't sound like it's coming from an out-of-touch corporation.
- **Brand Mentions & Health:** Who is talking about you, what are they saying, and where? Tools like Brand24 offer AI-powered access to mentions across a wide array of online sources, helping you protect your brand reputation and understand your share of voice. They specifically mention using sentiment analysis to check how the target audience feels about a brand. This allows for rapid response to negative feedback and amplification of positive mentions.
- **Competitive Insights:** What are your competitors doing well? Where are they falling short? AI social listening can track their activities and audience reactions, giving you valuable competitive intelligence. You might discover that a competitor's new marketing campaign is receiving a lot of negative sentiment due to a perceived lack of authenticity, providing an opportunity for your brand to highlight its own genuine approach.

Several AI tools excel in social listening. For instance, Zapier's review of AI social media management tools mentions platforms like **FeedHive**, which offers AI-powered performance predictions, and **ContentStudio**, which helps in staying on top of content topics. While not purely listening tools, their AI features contribute to understanding audience engagement. Dedicated listening platforms like **Sprinklr** boast of tapping into hundreds of millions of daily conversations to transform unstructured data into actionable insights. **Digimind** also positions itself as a leading social media monitoring and analytics platform to listen, engage, analyze, and report.

Simple Secret: **Use AI listening to find out what your audience *really* wants to talk about, not just what you *think* they want to talk about. It's like having a direct line to their collective consciousness, guiding your content strategy with real data, not guesswork. For example, a small coffee shop owner might *think* their audience wants to hear about new exotic bean origins, but AI listening might reveal that the dominant conversation among local coffee drinkers is actually about finding quiet places to work remotely or the best non-dairy milk alternatives. This insight allows the coffee shop to tailor its social media content (and perhaps even its offerings) to what the audience is actively discussing and seeking.**

AI for Analyzing Audience Demographics & Psychographics: Going Deeper Than Surface-Level Stats

While social listening gives you a broad view of conversations and sentiment, AI can also help you zoom in on the specific characteristics of your audience members. Traditional social media analytics on platforms like Facebook or Instagram provide basic demographic data – age, gender, location. This is useful, but it only scratches the surface. To truly connect, you need to understand the *why* behind their actions, which is where psychographics come in. It's the difference between knowing *who* your audience is and knowing *how they think and feel.*

Psychographics delve into your audience's lifestyle, values, interests, attitudes, opinions, and personality traits. Are they early adopters of technology? Do they prioritize sustainability? Are they motivated by status or by value? Are they adventure-seekers or homebodies? Knowing this allows you to tailor your messaging, content style, and even product offerings much more effectively. For instance, your course content on "Practical Uses of ChatGPT at Work" implicitly targets individuals interested in efficiency, skill enhancement, and problem-solving – these are psychographic traits.

AI supercharges this analysis. By processing vast amounts of data from social media profiles (bios, posts, shared content), online behavior (likes, shares, comments, group memberships, followed accounts), and even purchase history (where available and ethically accessed), AI algorithms can identify patterns and build detailed audience segments based on both demographic and psychographic factors. For example, an article from DisruptorTraining.co.uk highlights that AI excels in gathering and analyzing psychographic elements by looking at social media activity (likes, shares, comments) to uncover customer interests and values, and using Natural Language Processing (NLP) for sentiment analysis from feedback and reviews. This allows for a much richer understanding than simple demographics alone.

Imagine you sell eco-friendly coffee. Basic demographics might tell you your audience is 25-45 and lives in urban areas. AI-driven psychographic analysis could reveal that a significant portion of this audience also follows minimalist lifestyle influencers, frequently discusses climate change online, values brands with transparent sourcing, and actively seeks out products that align with their ethical concerns. This deeper insight is gold. Now you know to create content that highlights your sustainable practices (perhaps even showing the journey of your beans from farm to cup), uses a clean and minimalist aesthetic in your visuals, and features language that resonates with their values (e.g., "conscious consumption," "earth-friendly"), rather than just generic coffee ads focusing on taste or price alone.

Case Study Snippet: The Boutique Travel Agency

A small boutique travel agency specializing in adventure travel was struggling to differentiate itself. Basic demographics showed their audience was broad (28-55, mixed gender). By using an AI tool to analyze the social media activity of their existing customers and those engaging with competitor content, they uncovered key psychographic clusters. One significant segment was highly interested in "transformative travel experiences," valued

authenticity, and often posted about personal growth and challenging oneself. Another segment was more focused on luxury adventure, interested in unique accommodations and exclusive experiences, often sharing visually stunning content. Armed with these psychographic insights, the agency tailored its social media content: for the first group, they shared inspiring stories of personal transformation through travel, user-generated content focusing on challenges overcome, and partnered with influencers known for their authentic storytelling. For the luxury adventure segment, they showcased breathtaking visuals of unique lodges, highlighted exclusive access opportunities, and used a more sophisticated, aspirational tone. This targeted approach led to a significant increase in engagement within both segments and a noticeable rise in qualified leads for their specialized travel packages.

Tools like **Symanto** and **Insight7** discuss how AI provides advanced insights into audience demographics, psychographics, and behaviors. **Jeda.ai** is mentioned as a tool that bridges the gap between demographics and psychographics by analyzing vast data to reveal comprehensive insights. Even platforms not solely dedicated to this, like some advanced Customer Data Platforms (CDPs) or even features within broader AI marketing suites, are increasingly incorporating these capabilities. They can help you move beyond assumptions and build data-backed profiles of who your ideal customers are and what truly motivates them. The key is to leverage these tools to ask deeper questions about your audience – not just *who* they are, but *what makes them tick.*

This level of understanding allows for hyper-personalization. Instead of one-size-fits-all social media posts, you can create content streams tailored to different psychographic segments within your broader audience, leading to higher engagement, stronger brand loyalty, and ultimately, better business outcomes. This aligns with the principles of effective content marketing and sales, where understanding the customer's core motivations is paramount for crafting messages that convert.

D. Setting Up and Managing AI Automation – Best Practices

Successfully leveraging AI for social media automation isn't just about choosing the right tools; it's about integrating them thoughtfully into your workflow and managing them with a strategic, human-centric approach. AI is a powerful assistant, but it's not a set-and-forget solution, especially when it comes to communication and brand representation. Here are some best practices to ensure your AI automation efforts enhance, rather than detract from, your social media success.

Integrating AI Tools into Your Workflow: Practical Steps for Seamless Operation

1. **Start with Clear Goals:** Before you automate anything, define what you want to achieve. Are you aiming to save time, increase posting consistency, improve engagement, or generate more leads? Your goals will dictate which tools you choose and how you configure them.
2. **Choose the Right Tools for Your Needs (and Budget):** There's a vast array of AI social media tools available, from free or freemium options to enterprise-level platforms. Research and select tools that align with your specific goals, the platforms you use, your team size, and your budget. Start small if needed; you don't have to automate everything at once.
3. **Develop a Content Strategy First:** AI can help execute your strategy, but it can't create one from scratch (at least not

a nuanced one). Know your target audience (your personas!), your key messages, your content pillars, and your brand voice before you start automating content creation or scheduling.

4. **Create a Content Calendar and Approval Process:** Even with AI assistance, maintain a content calendar. Plan your themes and key posts in advance. If you have a team, establish a clear approval process for AI-generated or AI-scheduled content before it goes live. This ensures quality control and brand alignment.
5. **Train Your Team (If Applicable):** If multiple people will be using the AI tools, provide adequate training on how to use them effectively and ethically, including how to write good prompts, review AI outputs, and manage automated interactions.
6. **Set Up Your Tools Methodically:** Take the time to properly configure your chosen AI tools. This includes connecting your social media accounts securely, setting up content categories, defining scheduling rules, inputting brand voice guidelines (if the tool supports it), and configuring any automation triggers.
7. **Start with Partial Automation and Scale Up:** Don't try to automate everything overnight. Begin by automating simpler tasks, like scheduling pre-approved posts or using AI for initial content drafts. As you become more comfortable and see positive results, you can gradually expand your use of automation.
8. **Integrate with Other Marketing Tools:** Look for AI tools that can integrate with your existing marketing stack (e.g., CRM, email marketing platform, analytics tools) for a more holistic view of your customer journey and campaign performance.

The Crucial Role of Human Oversight: AI is an Assistant, Not a Replacement

This is perhaps the most important best practice. While AI can handle many tasks efficiently, it lacks human judgment, empathy, cultural understanding, and the ability to respond to unforeseen circumstances or nuanced conversations appropriately.

- **Review AI-Generated Content:** Always review and edit AI-generated content (captions, post ideas, visuals) before it goes live. Ensure it's accurate, on-brand, grammatically correct, and appropriate for your audience. AI is a great starting point, but your human touch adds the final polish and authenticity.
- **Monitor AI-Scheduled Posts:** Regularly check your scheduled posts to ensure they are still relevant and appropriate, especially in light of current events. A post scheduled weeks ago might become tone-deaf or insensitive due to unforeseen developments. Be prepared to pause or adjust your automated schedule quickly.
- **Oversee Automated Interactions:** If you're using AI chatbots or automated comment responses, closely monitor these interactions. Step in immediately if the AI is struggling, providing incorrect information, or if a user requires human assistance. Ensure escalation paths to humans are clear and effective.
- **Analyze AI Performance and Make Adjustments:** Don't just set up automation and forget it. Regularly review the performance of your AI-assisted efforts. Are the AI-suggested posting times actually yielding better engagement? Is the AI-curated content resonating with your audience? Use analytics to refine your AI settings and strategies.

Avoiding the Pitfalls of Over-Automation: Maintaining Authenticity and Genuine Connection

Automation, when overdone or poorly implemented, can make your brand appear robotic, impersonal, or out of touch. The goal is to use AI to enhance human connection, not replace it.

- **Don't Automate Everything:** Identify tasks that truly benefit from automation (e.g., scheduling, basic FAQs) and those that require a human touch (e.g., responding to complex customer service issues, engaging in nuanced conversations, building relationships with influencers).
- **Personalize Where Possible:** Even with automation, look for opportunities to personalize. If your AI tool allows for custom fields or dynamic content, use it. When a human steps in after an AI interaction, acknowledge the transition.
- **Prioritize Genuine Engagement:** Dedicate the time saved through automation to actively engaging with your audience – responding to comments and messages thoughtfully, participating in relevant conversations, and building real relationships.
- **Be Transparent (When Appropriate):** As mentioned with chatbots, letting users know they are interacting with an AI can manage expectations. Authenticity is key.
- **Listen to Feedback:** Pay attention to how your audience responds to your automated efforts. If you receive feedback that your interactions feel too robotic, take it seriously and adjust your approach.
- **Stay Flexible:** The social media landscape is constantly changing. Be prepared to adapt your automation strategies and tools as platforms evolve and audience expectations shift.

By following these best practices, you can harness the power of AI to make your social media marketing more efficient and effective, while still maintaining the authentic human connection that is vital for building a loyal community and a strong brand.

Creating Data-Driven Audience Personas with AI: Bringing Your Ideal Customer to Life

Once you've used AI to listen to social conversations and analyze the demographics and psychographics of your audience, the next logical step is to consolidate these insights into something actionable: data-driven audience personas. A persona is a semi-fictional representation of your ideal customer, based on real data and educated assumptions. They give a face and a story to the data, making it easier for you and your team to empathize with and create for your target audience. Traditionally, creating these involved a lot of manual research – surveys, interviews, sifting through analytics – and sometimes, quite a bit of guesswork. AI, however, allows you to build personas that are much more detailed, accurate, and dynamic, moving beyond broad generalizations to specific, actionable archetypes.

Instead of a generic persona like "Millennial Mark, aged 30, likes tech," AI can help you create a persona like: **"Eco-Conscious Emily, 32, urban dweller, works as a freelance graphic designer (values flexibility and creativity), prioritizes sustainability and ethical brands (evidenced by her social media engagement with environmental NGOs, B-corps, and brands with transparent supply chains). She actively seeks out information on reducing her carbon footprint, researches products thoroughly before purchasing, prefers experiences over material possessions, and is influenced by micro-influencers in the zero-waste and sustainable living communities. Her pain points include finding truly eco-friendly products that are also aesthetically pleasing and high-quality, and she often feels overwhelmed by greenwashing. She uses Instagram and Pinterest for inspiration and product discovery, and values authentic, non-salesy communication from brands."**

This level of detail is invaluable. It tells you not just *who* Emily is, but *what she cares about, where she spends her time online, what influences her decisions,* and *what problems she's trying to solve.* This directly informs your social media strategy – from the content you create to the platforms you use and the tone you adopt.

How does AI achieve this? By synthesizing the vast amounts of data gathered through social listening and audience analysis. AI algorithms can:

- **Identify Common Clusters:** Group individuals with similar behaviors, interests, values, and demographic profiles into distinct segments. AI can sift through thousands, even millions, of data points to find these natural groupings that a human analyst might miss.
- **Extract Key Attributes:** For each segment, AI can pinpoint the most defining characteristics, pain points, motivations, communication preferences, and even the specific language they use. This is where NLP plays a crucial role in understanding the nuances of online conversations.
- **Visualize Personas:** Some tools can even help generate visual representations or detailed narrative descriptions for each persona, making them easier for your team to understand and empathize with. This might include stock photos that represent the persona, or even AI-generated images based on the persona's characteristics.
- **Update Personas Dynamically:** Audiences evolve, and so should your personas. AI can continuously monitor data and suggest updates to your personas as new trends emerge or audience behaviors shift, ensuring they remain relevant. This is a significant advantage over static personas that quickly become outdated.

While dedicated "AI persona creation tools" might still be emerging as a distinct category for small businesses, the capabilities are often embedded within broader AI-powered marketing platforms, Customer Data Platforms (CDPs), or advanced analytics suites. The key is to leverage tools that can segment your audience based on the rich data AI uncovers and then help you articulate those segments as detailed personas. For example, the insights gleaned from tools like **Sprout Social** (for listening and sentiment), **Brand24** (for brand mentions and reputation), or platforms that analyze psychographics (as discussed by DisruptorTraining.co.uk and **Symanto**) all feed directly into building these robust personas. Even general AI tools like

ChatGPT can be used in a guided way to help synthesize research data into a persona format, once you've gathered the raw insights from other specialized AI tools.

Practical Example: Using AI Insights to Build a Persona for a SaaS Product

A company launching a new AI-powered productivity tool for remote teams uses social listening to track conversations around remote work challenges, productivity hacks, and competitor tools. AI analysis reveals a significant cluster of conversations from project managers in small to medium-sized tech companies who express frustration with tool overload and communication silos. Further psychographic analysis of this group (based on their LinkedIn profiles, shared articles, and forum discussions) shows they value efficiency, data-driven decision-making, and tools that integrate seamlessly. They are often early adopters of new technology but are also skeptical of hype and need to see clear ROI.

Based on this, the company uses AI-assisted insights to create the persona "**Strategic Samira, 38, Project Manager at a growing tech startup. Manages a remote team of 10-15 engineers and designers. Key pain points: juggling multiple project management and communication tools, difficulty tracking progress across disparate platforms, and ensuring team alignment on priorities. Values: efficiency, clear communication, tools that provide actionable insights, and solutions that empower her team rather than adding to their workload. Online behavior: active on LinkedIn, follows industry thought leaders on X/Twitter, reads tech blogs, and participates in online forums about project management best practices.**"

Having these AI-informed personas is incredibly valuable for your social media strategy. They guide:

- **Content Creation:** You know exactly what topics (e.g., "Streamlining Remote Team Communication," "Avoiding Tool Fatigue for Project Managers"), formats (e.g., case studies, short video demos, insightful LinkedIn articles), and tones (e.g., professional, solution-oriented, empathetic to their challenges) will resonate with each persona like Samira.

- **Platform Choice:** You understand which social media platforms each persona frequents most (e.g., LinkedIn and X/Twitter for Samira, rather than perhaps TikTok or Facebook).
- **Ad Targeting:** You can create highly specific ad campaigns on LinkedIn targeting project managers in tech, using messaging that speaks directly to Samira's pain points and values, improving ROI.
- **Product Development:** Insights from personas can even inform how you develop or refine your products and services. Samira's desire for seamless integration might become a key feature in the product roadmap.

By using AI to build these data-rich personas, you move from broadcasting generic messages to having targeted, meaningful conversations with the specific groups of people who are most likely to become loyal customers. It's about understanding not just *who* they are, but *what makes them tick*, and AI provides the key to unlocking that understanding at scale, making your social media efforts far more strategic and effective.

3.3 Analyzing Social Media Data with AI

In the world of social media marketing, data is abundant. Every like, share, comment, click, and follow generates a data point. Native analytics dashboards on platforms like Facebook, Instagram, and LinkedIn provide a basic overview of these metrics – follower growth, reach, engagement rates. While this information is useful, it often only scratches the surface, presenting a picture of *what* happened, but not necessarily *why* it happened or *what you should do next*. This is where Artificial Intelligence steps in, transforming raw social media data from a confusing deluge into a stream of actionable intelligence. AI can help you move beyond vanity metrics to truly understand your audience, measure your impact, and make data-driven decisions that fuel business growth.

In this section, we'll delve into how AI is revolutionizing social media analytics. We'll explore the limitations of traditional analytics and how AI uncovers deeper patterns and trends. We'll look at powerful AI applications like sentiment analysis to understand audience emotion, competitive analysis to benchmark your performance, and advanced ROI measurement to prove the value of your social media efforts. We'll also touch upon how AI can even assist in identifying the right influencers to partner with. Get ready to unlock the hidden stories within your social media data and turn insights into impactful strategies.

B. AI-Powered Content Ideation – Never Run Out of Ideas Again

One of the biggest hurdles in social media marketing is the relentless need for fresh content ideas. Staring at a blank content calendar can be intimidating, even for the most creative minds. What should you post today? What will capture your audience's attention? How can you keep your feed interesting and varied, especially when you're juggling multiple other business responsibilities? This is where AI steps in as an invaluable brainstorming partner, capable of generating a wealth of ideas, helping you tap into current trends, and ensuring your content pipeline never runs dry. This aligns perfectly with the course material that highlights using ChatGPT for generating blog posts and social media posts, which inherently starts with ideation.

Generating Post Ideas with AI Tools: Your Creative Spark

Numerous AI tools are designed specifically to combat creative block and fuel your content engine. These tools work in various ways, often by analyzing vast amounts of online content (blogs, articles, social media posts, forums), identifying patterns, understanding what resonates with specific audiences, and even processing your own existing content to suggest related topics. You can typically provide them with keywords relevant to your niche (e.g., "sustainable fashion," "healthy recipes for busy moms," "AI for small business"), information about your target audience (drawing from your AI-generated personas), links to your existing content, or even just a general theme, and they will generate a list of potential post ideas.

These suggestions can range from:

- **Topic Ideas:** Broad themes or specific subjects that your audience is likely to be interested in. For example, if your niche is home organization, AI might suggest topics like "Decluttering Tips for Small Apartments," "Eco-Friendly Storage Solutions," or "Creating a Minimalist Kids' Playroom."
- **Content Angles:** Different perspectives or hooks to make a common topic more unique and engaging. Instead of just "Benefits of Yoga," AI might suggest angles like "How Yoga Helped Me Overcome Burnout: A Personal Story," "5 Surprising Ways Yoga Boosts Productivity," or "Yoga Poses You Can Do at Your Desk."
- **Format Suggestions:** Recommendations for whether a particular idea is best suited for a text post, an image with a caption, a short video, a poll, a quiz, a carousel post, or even a longer-form blog post that can be summarized for social media. This is crucial as different platforms favor different formats.
- **Headline and Caption Starters:** Initial drafts or compelling phrases to get your writing process going. This can be a huge time-saver, especially when you're feeling uninspired.

For example, tools like **Buffer's AI Assistant** are highlighted for their ability to help with endless post variations and content repurposing, which inherently involves generating new takes on existing ideas. **Narrato AI Content Genie**, as mentioned in Buffer's resources, can auto-generate social media and blog content weekly based on a website URL and themes, effectively serving as an idea generator. **Sprout Social** also discusses how AI tools can streamline workflows and generate ideas, with features like their "Recommend by AI Assist" suggesting effective keywords for Listening topics, which can then inspire content. Semrush offers a "Social Content Ideation tool" that claims to generate over 100 post ideas per day categorized by topic, just by adding a URL. Free tools like **Copy.ai's Content Idea Generator** also promise to help users come up with their next blog or social media post.

Many general-purpose AI writing assistants like **ChatGPT, Jasper (formerly Jarvis)**, and others can also be prompted to brainstorm social media content ideas. The key is to provide them with clear context about your business, audience (your personas!), and content goals. For instance, you could prompt ChatGPT: "I run a local bookstore targeting young adult readers. Generate 10 engaging Instagram post ideas for a new fantasy novel release, focusing on themes of adventure and magic. Include suggestions for visuals."

Simple Secret: **Let AI be your brainstorming partner for endless content inspiration. Don't think of it as a replacement for your creativity, but as a powerful assistant that can bring new perspectives, overcome mental blocks, and ensure you always have a starting point for your next great post. Think of it as having a focus group and a team of creative writers available 24/7.**

AI for Identifying Viral Trends and Hot Topics: Riding the Wave

Timing can be everything on social media. Posting about a topic just as it's gaining traction can significantly boost your visibility and engagement. AI excels at sifting through the noise of the internet – social media chatter, news articles, blog posts, search queries – to identify emerging trends, viral content, and hot topics relevant to your industry or niche, often before they hit the mainstream.

Social listening tools with advanced AI capabilities (as discussed in the previous section) play a crucial role here. They monitor social chatter, news sites, and blogs in real-time, looking for spikes in conversation around specific keywords or themes. For instance, **Trend Hunter AI** is a platform specifically designed to accelerate trend research using artificial intelligence. Many comprehensive social media management platforms also incorporate trend identification features. By flagging these emerging trends, AI helps you:

- **Create Timely Content:** Develop posts that tap into current conversations and show your brand is relevant and up-to-date. If a particular meme format is going viral and it aligns with your brand voice, AI can help you quickly adapt it for your own message.
- **Join the Conversation Authentically:** Understand the context of a trend before jumping in, ensuring your contribution is meaningful and not just a forced attempt to be relevant. AI can help analyze the sentiment and nuances around a trend.
- **Predict Content Performance:** Some tools may even offer insights into the potential virality of a topic or the likely engagement of a particular content format related to a trend, helping you prioritize your content creation efforts.

Practical Example: The Local Coffee Roaster and the Dalgona Coffee Craze

During the early days of the COVID-19 pandemic, Dalgona coffee (whipped coffee) became a massive viral trend on TikTok and Instagram. A small, local coffee roaster, using AI-powered social listening and trend-spotting tools, noticed the rapid surge in mentions and searches for "Dalgona coffee" and related terms within their geographic area. Instead of just observing, they quickly:

1. **Created Content:** Posted a simple, visually appealing video tutorial on their Instagram and Facebook pages showing how to make Dalgona coffee using their own roasted beans, emphasizing the quality of their coffee for the best flavor.
2. **Offered a Promotion:** Bundled their best-selling espresso roast with a small whisk as a "Dalgona Coffee Starter Kit" available for local delivery.

3. **Engaged with User-Generated Content:** Encouraged customers to share their Dalgona coffee creations made with their beans, using a branded hashtag.

The result? A significant spike in online engagement, a boost in local sales (especially for the starter kit), and increased brand visibility as they tapped into a highly relevant and timely trend. The AI didn't create the coffee, but it alerted them to the opportunity and provided the data to act fast.

Crafting Engaging Questions and Polls with AI: Sparking Interaction

Engagement isn't just about likes and shares; it's about interaction – getting your audience to talk back, share their opinions, and feel like part of a community. Asking questions and running polls are fantastic ways to do this. But coming up with interesting and relevant questions that don't feel forced can be challenging. AI can assist here too.

AI tools can analyze your existing content, your audience personas (their interests, pain points, and values), and trending topics to suggest questions or poll ideas that are likely to provoke a response. For example, if you're a financial advisor targeting millennials, and AI identifies that a common concern in this demographic is saving for a down payment on a house, it might suggest poll questions like:

- "What's your biggest hurdle when it comes to saving for a down payment? A) Student Loans B) High Rent C) Lack of a Clear Plan D) Other (Comment below!)"
- Or open-ended questions like: "If you could ask a financial expert one question about buying your first home, what would it be?"

Some AI writing assistants can be prompted to generate lists of engaging questions related to a specific topic. For example, you could ask ChatGPT: "Generate 5 thought-provoking questions about the future of remote work to ask my LinkedIn audience of HR professionals."

The key is to use these AI-generated prompts as a starting point and then refine them to perfectly match your brand voice and the specific context of your social media platform.

By leveraging AI for content ideation, trend spotting, and crafting interactive prompts, you can ensure your social media feed remains vibrant, relevant, and, most importantly, engaging for your audience, turning passive scrollers into active participants in your brand's conversation.

A. The Power of AI in Social Media Analytics – Deeper Dives, Clearer Insights

Native analytics dashboards provided by social media platforms like Facebook Insights, Instagram Analytics, or LinkedIn Page Analytics offer a starting point for understanding your performance. They can show you follower growth, post reach, impressions, likes, comments, shares, and basic demographic data about your audience. While this information is valuable for a quick snapshot, it often has significant limitations when it comes to providing deep, actionable insights that can truly transform your strategy.

Limitations of Native Platform Analytics: What They Don't Always Tell You

Native analytics often fall short in several key areas:

- **Surface-Level Metrics:** They tend to focus on vanity metrics (like follower count or likes) which don't always correlate with business objectives like lead generation, sales, or customer loyalty. It"s hard to see the direct ROI from these basic numbers alone.
- **Lack of Context (The "Why"):** While they show *what* happened (e.g., a spike in engagement), they rarely explain *why* it happened. Was it the topic, the visual, the time of day, an external event, or a combination of factors? Understanding the drivers of performance is crucial for replication and improvement.

- **Limited Sentiment Analysis:** Most native tools don't offer sophisticated sentiment analysis. They can count comments, but they can't easily tell you the overall feeling or emotion behind those comments at scale.
- **Siloed Data:** Each platform provides its own analytics, making it difficult to get a holistic view of your overall social media performance across all channels without manually exporting and consolidating data.
- **Basic Audience Segmentation:** While some demographic data is available, it's often not granular enough to understand the nuances of different audience segments and how they interact with your content differently.
- **Weak Competitive Benchmarking:** Native tools typically don't offer robust features for comparing your performance against competitors in a detailed way.
- **Difficulty in Tracking Complex Customer Journeys:** It can be challenging to connect social media activity to off-platform conversions or to understand how social media touchpoints contribute to the overall customer journey.

How AI Uncovers Hidden Patterns and Trends: Processing Vast Amounts of Data for Richer Insights

This is where AI-powered analytics tools step in to fill the gaps. AI excels at processing and analyzing vast and complex datasets far beyond human capability, uncovering hidden patterns, correlations, and predictive insights that would otherwise remain buried. Here's how AI supercharges social media analytics:

- **Advanced Data Processing:** AI algorithms can ingest and process data from multiple social media platforms simultaneously, along with data from your website analytics, CRM, and sales platforms, to create a unified view of your customer and campaign performance.

- **Sophisticated Pattern Recognition:** Machine learning models can identify subtle patterns in user behavior, content performance, and audience engagement that are not obvious through manual analysis. For example, AI might discover that a particular combination of content type, posting time, and visual style consistently leads to higher conversion rates for a specific audience segment.
- **Predictive Analytics:** By analyzing historical data, AI can forecast future trends, predict which content is likely to perform well, or even anticipate potential shifts in audience sentiment or behavior. This allows for more proactive and strategic decision-making.
- **Natural Language Processing (NLP) for Deeper Text Analysis:** AI uses NLP to understand the meaning, context, and sentiment of text-based social media content (posts, comments, reviews) at scale, providing much richer insights than simple keyword counting.
- **Automated Anomaly Detection:** AI can automatically flag unusual spikes or dips in your metrics, alerting you to potential issues (e.g., a sudden drop in engagement, a negative viral comment) or opportunities (e.g., a piece of content unexpectedly taking off) that require attention.
- **Intelligent Data Visualization:** AI-powered tools often present complex data in intuitive dashboards and reports, using smart visualizations to highlight key insights and make them easily understandable for non-analysts.

Simple Secret: **Let AI be your data detective, finding clues your competitors miss. While native analytics show you the tip of the iceberg, AI dives deep to reveal the full picture, uncovering the underlying currents and hidden treasures in your social media data that can guide you to more effective strategies and better results.**

By moving beyond basic platform analytics and embracing AI-powered solutions, businesses can gain a much deeper and more nuanced understanding of their social media performance, their audience, and the competitive landscape. This enables them to optimize their strategies, allocate resources more effectively, and ultimately achieve a greater return on their social media investment.

C. AI for Crafting Compelling Social Media Copy – Words that Convert

Once you have your audience understood (thanks to your AI-powered personas!) and a pipeline of content ideas, the next challenge is crafting the actual words – the captions, headlines, and ad copy that will grab attention, convey your message effectively, and drive action. Writing compelling copy consistently, especially when tailored for different social media platforms and their unique audiences, can be incredibly time-consuming and mentally taxing. This is where AI writing assistants shine, acting as your tireless, 24/7 copy-crafting partner, ready to help you generate everything from witty one-liners to persuasive ad campaigns. This directly aligns with the course content that emphasizes using ChatGPT for social media marketing, copywriting, and even generating marketing copy for advertising campaigns.

AI Writing Assistants for Social Media: Your 24/7 Wordsmith

AI writing assistants are tools specifically designed to generate human-like text based on prompts and data. For social media, they can be incredibly versatile, helping you create:

- **Engaging Captions:** From witty, short captions for Instagram or X/Twitter to more informative and detailed descriptions for LinkedIn posts or Facebook updates. For example, you could ask an AI to generate three different Instagram caption options for a photo of your new product, specifying a playful tone and including a call to action to visit your website.

- **Click-Worthy Headlines:** For your blog posts shared on social media, for social media ads, or even for the titles of your YouTube videos or podcast episodes promoted on social channels. A compelling headline is often the difference between a scroll-past and a click-through.
- **Persuasive Ad Copy:** Crafting text for Facebook, Instagram, LinkedIn, or X/Twitter ads that are designed to convert. This includes the headline, body copy, and call to action. Your course notes mention using ChatGPT for PPC Ad campaign copy, and AI tools excel at generating multiple variations for A/B testing.
- **Post Variations:** Quickly generating multiple versions of a post to A/B test different messaging, to keep your content fresh without starting from scratch, or to tailor a core message for different platforms. For instance, take a key announcement and ask the AI to create a concise version for X/Twitter, a professional version for LinkedIn, and a more visual-storytelling version for Instagram.
- **Product Descriptions for Social Commerce:** If you're selling directly on platforms like Instagram Shops or Facebook Shops, AI can help write engaging and informative product descriptions, as highlighted in the course material regarding e-commerce and product descriptions using ChatGPT.

Many tools are available in this space. **Jasper (formerly Jarvis)** is frequently mentioned as a powerful AI writing assistant adept at creating engaging social media captions, ad copy, and blog posts, understanding the nuances of different platforms. **Copymatic** positions itself as an AI copywriter that can write digital ads, website copy, and blog content in seconds. **Rytr** offers a free AI writing assistant for crafting high-quality content quickly. **Writesonic** is another popular option, often highlighted for its ability to generate SEO-optimized content and various marketing copy. **Hootsuite's OwlyWriter AI** is specifically designed to generate social media captions and content ideas. Buffer's article on AI writing tools also extensively covers its own **Buffer AI Assistant**, emphasizing its integration within the Buffer platform for seamless content creation and scheduling, and its understanding of platform-specific nuances (e.g., character limits for X/Twitter, professional tone for LinkedIn).

These tools typically work by you providing a prompt – this could be a topic, a few keywords, a desired tone (e.g., witty, formal, empathetic, urgent), the target audience (referencing your personas!), the specific social media platform, and the desired output (e.g.,

caption, ad copy, headline). The AI then generates text based on its training data and your input.

Simple Secret: **Use AI to write faster, not just to write *for* you. Think of AI as an assistant that provides a solid first draft, helps overcome writer's block, or suggests alternative phrasing. Always review, edit, and inject your unique brand personality into AI-generated copy to ensure authenticity and quality. Your unique insights, brand voice, and understanding of your audience's nuances are irreplaceable; AI is there to enhance, not replace, your creative input.**

Optimizing Copy for Platform Nuances: Speaking the Right Language

What works on LinkedIn won't necessarily fly on TikTok, and an effective X/Twitter post is very different from an engaging Facebook update. Each social media platform has its own unwritten rules, optimal post lengths, content styles, audience expectations, and even preferred use of emojis or hashtags. AI can be a great help in tailoring your copy accordingly, saving you the mental gymnastics of constantly switching gears.

Many advanced AI writing tools allow you to specify the target social media platform when generating copy. The AI will then adjust the generated text in terms of:

- **Length:** Ensuring it fits character limits (e.g., X/Twitter's 280 characters) or optimal readability for the platform (e.g., shorter paragraphs for mobile-first platforms like Instagram).
- **Tone:** Adapting the language to be more professional and insightful for LinkedIn, more casual and visual for Instagram, more concise and news-oriented for X/Twitter, or more community-focused for Facebook.
- **Formatting:** Suggesting the use of emojis (and which ones are appropriate), line breaks for readability, or the number and type of hashtags suitable for the platform.
- **Call to Actions (CTAs):** Crafting CTAs that are effective for the specific platform's user behavior and features (e.g., "Link in bio" for Instagram, "Learn More" button for Facebook ads, direct questions for LinkedIn engagement).

For example, **Buffer's AI Assistant** is explicitly mentioned for its ability to understand and adapt to the nuances of each social media platform, generating content suitable for X (formerly Twitter), LinkedIn, Instagram, etc., by adjusting tone and length automatically. This means you can take a core message and quickly get platform-optimized versions, ensuring your content feels native to each environment.

Maintaining Brand Voice and Tone with AI: Consistency is Key

A crucial aspect of effective social media marketing is a consistent brand voice. Whether your brand is quirky and humorous, authoritative and informative, or warm and empathetic, your social media copy should reflect that personality in every post. This consistency builds recognition and trust. A common concern with AI-generated content is that it might sound generic, robotic, or simply not like *your* brand.

However, many AI writing tools are becoming increasingly sophisticated in their ability to learn and adapt to a specific brand voice. Some tools allow you to:

- **Input Brand Guidelines:** Provide information about your brand's personality, core values, mission, target audience, and specific do's and don'ts for language (e.g., "always use optimistic language," "avoid industry jargon," "use a conversational and friendly tone").
- **Upload Existing Content:** Feed the AI samples of your past successful content – your best-performing blog posts, social media updates, or email newsletters. The AI can analyze this content to learn your style, common phrases, and overall tone.
- **Iterative Refinement and Feedback:** Guide the AI through feedback. If a generated piece of copy isn't quite right, you can ask it to make it "more formal," "more playful," "more empathetic," or to "rewrite this in the style of [a brand you admire, or your own previous successful post]." The more you guide and refine, the better the AI becomes at mimicking your desired style. Some tools even allow you to create a "brand voice profile" that the AI will then use for all future generations.

B. AI for Sentiment Analysis – Understanding the "Why" Behind the Numbers

Beyond just counting likes, comments, and shares, understanding the *emotion* and *opinion* behind these interactions is crucial for truly grasping how your audience feels about your brand, products, services, or content. This is where sentiment analysis, powered by Artificial Intelligence, becomes an invaluable tool. It helps you look past the quantitative data to understand the qualitative nuances of social conversations, providing the "why" behind the numbers.

What Sentiment Analysis Is and How It Works on Social Data

Sentiment analysis, also known as opinion mining, is a subfield of Natural Language Processing (NLP) that uses AI algorithms to automatically identify, extract, and quantify the emotional tone or subjective opinion expressed in a piece of text. In the context of social media, this means analyzing posts, comments, reviews, mentions, and messages to determine whether the sentiment expressed is positive, negative, or neutral.

Here's a simplified overview of how it generally works:

1. **Data Collection:** AI tools gather text data from various social media sources (e.g., X/Twitter, Facebook, Instagram comments, blog comments, forum discussions, product reviews).
2. **Text Preprocessing:** The raw text is cleaned and prepared for analysis. This involves removing irrelevant characters, correcting typos (to some extent), and sometimes breaking down text into smaller units like sentences or phrases.
3. **Feature Extraction:** The AI identifies key words, phrases, emojis, and other linguistic features that are indicative of sentiment.
4. **Sentiment Classification:** Using machine learning models (often trained on vast datasets of text labeled with sentiment), the AI classifies the text into predefined sentiment categories:
    - **Positive:** Expressing happiness, satisfaction, approval, praise, etc.
    - **Negative:** Expressing dissatisfaction, anger, frustration, criticism, etc.
    - **Neutral:** Expressing objective information, questions without strong emotion, or ambiguous sentiment.
    - Some advanced models can even detect more granular emotions like joy, sadness, anger, fear, surprise, or identify specific aspects of a product/service that are being discussed positively or negatively (aspect-based sentiment analysis).
5. **Aggregation and Reporting:** The results are aggregated to provide an overall sentiment score for a brand, product, campaign, or topic, often visualized in dashboards.

Many social listening platforms and dedicated analytics tools incorporate AI-powered sentiment analysis. Examples include **Brandwatch**, **Talkwalker**, **Sprout Social**, **Hootsuite Insights**, and **NetBase Quid**. Some tools offer real-time sentiment tracking, allowing businesses to monitor shifts in public opinion as they happen.

Gauging Brand Perception and Customer Satisfaction: Real-World Examples

Sentiment analysis provides a powerful lens through which to view your brand perception and customer satisfaction levels.

- **Brand Health Monitoring:** By continuously tracking the sentiment of brand mentions, you can get a real-time pulse on how your brand is perceived in the market. A sudden dip in positive sentiment or a spike in negative sentiment can be an early warning sign of a PR issue, a problem with a product, or a poorly received marketing campaign.
    - **Example:** A restaurant chain launches a new menu item. AI sentiment analysis of social media comments reveals that while some customers praise the taste (positive), a significant number complain about the price being too high (negative). This insight allows the chain to quickly address pricing concerns or highlight the value proposition more effectively.
- **Customer Satisfaction Tracking:** Analyzing sentiment in customer reviews, support interactions (if logged and accessible), and direct messages can provide a more nuanced understanding of customer satisfaction than traditional surveys alone. It can highlight specific areas of delight or frustration.
    - **Example:** An e-commerce company uses AI to analyze sentiment in product reviews. They discover that while most reviews for a new dress are positive regarding the design, many negative comments mention inconsis-

tent sizing. This prompts them to review their sizing charts and quality control for that product.

- **Campaign Performance Measurement:** Sentiment analysis can help you understand how your audience is reacting to a specific marketing campaign beyond just reach and engagement numbers. Are people genuinely excited by your new ad, or are they finding it annoying or confusing?

    - **Example:** A software company runs a social media contest. While engagement numbers (likes, shares) are high, AI sentiment analysis of comments reveals that many participants are confused about the entry rules, leading to frustration. The company can then clarify the rules to improve the experience.

Identifying Potential Crises or Opportunities Early

One of the most valuable aspects of AI-driven sentiment analysis is its ability to act as an early warning system or an opportunity spotter.

- **Crisis Management:** A sudden surge in negative sentiment around your brand or a specific topic related to your industry can indicate an emerging crisis. AI can flag this rapidly, allowing your PR and social media teams to investigate and respond proactively before the situation escalates. For instance, if a product recall is announced by a competitor, AI can track if your brand is being mistakenly associated with the issue or if customers are expressing concerns about similar products you offer.
- **Identifying Unmet Needs or Product Improvement Ideas:** Negative sentiment isn't always bad; it can be a rich source of feedback. If customers are consistently expressing frustration about a particular feature of your product or a gap

in your service, this is valuable information that can drive innovation and improvement.

- **Spotting Positive Trends and Advocates:** Conversely, a spike in positive sentiment around a particular aspect of your business or a piece of content can highlight what you're doing well and what resonates most with your audience. It can also help identify brand advocates or influencers who are organically praising your brand, creating opportunities for collaboration.

***Simple Secret:* Use AI sentiment analysis to listen to the *emotions* behind the words. It's like having a superpower that tells you how people truly feel, allowing you to be more empathetic, responsive, and strategic in your social media communications and overall business decisions.**

By leveraging AI for sentiment analysis, businesses can move beyond simply counting mentions to understanding the true voice of the customer. This deeper emotional intelligence allows for more informed decision-making, better brand management, improved customer experiences, and the ability to navigate the dynamic social landscape with greater agility and insight.

C. AI for Competitive Analysis on Social Media

Understanding your own social media performance is vital, but to truly gain an edge, you also need to understand what your competitors are doing, how they are performing, and where opportunities might lie for you to differentiate and excel. Manually tracking competitor activity across multiple platforms, analyzing their content, and benchmarking your performance against theirs can be an incredibly laborious and often superficial process. Artificial Intelligence provides a powerful toolkit to automate and deepen your competitive analysis on social media, giving you actionable insights to refine your own strategy.

Benchmarking Your Performance Against Competitors: Using AI to Track Strategies, Content, and Engagement

AI-powered competitive analysis tools can monitor your competitors" social media presence and provide you with valuable comparative data. Here's how AI helps:

- **Automated Competitor Tracking:** You can define a list of key competitors, and AI tools will automatically track their social media activity, including their posts, engagement rates (likes, comments, shares), follower growth, posting frequency, and content types.
- **Content Strategy Analysis:** AI can analyze the types of content your competitors are publishing (e.g., blog links, videos, images, questions, promotions), the topics they focus on, the tone of their messaging, and the hashtags they use. This can reveal their content pillars and areas of emphasis.
    - **Example:** A new artisanal coffee shop uses an AI tool to analyze the social media content of established local cafes. The AI reveals that successful competitors frequently post high-quality images of their latte art, share customer testimonials, and run weekly polls about new drink flavors. This gives the new shop ideas for its own content strategy.
- **Engagement Benchmarking:** AI tools can compare your engagement rates (per post or overall) with those of your competitors, providing context for your own performance. Are you outperforming them, or are there areas where they are achieving better connection with their audience?
- **Audience Overlap and Growth Comparison:** Some advanced tools can help identify the overlap between your audience and your competitors" audiences. They can also track competitor follower growth rates and sources, helping you understand where they might be gaining traction.

- **Share of Voice (SOV):** AI can help measure your brand's share of voice within your industry or for specific keywords compared to your competitors. This indicates how much of the online conversation around relevant topics is about your brand versus others.

    - **Example:** A SaaS company in the project management space uses AI to track its SOV for keywords like "best project management software" and "team collaboration tools" against its top three competitors. They notice a competitor gaining SOV rapidly due to a successful influencer campaign, prompting them to consider a similar strategy.

Identifying Gaps and Opportunities in Your Niche

Beyond just tracking what competitors *are* doing, AI can help you identify what they *aren"t* doing, or where their efforts might be falling short, revealing strategic opportunities for your brand.

- **Content Gap Analysis:** By analyzing the topics your competitors cover and comparing them to the topics your target audience is discussing (through social listening and sentiment analysis), AI can help identify content gaps – relevant topics that your audience cares about but that aren"t being adequately addressed by you or your competitors. This is a prime opportunity to create valuable content that fills that void and positions you as a thought leader.

    - **Example:** A financial advisor targeting millennials uses AI to analyze competitor content and audience conversations. The AI identifies a lack of simple, engaging content about sustainable investing, despite high interest from the target demographic. The advisor creates a series of short videos and infographics on this topic, quickly gaining traction.

- **Sentiment on Competitor Mentions:** Analyzing the sentiment of comments on your competitors" posts or mentions of their brand can reveal their strengths and weaknesses from the customer"s perspective. Are customers consistently praising a competitor"s customer service but complaining about their product"s ease of use? This insight can inform your own product development or marketing messaging, highlighting your strengths in areas where competitors are weak.
- **Identifying Underserved Audience Segments:** AI might reveal that your competitors are primarily focusing on one segment of the potential market, leaving other segments underserved. This could be an opportunity for you to tailor your messaging and content to attract those neglected groups.
- **Spotting Emerging Trends Before Competitors:** By combining social listening with competitive analysis, AI can help you spot emerging trends or shifts in consumer preferences within your niche that your competitors haven"t yet capitalized on, giving you a first-mover advantage.

Tools that often include AI-powered competitive analysis features are typically part of broader social listening or social media management suites like **Sprout Social**, **Brandwatch**, **Talkwalker**, or **SEMrush** (which has strong social media tracking capabilities). When choosing a tool, consider its ability to track specific competitors, the depth of its content and engagement analysis, and its reporting capabilities.

Simple Secret: **Use AI to be a smart observer of your competition, not just a casual lurker. Let AI systematically track their moves, analyze their content's reception, and pinpoint the gaps they're leaving in the market. This isn't about copying; it's about learning, differentiating, and strategically positioning your brand to win.**

By leveraging AI for competitive analysis on social media, you can move from guesswork to data-driven insights about your competitive landscape. This allows you to make more informed decisions about your own content strategy, positioning, and areas for innovation, ultimately helping you to stand out and capture a greater share of your target market.

D. AI for Eye-Catching Visual Content – Stopping the Scroll

In the fast-paced, visually-driven world of social media, text alone often isn't enough to capture attention. Platforms like Instagram, Pinterest, TikTok, and even increasingly Facebook and LinkedIn, prioritize visual content. Eye-catching visuals – images, graphics, infographics, and videos – are crucial for stopping the scroll, conveying messages quickly, evoking emotion, and making your content memorable. However, creating high-quality visual content consistently can be a significant challenge, especially for small business owners and entrepreneurs who may not have dedicated design teams, expensive software, or extensive budgets. This is where AI-powered visual creation tools are becoming game-changers, democratizing design and video production and making professional-looking visuals accessible to everyone. Your course outline specifically mentions "Creating AI images using Midjourney & Dall-E 2" and "AI video creation & script writing using Chat GPT," highlighting the importance of these capabilities.

AI Image Generation for Social Media: Your Personal Digital Artist

Imagine being able to describe an image in words – no matter how fantastical or specific – and have AI bring it to life in seconds. That's the power of AI image generation tools. These platforms, often based on sophisticated models like OpenAI's **DALL-E 2**, **Midjourney**, or **Stable Diffusion**, use complex algorithms to create unique graphics, illustrations, banners, ad creatives, stylized product photos, and even abstract art from simple text prompts. You can specify the subject, style (e.g., photorealistic, cartoon, abstract, watercolor, pixel art,

3D render), colors, mood, lighting, composition, and even artistic influences, and the AI will generate visuals to match.

This capability is incredibly useful for social media because it allows you to:

- **Create Unique Branding Elements:** Generate custom icons, patterns, textures, or background images that perfectly align with your brand identity, without needing to hire a graphic designer for every small element.
- **Illustrate Concepts:** Create visuals for abstract ideas, services, or complex data that are difficult to photograph. For example, a consultant could generate an image representing "synergy" or "innovation."
- **Design Ad Creatives:** Quickly produce multiple variations of images for A/B testing your social media ads. You could test different backgrounds, color schemes, or character styles for the same ad concept to see what performs best.
- **Enhance Blog Post Shares:** Generate compelling header images or in-post illustrations for links shared on social platforms, making your shared content more clickable and visually appealing.
- **Produce Product Mockups or Stylized Shots:** Visualize products in different settings or styles without expensive photoshoots. For instance, an e-commerce store selling t-shirts could generate images of their designs on various models in diverse environments.
- **Generate Social Media Banners and Profile Pictures:** Create unique and eye-catching visuals for your social media profiles and cover photos.

Several tools are emerging in this space. While some are standalone AI art generators like Midjourney (often accessed via Discord) and DALL-E 2, others are being integrated into broader design platforms like Canva (which has its own AI image generator, Text to Image) or social media management tools. For example, Buffer's list of AI social media content creation tools mentions **Narrato AI Content Genie** which includes an AI image generator. Piktochart, known for visual design, is also incorporating AI, as seen with their AI Carousel Maker which can generate images for slides. Sprinklr's blog on AI tools for social media content creation also mentions AI-powered image editing tools that streamline content creation. The key is to experiment with different tools and, crucially, with your prompting techniques to achieve the desired visual style for your brand.

Simple Secret: **Create unique visuals without needing a design degree using AI image tools. Start with clear, descriptive prompts, and don't be afraid to iterate and refine until you get an image that perfectly captures your message and brand aesthetic. For example, instead of just prompting "a cat," try "a photorealistic image of a fluffy ginger cat wearing a tiny blue bowtie, sitting on a stack of old books in a cozy library, soft window light, detailed fur." The more detail, the better the result.**

AI Video Creation and Editing: Making Video More Accessible

Video content consistently drives high engagement on social media, but production can be complex, time-consuming, and expensive. AI is simplifying this process in several ways, making video a more attainable medium for small businesses. Your course notes highlight the use of ChatGPT for script writing, which is often the first step in video creation.

- **Text-to-Video Generation:** Some AI tools can take a script (perhaps one drafted with ChatGPT!), a blog post, or even just a text prompt and generate a video. These tools often use libraries of stock footage and images, AI-generated voiceovers, and animated text overlays. This is great for creating short informational videos, animated explainers, social media ads, or summaries of articles quickly.

- **Automated Video Editing:** AI can analyze raw video footage and automatically identify key moments, remove awkward pauses or filler words (like "um" and "uh"), add captions and subtitles (crucial for accessibility and silent viewing), resize videos for different social media formats (e.g., square for Instagram feed, vertical 9:16 for TikTok/Reels/Shorts), and even suggest or automatically add royalty-free background music.
- **AI Avatars and Voiceovers:** Create videos featuring AI-generated avatars that speak your script, or use AI voiceovers to narrate your content in various languages and accents. This can be useful for creating consistent video content without needing to be on camera yourself or hiring voice actors for every project.
- **Short-Form Video Creation & Repurposing:** Tools are emerging that specialize in helping create engaging short-form videos for platforms like TikTok, Instagram Reels, and YouTube Shorts. Often, these tools can take longer videos (like a webinar or a lengthy YouTube tutorial) and automatically identify the most engaging snippets, reformatting them into multiple short, shareable clips.

Platforms like **Pictory** are known for creating AI-generated videos for social media, often from text or long-form video content. **Lumen5** is another popular tool that transforms blog posts and articles into videos. **Descript**, mentioned by Hootsuite, is an AI-powered audio and video editing tool that simplifies editing long-form and short-form videos, including features like automatic transcription and overdubbing. Media A La Carte mentions **Kaiber AI** for making music videos and animated social media clips from static images or prompts, and **Opus Clip** for turning long videos into viral short clips. These tools can significantly reduce the technical barriers and time investment traditionally associated with video production.

Practical Example: The SaaS Company Explainer Video

A small SaaS company wants to create a short explainer video for their new software feature to share on LinkedIn and X/Twitter. Instead of a costly and time-consuming traditional video shoot, they:

1. Use **ChatGPT** to draft a concise and engaging 60-second video script highlighting the problem the feature solves and its key benefits.
2. Feed this script into an AI text-to-video tool like **Pictory** or **Lumen5**. The tool automatically selects relevant stock footage and animations, adds text overlays for key points, and generates an AI voiceover.
3. Use the AI tool's editing features to make minor tweaks, adjust the pacing, and add their brand logo and colors.
4. Generate versions in both landscape (for LinkedIn) and square (for X/Twitter) formats.

In a matter of hours, rather than days or weeks, they have a professional-looking explainer video ready to share, at a fraction of the traditional cost.

Ethical Considerations and Best Practices for AI-Generated Visuals

As with any powerful technology, the use of AI for visual content creation comes with ethical considerations and best practices that businesses should keep in mind. This is a key theme in your course outline under "Ethical implications of AI."

- **Authenticity and Disclosure:** While AI can create stunning visuals, it's important to be transparent with your audience, especially if the content could be misleading. Consider disclosing when an image or video is significantly AI-generated, particularly if it depicts realistic scenes or people that don't exist (e.g., using a small disclaimer like #AIgenerated or "Image created with AI"). This builds trust and manages expectations.

- **Copyright and Ownership:** The legal landscape around AI-generated art is still evolving. Be aware of the terms of service of the AI tools you use regarding copyright ownership of the generated visuals. Avoid using AI to generate images that infringe on existing copyrights (e.g., creating images in the distinct style of a living artist without permission or using trademarked characters directly in your prompts in a way that aims to replicate protected IP).
- **Misinformation and Deepfakes:** AI can be used to create highly realistic but fake images or videos (deepfakes). As a responsible business, it's crucial to avoid creating or spreading content that could be deceptive or harmful. Focus on using AI to enhance creativity and communication, not to mislead.
- **Bias in AI Models:** AI models are trained on vast datasets, and if these datasets contain biases (e.g., underrepresentation or stereotypical representation of certain demographics), the AI may generate biased visuals. Be mindful of this and strive to create inclusive and representative content. Critically evaluate the outputs and guide the AI towards more diverse and equitable representations if needed by adjusting your prompts or choosing different models.
- **User Privacy (Especially with Video Editing):** When using AI tools to edit videos featuring real people, ensure you have their consent, especially if the AI is analyzing or altering their likeness or voice significantly. Adhere to data privacy regulations.
- **Maintaining Brand Consistency:** While AI offers endless creative possibilities, ensure the visuals you generate still align with your overall brand identity, style, and messaging. Don't let the novelty of AI distract from your core brand values. Develop clear guidelines for how AI-generated visuals should look and feel for your brand.

By thoughtfully integrating AI visual tools and adhering to ethical best practices, businesses can significantly enhance their social media presence, creating more engaging and visually appealing content while saving time and resources, and truly stopping the scroll.

D. AI for Measuring Social Media ROI and Campaign Effectiveness

One of the most persistent challenges for marketers is proving the return on investment (ROI) of their social media efforts. While likes, shares, and follower growth are visible, connecting these activities to tangible business outcomes like leads, sales, and customer lifetime value can be complex. Artificial Intelligence is increasingly playing a crucial role in helping businesses move beyond surface-level metrics to more accurately measure social media ROI and understand true campaign effectiveness.

Tracking Key Performance Indicators (KPIs) with AI: Beyond Likes and Shares – Focusing on Conversions, Leads, and Sales Attribution

To measure ROI, you need to track Key Performance Indicators (KPIs) that align directly with your business objectives. AI helps in tracking and analyzing these more meaningful KPIs:

- **Conversion Tracking and Attribution:** AI-powered analytics tools can integrate with your website analytics (e.g., Google Analytics) and CRM systems to track how social media interactions lead to specific conversion events, such as newsletter sign-ups, demo requests, ebook downloads, or actual purchases. AI algorithms can help with attribution modeling, determining which social media touchpoints or campaigns contributed most effectively to these conversions, especially in complex customer journeys involving multiple interactions.
  - **Example:** An e-commerce store uses AI to analyze its sales data alongside its social media campaign data. The AI identifies that Instagram story ads featuring user-gen-

erated content have a significantly higher conversion rate to sales than standard product posts on Facebook, even if the Facebook posts get more likes. This allows them to reallocate their ad spend more effectively.

- **Lead Generation and Quality Analysis:** If lead generation is a key goal, AI can help track the number of leads generated from social media channels. More importantly, it can analyze the quality of these leads by integrating with CRM data to see which leads progress through the sales funnel and eventually become customers. This helps in optimizing campaigns not just for lead quantity, but for lead quality.
- **Customer Lifetime Value (CLV) Insights:** By analyzing long-term customer data, AI can help identify if customers acquired through specific social media channels or campaigns tend to have a higher CLV. This provides a more strategic view of ROI beyond initial purchases.
- **Website Traffic and Engagement from Social:** AI can provide deeper insights into the quality of website traffic driven by social media – not just the number of clicks, but also metrics like bounce rate, time on site, and pages per visit for users coming from social channels. This indicates how engaged the social media audience is once they land on your website.

AI-Powered Reporting and Dashboards: Making Data Understandable and Actionable

Raw data, no matter how comprehensive, is only useful if it can be understood and acted upon. AI-powered analytics platforms excel at transforming complex data into clear, intuitive, and actionable reports and dashboards.

- **Automated Reporting:** AI can automate the generation of regular performance reports, saving significant time and effort. These reports can be customized to highlight the KPIs that matter most to your business and stakeholders.

- **Intelligent Data Visualization:** AI tools often use advanced visualization techniques (interactive charts, graphs, heatmaps) to present data in a way that makes it easy to spot trends, patterns, and outliers. This is far more effective than sifting through spreadsheets.
- **Natural Language Generation (NLG) for Insights:** Some advanced AI tools use NLG to provide plain-language summaries and explanations of key findings in reports. Instead of just showing a chart, the AI might write a sentence like, "Engagement on LinkedIn increased by 15% this month, primarily driven by video content targeting senior professionals, resulting in a 10% uplift in demo requests from this platform."
- **Customizable Dashboards:** AI platforms often allow you to create customized dashboards that display the specific metrics and insights relevant to different team members or business goals, providing a real-time view of performance.
- **Predictive ROI Forecasts:** Some AI tools can even use historical data and predictive modeling to forecast the potential ROI of future campaigns or to suggest budget allocations for maximizing returns.

Platforms like **Google Analytics** (with its AI-powered insights), **HubSpot**, **Sprout Social**, **Hootsuite Impact**, and various specialized marketing analytics platforms (e.g., **Funnel.io**, **Supermetrics** which help consolidate data for analysis) leverage AI to provide deeper ROI insights. The key is the ability to connect social media data with business outcome data (sales, leads) and then use AI to find the correlations and causal links.

Simple Secret: **Use AI to connect the dots between your social media activity and your bottom line. Move beyond guessing the value of your social efforts by letting AI track conversions, attribute sales, and present the data in a way that clearly demonstrates ROI to you and your stakeholders.**

By employing AI to measure social media ROI and campaign effectiveness, businesses can gain a much clearer understanding of what's working, what's not, and how to optimize their strategies for better financial outcomes. This data-driven approach not only justifies social media spend but also guides future investments and helps in building a more accountable and results-oriented social media presence.

E. AI for Hashtag Strategy – Boosting Discoverability

Hashtags are the signposts of social media, the invisible threads that connect conversations, content, and communities. They are essential for helping users discover content relevant to their interests and for brands to increase the visibility and reach of their posts. A well-thought-out hashtag strategy can significantly boost your content's performance. However, finding the *right* hashtags – those that are relevant to your content, popular enough to be searched by your target audience, but not so oversaturated that your content gets instantly buried – can be a time-consuming guessing game. This is where AI comes in to take the guesswork out of your hashtag game, transforming it from a chore into a strategic advantage.

AI-Powered Hashtag Suggestion Tools: Finding Your Niche Navigators

AI-powered hashtag suggestion tools analyze your content (text and sometimes even images), your industry, your target audience (your personas!), and current trends to recommend a list of relevant and potentially effective hashtags. These tools go beyond simple keyword matching; they leverage Natural Language Processing (NLP) to understand context, semantic relationships, and even the sentiment of your content to suggest truly pertinent tags.

Here's how they typically work and what to look for:

- **Content Analysis:** Many tools allow you to input your post caption, a URL to your content, or even an image, and the AI will analyze it to suggest relevant hashtags. For example, if you post an image of a latte art, the AI won't just suggest #coffee, but might also suggest #latteart, #coffeeshopvibes, #morning-brew, or even more niche tags related to the specific style of art or coffee.

- **Relevance Scoring:** AI can assess how relevant a hashtag is to your specific content, helping you avoid using overly broad or irrelevant tags that might attract the wrong audience or make your content look spammy.
- **Volume and Competition Metrics:** Good AI hashtag tools often provide data on how popular a hashtag is (e.g., estimated search volume or number of posts using it) and how much competition there is for it. This helps you find a sweet spot – hashtags that people are searching for but where your content still has a chance to stand out and not get lost in a sea of millions of other posts.
- **Trend Identification:** Some tools can identify trending hashtags relevant to your niche or even broader viral trends that you might be able to creatively and appropriately incorporate into your content, allowing you to tap into current conversations.
- **Niche Hashtag Discovery:** This is where AI truly shines. It can uncover less obvious, long-tail, or niche-specific hashtags that your target audience might be following. These often have lower volume but much higher intent and can lead to more qualified engagement.
- **Platform-Specific Suggestions:** Hashtag usage and best practices can vary significantly by platform (e.g., Instagram often uses a larger number of hashtags, including very niche ones, while X/Twitter might use fewer, more focused tags, and LinkedIn hashtags tend to be more professional and topic-oriented). Some AI tools may offer platform-specific recommendations or allow you to specify the target platform.
- **Related Hashtag Groups:** Some AI tools can suggest groups of related hashtags that work well together, helping you

build out a comprehensive set for a particular post or content pillar.

Several platforms offer AI-driven hashtag assistance. For instance, **Flick** is often highlighted by sources like Socialinsider for its AI hashtag generator and advanced hashtag analytics, helping users find relevant, low-competition hashtags. **Hootsuite** offers a free Social Media Hashtag Generator that can instantly generate caption ideas and presumably relevant hashtags for various platforms. Many comprehensive social media management tools like **Buffer** and **Sprout Social**, as mentioned in various articles, are incorporating AI features that extend to suggesting hashtags or optimizing posts, which would naturally include hashtag strategy. **FeedHive**, noted by Zapier and Reddit users, also offers AI features that likely include hashtag suggestions as part of its AI Writing Assistant and performance prediction capabilities. Even general AI writing assistants like **ChatGPT** can be prompted to suggest hashtags if you provide them with the content of your post, your target audience, and the target platform. For example, you could prompt: "I'm posting an Instagram reel about a 5-minute morning yoga routine for beginners. Suggest 15 relevant hashtags, including a mix of popular and niche ones."

Optimizing Hashtag Mix: The Art and Science of Balance

An effective hashtag strategy isn't just about finding individual good hashtags; it's about creating the right mix to maximize reach and relevance. AI can help you achieve this balance by suggesting a combination of:

- **Broad/Popular Hashtags:** These have high search volume and can give your content initial visibility (e.g., #marketing, #smallbusiness, #foodie). Use these sparingly as competition is fierce.
- **Niche-Specific Hashtags:** These are more targeted to your specific industry, topic, or audience and can attract more qualified engagement (e.g., #sustainablecoffeeshops, #AIforSMBs,

#veganbakingrecipes). These are often where you'll find your most engaged audience.

- **Branded Hashtags:** Unique to your business, used to build community, track user-generated content (UGC), and promote campaigns (e.g., #YourBrandNameHere, #YourCampaign-Name, #YourBrandCommunity).
- **Community Hashtags:** Hashtags used by specific online communities your target audience belongs to (e.g., #bookstagram for book lovers, #womenintech for women in the technology sector).
- **Location-Based Hashtags:** If you're a local business or targeting a specific geographic area, these are crucial (e.g., #LondonCafe, #NYCMarketing, #ParisianBoutique).
- **Content-Descriptive Hashtags:** Tags that accurately describe what your post is about (e.g., #tutorial, #behindthescenes, #productreview).

AI tools can analyze the performance of different hashtag combinations over time (if integrated with your analytics), helping you understand what works best for your specific content and audience. Some tools might even allow you to save sets of effective hashtags for different types of content.

Simple Secret: **Let AI find the hidden gem hashtags that get your content seen by the *right* people. Don't just rely on the obvious or most popular tags where your content will likely drown. Use AI to uncover those niche, high-intent hashtags that connect you directly with your ideal audience and help you stand out from the crowd. For example, a handmade soap maker might use AI to discover that while #soap is too broad, niche tags like #artisansoapmaking, #coldprocesssoaplover, or #naturalhandmadesoap attract highly engaged buyers looking for exactly what they offer. AI can help identify these by analyzing the hashtags used by successful competitors or by accounts their target audience frequently engages with.**

By integrating AI into your hashtag research and selection process, you can save significant time, improve the discoverability of your social media content, reduce the trial-and-error, and ultimately drive more meaningful engagement and growth for your business. It's about working smarter, not just harder, to ensure your valuable content reaches the audience it's intended for.

E. AI for Influencer Marketing – Finding the Right Partners

Influencer marketing has become a significant component of many social media strategies. Partnering with the right influencers can help brands reach new, targeted audiences, build trust, and drive conversions. However, identifying truly relevant and authentic influencers amidst a sea of self-proclaimed gurus and accounts with inflated follower counts can be a daunting and time-consuming task. Artificial Intelligence offers a more data-driven and efficient approach to discovering, vetting, and even managing influencer relationships.

AI Tools for Identifying Relevant and Authentic Influencers: Looking Beyond Follower Counts

Simply choosing influencers based on their follower count is a common mistake that can lead to wasted budgets and ineffective campaigns. AI-powered influencer discovery platforms go much deeper, analyzing a multitude of factors to identify the best fit for your brand:

- **Audience Demographics and Psychographics:** AI can analyze an influencer's audience to ensure it aligns with your target customer profile. This includes not just age, gender, and location, but also interests, values, brand affinities, and purchasing behaviors. It's about reaching the *right* people, not just a lot of people.
- **Content Relevance and Quality:** AI algorithms can analyze the influencer"s content (text, images, videos) for relevance to your brand, industry, and campaign themes. They can also assess the quality of the content, its tone, and whether it aligns with your brand values.

- **Engagement Rate and Authenticity:** High follower counts mean little if the audience isn"t genuinely engaged. AI tools scrutinize true engagement rates (likes, comments, shares, saves relative to follower count), looking for patterns that indicate authentic interaction rather than just passive following. They can differentiate between meaningful comments and generic bot-like responses.
- **Brand Fit and Affinity:** AI can assess an influencer's past brand collaborations and organic brand mentions to determine if they have a genuine affinity for brands like yours or if they frequently promote competitors, which might create a conflict of interest.
- **Niche Influence and Authority:** AI can identify micro-influencers or nano-influencers who may have smaller followings but possess very high authority and engagement within a specific niche. These influencers often have a more dedicated and trusting audience, leading to better results for certain campaigns.
- **Performance Prediction:** Some advanced AI tools can even predict the potential reach, engagement, and even conversion rates an influencer might generate for your specific campaign based on their past performance and audience characteristics.

Detecting Fake Followers and Engagement: Ensuring You're Paying for Real Influence

One of the biggest plagues in influencer marketing is the prevalence of fake followers, bot-driven engagement, and inflated metrics. AI is instrumental in combating this issue:

- **Follower Audit Algorithms:** AI tools can analyze an influencer's follower list for suspicious patterns, such as accounts with no profile pictures, no posts, generic names, or a high ratio of following to followers. They can identify batches of followers acquired suddenly, which might indicate purchased followers.

- **Engagement Pattern Analysis:** AI can detect unnatural engagement patterns, such as a sudden spike in likes from low-quality accounts immediately after a post, or comments that are generic and repetitive across many posts. Authentic engagement tends to be more organic and varied.
- **Audience Credibility Scoring:** Many AI platforms provide an audience credibility score or a percentage of likely fake followers, helping you filter out influencers with artificially inflated numbers.
- **Comment Sentiment and Relevance:** AI can analyze the sentiment and relevance of comments on an influencer's posts. A high volume of irrelevant or spammy comments can be a red flag.

Platforms like **Grin**, **Upfluence**, **Aspire (formerly AspireIQ)**, **CreatorIQ**, and **HypeAuditor** are well-known in the influencer marketing space and leverage AI extensively for discovery, vetting (including fraud detection), and campaign management. These tools often allow you to search for influencers based on specific criteria, analyze their profiles in detail, and manage communication and payments.

Simple Secret: **Use AI to find influencers whose audience genuinely matches yours and whose engagement is real. Don't be swayed by big numbers alone; let AI dig deeper to uncover authentic partners who can truly champion your brand to the right people.**

By incorporating AI into your influencer marketing efforts, you can make more informed decisions, avoid costly mistakes by partnering with inauthentic influencers, and build more effective, data-driven campaigns. This leads to more genuine connections with your target audience and a better return on your influencer marketing investment.

3.4 Case Studies: AI-Powered Social Media Success

Theory and explanations are valuable, but seeing how these AI strategies play out in the real world can provide even greater clarity and inspiration. In this section, we'll look at a couple of examples (hypothetical, but based on common applications and results) of how businesses, particularly small to medium-sized ones, might leverage AI to achieve significant improvements in their social media marketing efforts. These case studies will illustrate how the "simple AI secrets" we've discussed can be practically applied to overcome common challenges and drive tangible results.

3.2 Automating Social Media Posting with AI

Consistency is king in the realm of social media. Regularly sharing valuable content keeps your audience engaged, your brand top-of-mind, and the ever-watchful algorithms happy. A sporadic or inconsistent posting schedule can lead to your content being deprioritized by platform algorithms, meaning fewer of your followers will see it, and your overall reach will diminish. But who has the time to manually post across multiple platforms, multiple times a day, all while trying to hit those elusive "optimal posting times" for each specific audience and platform? For busy small business owners and entrepreneurs, this can be a major drain on precious time and resources, often leading to social media falling by the wayside despite its importance. This is where AI-powered automation steps in, not just as a simple scheduler, but as an intelligent assistant that can help you maintain a powerful and consistent online presence with far less manual effort, freeing you to focus on strategy, engagement, and other core business activities.

In this section, we'll explore how AI is revolutionizing social media automation. We'll look beyond basic scheduling to uncover the strategic benefits of letting AI handle your posting, how AI tools can intelligently curate relevant third-party content to supplement your own, and even how they can assist with some aspects of engagement, such as responding to common queries or categorizing incoming messages. We'll also cover the best practices for setting up and managing this automation, ensuring that AI acts as a powerful amplifier for your authentic voice and human touch, rather than a robotic replacement that alienates your audience. The goal is to use automation to enhance efficiency and effectiveness, not to remove the genuine connection that social media thrives on.

Case Study 1: Fringe - Overcoming Writer's Block and Scaling Content with AI

Background: Fringe, a small brand design company, prided itself on its creative output and unique branding solutions for its clients. However, like many creative agencies, the team, including the owner, often faced the dreaded writer"s block, especially when it came to generating fresh, engaging copy for their own social media channels and for their diverse range of clients. Crafting compelling Instagram captions, snappy Facebook ad copy, website landing page text, and even product descriptions consistently was a time-consuming challenge. The owner initially believed that AI writing tools weren"t necessary for a team of creative professionals.

The Challenge: Fringe"s primary challenges were:

1. **Writer's Block:** The creative team would get stuck for hours, sometimes days, trying to find the right words for a social media post or a client's new product launch, leading to delays and frustration.
2. **Content Scalability:** As the agency grew, the demand for high-quality written content for various social media platforms and client projects increased, making it difficult to keep up without burning out the team or hiring more writers.
3. **Maintaining Freshness:** Consistently producing unique and engaging copy that didn't sound repetitive, especially for ongoing social media campaigns, was becoming increasingly difficult.

The AI Solution Implemented: Skeptical at first, the owner of Fringe decided to try **Copy.ai**, an AI-powered copywriting tool. Copy.ai works by taking a company or brand name and a short description as input. Based on this, its algorithm can generate various types of marketing copy, including social media content, ad headlines, product descriptions, and more. The Fringe team began using Copy.ai for several specific social media related tasks:

- **Generating Initial Drafts for Social Media Captions:** For their own agency's Instagram and LinkedIn posts, they would input the topic or image concept and let Copy.ai generate several caption options. This provided a starting point, breaking through the initial writer"s block.
- **Brainstorming Ad Copy Variations:** When creating Facebook and Instagram ad campaigns for clients, they used Copy.ai to quickly generate multiple versions of ad headlines and body text, allowing for A/B testing and optimization.
- **Developing Product Descriptions for E-commerce Clients:** For clients selling products online, Copy.ai helped create engaging and benefit-driven product descriptions that could be used on their websites and in social media shopping posts.
- **Overcoming Creative Blocks for Blog Post Ideas (to be shared on social):** While not directly social copy, they also used it to brainstorm blog post titles and introductions, which would then be promoted across their social channels.

Results and Key Takeaways:

- **Significant Time Savings & Increased Efficiency:** The owner of Fringe reported that what used to take hours of brainstorming and drafting could now be accomplished much faster. The AI provided a solid foundation that the team could then refine and customize. This was particularly true for repetitive tasks like generating multiple ad variations.

- **Overcoming Writer's Block:** Copy.ai became an invaluable tool for breaking through creative ruts. Even if the AI-generated copy wasn"t perfect, it often sparked new ideas or provided a different angle that the team hadn"t considered. The owner mentioned solving instances of writer's block that he and his team had been dealing with for months.
- **Improved Content Quality and Variety:** The tool helped generate a wider variety of phrasing and approaches than the team might have come up with on their own, leading to fresher and more diverse social media content for both Fringe and its clients.
- **Enhanced Scalability:** Fringe was able to take on more client work requiring written content without a proportional increase in staff or stress. They could generate rows of copy options quickly.
- **AI as an Assistant, Not a Replacement:** Crucially, the owner realized that Copy.ai wasn"t there to replace his creative team but to augment their abilities. The AI handled the initial heavy lifting or provided inspiration, and the human designers and copywriters then added their expertise, brand understanding, and final polish.

Simple AI Secret Illustrated: This case study perfectly illustrates the secret: **Use AI to write faster and overcome creative blocks, not just to write *for* you.** Fringe leveraged AI as a brainstorming partner and a first-draft assistant. This allowed their skilled human team to focus on refining, strategizing, and adding the unique creative touches that set their clients" brands apart, all while significantly boosting their content output for social media and other marketing channels. The AI tool helped eliminate the busy work and mental hurdles, freeing up human creativity.

(This case study is adapted from information provided by Marketing AI Institute regarding Copy.ai and Fringe.)

A. The Strategic Benefits of AI-Powered Social Media Automation

Automating your social media posting with AI isn't just about saving a few minutes here and there; it's a strategic move that can yield significant benefits for your business, transforming your social media from a reactive chore into a proactive growth engine. When AI takes over the more repetitive aspects of social media management, it frees you and your team to focus on higher-value activities like strategy development, deeper customer engagement, creative content ideation, and analyzing the results of your campaigns. Let's explore some of the key strategic advantages that make AI automation a non-negotiable for savvy businesses today.

Time and Resource Savings: Reclaiming Your Most Valuable Assets

This is perhaps the most immediate and tangible benefit, and one that resonates deeply with busy entrepreneurs and small business owners. Manually logging into multiple social media platforms (Facebook, Instagram, X/Twitter, LinkedIn, Pinterest, TikTok, etc.), crafting or adapting posts for each platform's unique format in real-time, and ensuring they go out at optimal intervals is incredibly time-consuming. It's a recipe for burnout and can easily consume hours each week that could be better spent on activities that directly drive revenue, enhance customer satisfaction, or foster innovation.

AI-powered automation tools allow you to schedule weeks or even months of content in advance, across all your chosen platforms, from a single dashboard. Imagine dedicating a few hours at the beginning of the month to plan and schedule your core social media content, and then letting AI handle the execution. This dramatically reduces the daily administrative burden. Those reclaimed hours can be reinvested into:

- **Core Business Functions:** Product development, sales calls, customer service, financial management.

- **Strategic Marketing Planning:** Analyzing market trends, refining your overall marketing strategy, exploring new channels.
- **Creating More In-Depth, High-Quality Content:** Developing pillar blog posts, producing engaging videos, designing comprehensive lead magnets – content that AI can then help you promote.
- **Networking and Relationship Building:** Engaging in meaningful one-on-one conversations on social media, attending industry events, or building partnerships.

Case Study Snippet: The Solopreneur Consultant

A business consultant, operating as a solopreneur, found herself spending nearly 10 hours a week manually posting industry insights and tips across LinkedIn, X/Twitter, and a Facebook Business Page. This left little time for client work and business development. By implementing an AI-powered social media automation tool, she was able to batch-create her content for the month (using AI writing assistants to help draft posts) and schedule it all in about 3 hours. The AI tool also helped identify optimal posting times. This freed up nearly 7 hours a week, which she then dedicated to personalized outreach to potential clients on LinkedIn and developing a new online workshop, significantly boosting her lead generation and revenue.

Consistent Online Presence: Staying Top-of-Mind, Effortlessly

Consistency is crucial for building brand awareness, fostering audience engagement, and maintaining favor with social media algorithms. Sporadic posting – a flurry of activity one week and then silence the next – can lead to your content being deprioritized by platform algorithms (meaning fewer of your followers see it) and can make your brand appear unreliable or inactive to your audience. Potential customers might wonder if you're still in business or if you're serious about your online presence.

AI automation ensures that your brand maintains a regular, consistent posting schedule, even when you're swamped with other tasks, on vacation, or asleep. This steady stream of valuable content keeps your brand visible in your audience\s feeds, reinforces your messaging, builds anticipation for your posts, and helps to cultivate a reliable online presence that your followers can count on. This consistent activity signals to algorithms that your account is active and valuable, which can potentially increase your organic reach and make it easier for new followers to discover you.

Optimized Posting Times for Maximum Impact: Hitting the Sweet Spot

Posting content when your target audience is most active and receptive can significantly increase its visibility, engagement (likes, comments, shares), and click-through rates. But how do you know when those optimal times are? They can vary greatly depending on the platform (e.g., LinkedIn usage peaks during business hours, while Instagram might see more activity in the evenings and on weekends), your specific audience demographics (e.g., students might be active at different times than working professionals), their geographic location, and even the day of the week or time of year.

Manually trying to figure this out and then being available to post at those exact times is a logistical nightmare. AI-powered social media automation tools often come with built-in analytics that can analyze your past engagement data (which posts got the most interaction and when) and your audience's activity patterns to determine the best times to post for maximum impact on each specific platform. Some tools can automatically schedule your content to go out at these AI-determined optimal times, or provide you with a suggested schedule. This takes the guesswork out of your scheduling and ensures your valuable content has the best possible chance of being seen and interacted with by the largest segment of your target audience.

***Simple Secret:* Post when your audience is listening, not just when you have time, with AI-driven scheduling. Let AI analyze the data to pinpoint those golden windows of opportunity**

across different platforms, ensuring your messages land when they're most likely to make an impact and spark engagement. This is like having a data scientist constantly optimizing your social media timing.

By leveraging these strategic benefits, AI-powered social media automation transforms your social media efforts from a reactive, time-intensive chore into a proactive, efficient, and more impactful component of your overall marketing strategy. It allows you to work smarter, not just harder, in building and maintaining a strong and engaging online presence that contributes directly to your business goals.

Case Study 2: Ad-Flex Communications - Optimizing Social Ad Spend with AI

Background: Ad-flex communications, a marketing agency, was tasked with running social media advertising campaigns on Facebook and Instagram for one of its clients. Like many agencies, they relied on historical market research, past campaign performance, and the experience of their ad specialists to design ad creatives (images, videos, copy) and set campaign parameters. However, the dynamic nature of social media advertising meant that what worked yesterday might not work today, and manually optimizing campaigns in real-time was challenging and resource-intensive.

The Challenge: Ad-flex communications faced several key challenges in delivering optimal results for their client"s social ad campaigns:

1. **Guesswork in Creative Performance:** It was difficult to predict with certainty which ad creatives (combinations of visuals, headlines, copy, calls-to-action) would perform best before launching a campaign and spending a significant portion of the budget.
2. **Manual and Time-Consuming Optimization:** Continuously monitoring ad performance, identifying underperform-

ing assets, and reallocating budget to better-performing ads required constant human intervention and analysis.

3. **Maximizing ROI on Ad Spend:** The agency was under pressure to deliver the highest possible conversion rates and the lowest cost per result for their client, ensuring the ad budget was spent as efficiently as possible.
4. **Adapting to Market Changes:** Social media trends and audience behavior can shift rapidly. Manually adjusting campaigns to account for these real-time changes was a slow process.

The AI Solution Implemented: Ad-flex communications decided to use **Pattern89** (now part of Shutterstock.AI), an AI platform designed to optimize advertising creative and performance on platforms like Facebook and Instagram. Pattern89's AI analyzes ad creatives across thousands of dimensions (e.g., image elements, colors, copy length, sentiment, calls-to-action) to predict performance and provide optimization recommendations. Ad-flex utilized Pattern89's solutions – Analyze, Predict, and Optimize – for one of their client"s campaigns and ran a comparative campaign for the same client without AI assistance over a two-week period.

- **Analyze & Predict:** Before launching the AI-assisted campaign, Pattern89's AI analyzed the planned ad creatives, predicting how different elements would likely perform based on its vast dataset of past ad performance.
- **Optimize:** During the campaign, the Pattern89 platform automatically and continuously adjusted and modified the AI-assisted campaign to account for market changes and performance data, reallocating budget to higher-performing ad variations and suggesting creative tweaks.

Results and Key Takeaways: The results from the two-week comparative test were striking:

- **Drastically Lower Cost Per Result:** The AI-assisted campaign managed by Pattern89 achieved an **81% lower cost per result** compared to the manually managed campaign. This meant the client was getting significantly more desired outcomes (e.g., clicks, leads, conversions) for their money.
- **Significantly Higher Conversion Rate:** The AI-optimized campaign had a **439% higher conversion rate** with an equal ad spend. This demonstrated the AI's effectiveness in not just reaching people, but reaching the *right* people with the most effective creatives to drive action.
- **Increased Impressions:** The AI-assisted campaign also garnered **11% more impressions**, indicating better reach and visibility.
- **Data-Driven Optimization Outperforms Manual Analysis:** The case study highlighted that human analysis of historical market research, while valuable, was no match for the AI's ability to process massive amounts of data, make predictions, and implement consistent, real-time optimizations.
- **Continuous Improvement:** The AI's ability to constantly learn and adjust meant the campaign was always striving for better performance, adapting to the dynamic social advertising environment.

Simple AI Secret Illustrated: This case study demonstrates the power of: **Let AI optimize your ad creatives and targeting in real-time for maximum impact.** Instead of relying solely on intuition or past experience, ad-flex communications used AI to make data-driven decisions about their ad creatives and to continuously refine the campaign while it was live. The AI acted as a tireless, hyper-efficient ad manager, constantly tweaking variables to achieve the best possible results, far exceeding what could be done manually within the same timeframe and budget.

(This case study is adapted from information provided by Marketing AI Institute regarding Pattern89 and ad-flex communications.)

B. AI Tools for Intelligent Scheduling and Content Curation

Beyond simply queuing up posts you've already created, modern AI-powered social media tools bring a new level of intelligence to both scheduling your own content and discovering and curating relevant third-party content to share with your audience. This ensures your feed remains active, valuable, diverse, and optimized for engagement without requiring constant manual intervention. It's about creating a smart, semi-autonomous content pipeline.

Overview of AI-Powered Scheduling Platforms: Smart Timing and Efficient Workflows

Many social media management platforms now incorporate AI to enhance their scheduling capabilities, moving far beyond basic date-and-time selection. These platforms offer features designed to maximize your content\s impact and streamline your workflow, making your social media management more strategic and less reactive. When evaluating these tools, look for:

- **Best-Time-to-Post Suggestions:** As discussed earlier, AI analyzes your audience's activity patterns on each platform and your historical engagement data to recommend the optimal times to publish your content. This isn\t a generic best practice; it\s tailored to *your* specific audience. Tools like **SocialBee** are noted for suggesting the best times to post based on past performance. Many comprehensive platforms like **Sprout Social**, **Hootsuite**, and **Buffer** also offer similar AI-driven scheduling optimization, often showing you a heatmap of when your audience is most engaged.
- **Content Queues and Categories:** Organize your approved content into categories (e.g., "Blog Posts," "Industry News," "Behind-the-Scenes," "User-Generated Content," "Promotional Offers," "Educational Tips"). AI can then help you create a balanced posting schedule, ensuring a good mix of content types goes out regularly, preventing your feed from becoming too monotonous or overly promotional. **SmarterQueue** is a tool

that emphasizes its intelligent content categorization and evergreen recycling features, allowing you to set rules for how often content from each category should be posted.

- **Bulk Scheduling with AI Optimization:** Upload multiple posts at once (e.g., from a spreadsheet or by connecting to a content library), and let the AI distribute them across your calendar at optimal times or according to predefined category schedules. This is a massive time-saver for campaigns or when you have a batch of content ready.
- **AI-Powered Performance Predictions:** Some advanced tools, like **FeedHive** (mentioned by Zapier), offer AI-powered performance predictions to help you tune your posts for maximum engagement *even before* they are scheduled. This might involve suggestions for improving copy, visuals, or hashtag choices based on what the AI predicts will perform well.
- **Content Recycling and Evergreen Posting:** Not all content has a short shelf life. AI can identify your top-performing past content (evergreen content like how-to guides, foundational industry insights, or popular case studies) and intelligently reschedule it to reach new audiences or remind existing followers, extending the lifespan of your best work. **FeedHive** is also highlighted for its AI-powered content recycling, ensuring your best pieces continue to deliver value.
- **Visual Calendar Interface:** A clear, drag-and-drop visual content calendar makes it easy to see your schedule at a glance, identify gaps, and make adjustments as needed. Most leading schedulers like **SocialPilot**, **Buffer**, and **Sprout Social** offer this, often color-coded by platform or content category.

Practical Example: The Busy Bakery Owner

A local bakery owner wants to maintain an active presence on Instagram and Facebook but has limited time. She uses an AI-powered scheduler to:

1. Create content categories: "New Products," "Customer Spotlights (UGC)," "Baking Tips," "Holiday Specials," and "Behind the Scenes."
2. Bulk uploads photos and pre-written captions (perhaps drafted with an AI writing assistant) for the month into these categories.
3. Lets the AI tool determine the optimal posting times for Instagram (e.g., evenings and weekends when people are looking for treats) and Facebook (e.g., lunchtimes and early evenings).
4. Sets rules for the AI to post one "New Product" shot every Monday, a "Customer Spotlight" every Wednesday, a "Baking Tip" every Friday, and sprinkle "Behind the Scenes" content throughout the week, ensuring a varied feed.
5. The AI also identifies her most popular past posts (e.g., a video on frosting techniques) and automatically re-shares them every few months to capture new followers.

This system allows her to spend just a few hours a month on social media planning, while AI ensures a consistent and optimized posting schedule.

AI for Content Curation: Keeping Your Feed Fresh and Valuable

Sharing only your own content can sometimes feel overly promotional or repetitive. Curating and sharing high-quality, relevant content from other reputable sources within your industry (e.g., articles, studies, infographics, videos from non-competing thought leaders) can add significant value for your audience, position you as a knowledgeable resource and hub of information, and help fill gaps in your content calendar. However, finding truly great content to curate can be as time-consuming as creating it yourself. AI can make this process much more efficient.

AI-powered content curation tools work by:

- **Monitoring Sources:** Scanning blogs, news sites, industry publications, academic journals, and even social media for content relevant to keywords, topics, or specific sources you specify.
- **Filtering and Relevance Scoring:** Using AI (often NLP and machine learning) to assess the quality, credibility, and relevance of potential content to your audience and brand. Some tools can even analyze sentiment to avoid sharing negatively skewed articles unintentionally.
- **Suggesting Content:** Presenting you with a feed of suggested articles, blog posts, or videos to share, often with a summary or key takeaways highlighted by the AI.
- **Automated Sharing (with review):** Some tools can even automatically add approved curated content to your posting schedule, often allowing you to add your own commentary or introductory text.

Platforms like **Quuu** are specifically known for curated content automation, finding relevant third-party content (often hand-curated by humans initially, then categorized by AI) and integrating with schedulers like Buffer or Hootsuite. **ContentStudio**, mentioned by Zapier, is strong in content discovery and staying on top of content topics, which aids curation by suggesting articles, videos, and GIFs. **SocialPilot** is also often cited as a cost-effective tool with comprehensive content curation features, allowing you to find and schedule relevant content from various sources. **Sprinklr**, in its blog, mentions that its platform helps find and share relevant content faster using AI, by sifting through millions of articles to surface the most relevant ones for your brand.

Simple Secret: **Use AI content curation to become a trusted resource, not just a broadcaster. Set up AI to monitor key industry blogs, news sites, and thought leaders. Review the AI's suggestions daily or weekly, add your own insightful comment or question to the curated piece, and schedule it. This shows**

your audience you're engaged with your industry and dedicated to bringing them value beyond your own products or services.

By using AI for intelligent scheduling of your own content and smart curation of external content, you ensure that your social media presence is not only consistent but also rich with a variety of valuable information, posted at times when your audience is most likely to see and engage with it. This strategic automation frees you to focus on creating high-impact original content and building deeper, more meaningful relationships with your followers.

Conclusion: Your Social Media, Supercharged by AI

Throughout this chapter, we've journeyed through the exciting landscape of AI-powered social media marketing, uncovering simple yet powerful secrets that can help you, as a small business owner or entrepreneur, transform your social media efforts from a source of stress into a strategic asset. We've seen how AI can be your tireless assistant in understanding your audience, crafting compelling content, automating tedious posting schedules, and analyzing performance with a depth you might not have thought possible.

Let's quickly recap the core "Simple AI Secrets" we've explored:

- **Understanding Your Audience:** Use AI listening to find out what your audience *really* wants to talk about and let AI be your data detective to build rich, actionable audience personas.
- **Content Creation:** Let AI be your brainstorming partner for endless content inspiration, help you write faster (not *for* you), create unique visuals without needing a design degree, and find those hidden gem hashtags that get your content seen.
- **Automation & Scheduling:** Post when your audience is listening, not just when you have time, with AI-driven scheduling. Use AI for quick answers to common questions via chatbots, but always keep a human touch for deeper engagement.

- **Analytics & Insights:** Let AI be your data detective, finding clues your competitors miss by going beyond surface metrics. Use AI sentiment analysis to listen to the *emotions* behind the words. Use AI to be a smart observer of your competition, and to connect the dots between your social media activity and your bottom line (ROI).
- **Influencer Marketing:** Use AI to find influencers whose audience genuinely matches yours and whose engagement is real, looking beyond just follower numbers.

It's crucial to remember that AI is a tool – an incredibly powerful one – but it's most effective when it augments human creativity, strategy, and empathy, not when it attempts to replace them entirely. The goal isn't to create a robotic, impersonal social media presence. Instead, it's to leverage AI's strengths in data processing, pattern recognition, and automation to free up your valuable time and mental energy. This allows you to focus on what you do best: building genuine relationships, understanding your customers on a deeper level, and injecting your unique brand personality into every interaction.

Don't be intimidated by the term "Artificial Intelligence." As we've seen, many AI tools are designed with user-friendliness in mind, offering intuitive interfaces and clear benefits. The key is to start small, experiment, and find the tools and strategies that best fit your specific business needs and goals. You don't need to implement everything at once. Perhaps begin by using an AI writing assistant to help with content ideation or an AI-powered scheduler to optimize your posting times.

As you integrate these AI secrets into your social media workflow, you'll likely find that you're not only saving time and resources but also achieving better results: more engagement, higher quality leads, increased brand awareness, and a clearer understanding of your impact. The landscape of AI and social media is constantly evolving, so a mindset of continuous learning and adaptation will serve you well.

So, take these insights, choose one or two areas where AI can make an immediate difference for you, and start experimenting. The power to supercharge your social media marketing is now more accessible than ever. Embrace AI as your partner, and watch your business grow.

Remember, the ultimate goal is to build meaningful connections and drive business results. AI is here to help you do that more effectively and efficiently. For more personalized guidance on implementing AI strategies in your business, don't hesitate to connect with me, Jason Fleagle, at thejasonfleagle.com.

In the next chapter, we'll explore another critical area where AI can provide a significant boost to your business: AI for Sales and Customer Relationship Management. Get ready to discover how AI can help you streamline your sales process, nurture leads more effectively, and build stronger, more profitable customer relationships.

C. Automating Engagement (Carefully!): The Human-AI Partnership

While AI can automate many aspects of social media posting and scheduling, automating direct engagement with your audience – the comments, messages, and conversations – requires a much more nuanced and careful approach. Genuine human connection is the cornerstone of strong community building on social media. People follow and interact with brands they feel a connection to, and overly robotic or impersonal automated responses can quickly erode trust and alienate your audience. However, AI can still play a valuable role in managing initial interactions, filtering communications, and providing quick answers to common questions, provided it's implemented thoughtfully and with clear human oversight. It's about creating a human-AI partnership where AI handles the volume and repetition, and humans handle the nuance and relationship-building.

AI Chatbots for Basic Social Media Interactions: Your First Line of Response

AI-powered chatbots can be integrated with your social media messaging platforms (like Facebook Messenger, Instagram DMs, or even X/Twitter DMs) to handle common, repetitive inquiries. This can be particularly useful for:

- **Answering Frequently Asked Questions (FAQs):** Chatbots can be trained on your business's FAQs (e.g., store hours, shipping policies, return procedures, basic product information, service areas) to provide instant answers to customers, 24/7, even outside of business hours. This immediate responsiveness can significantly improve customer satisfaction.
- **Initial Lead Qualification:** They can ask preliminary questions to gather information from potential leads (e.g., budget, timeline, specific needs) before passing them on to a human sales representative. This ensures that your sales team spends their time on more qualified prospects.
- **Directing Users to Resources:** Chatbots can guide users to relevant pages on your website, specific blog posts, help articles, video tutorials, or product pages, helping users find the information they need quickly without human intervention.
- **Taking Simple Orders or Bookings:** For some businesses, chatbots can be configured to handle basic transactions like booking an appointment or taking a simple order for a standardized product.

Platforms like **Chatfuel** are well-known for building AI chatbots for Facebook and Telegram, enabling businesses to provide instant replies and capture leads, as mentioned by Great Scott Social Media and Sprinklr. **Metricool** also notes that AI-driven chatbots can handle customer queries and recommend products. Many other platforms like **Tidio**, **ManyChat**, or even custom solutions using **Dialogflow** (from Google) or **Microsoft Bot Framework** allow for the creation of sophisticated chatbots. Your course notes also highlight "Generating content for chatbots" and "Generating customer service responses" as key uses for ChatGPT, which can be the engine behind some of these chatbot interactions.

When implementing chatbots, it"s crucial to:

- **Clearly Disclose It's a Bot:** Users should generally know when they are interacting with an AI to manage expectations. A simple "Hi, I'm [Brand Name]"s automated assistant! I can help with X, Y, and Z. If you need more help, just type "speak to a human"-"
- **Design Clear Escalation Paths:** Ensure there's an easy and obvious way for users to connect with a human if the bot can't help, if the query is complex, sensitive, or if the user simply prefers to speak to a person. Frustrating a user by trapping them in a bot loop is a sure way to lose them.
- **Train and Test Thoroughly:** Continuously train your chatbot with new information, common customer questions, and variations of how those questions are asked. Test its responses rigorously to ensure accuracy, a helpful tone, and that it aligns with your brand voice.
- **Focus on Simple, Repetitive Tasks:** Don't try to make chatbots handle nuanced, emotionally charged, or highly personalized conversations. Their strength lies in efficiency for straightforward interactions.
- **Monitor Interactions:** Regularly review chatbot conversations to identify areas for improvement, common pain points the bot can"t solve, and opportunities to update its knowledge base.

Simple Secret: **Use AI for quick answers to common questions and for guiding users, but always keep a human touch readily available for deeper engagement and complex issues. Think of chatbots as helpful receptionists or triage nurses who can handle the basics efficiently, freeing up your human team for more meaningful conversations and problem-solving that require empathy and critical thinking.**

AI for Comment Moderation (Basic Filtering): Maintaining a Healthy Community

Managing comments on your social media posts can be overwhelming, especially if you have a large or very active audience, or if your content touches on sensitive topics. Unfortunately, not all comments are positive or constructive; spam, abusive language, hate speech, or irrelevant self-promotion can detract from the community experience you're trying to build and can even damage your brand reputation. AI can assist in the initial filtering and management of these comments.

AI-powered comment moderation tools use Natural Language Processing (NLP) and machine learning to:

- **Identify Spam:** Automatically detect and hide or flag comments that are clearly spammy (e.g., repetitive links to unrelated websites, generic promotional messages, strings of emojis or gibberish).
- **Filter Potentially Harmful Content:** Flag comments containing profanity, hate speech, bullying language, or personal attacks based on predefined keyword lists, learned patterns, or sentiment analysis. **Tribe.AI** discusses how AI-powered moderation helps maintain safe online communities by identifying harmful content.
- **Categorize Comments:** Some tools might categorize comments by sentiment (positive, negative, neutral) or topic, helping you prioritize which ones need an urgent human response (e.g., a very negative comment or a customer complaint) versus those that can be addressed later (e.g., a simple positive comment).

Tools like **Smart Moderation** (mentioned by CommentGuard) allow real-time comment monitoring with customizable AI algorithms. **Sprinklr** also provides a robust social media moderation suite, leveraging AI for large enterprises, as noted by Social Factor.

Utopia Analytics offers AI content moderation software designed to protect platforms from toxic content. Many native social media platforms (like Facebook and Instagram) also have built-in moderation tools that use AI to filter certain types of comments, and you can often add your own keyword blocklists.

However, it is absolutely critical to emphasize the need for **human review and oversight** in comment moderation. AI is not perfect and can sometimes misinterpret context, sarcasm, cultural nuances, or slang. Relying solely on AI for comment deletion could lead to censoring legitimate (though perhaps critical) feedback, accidentally removing valuable user contributions, or failing to identify subtle forms of abuse. Instead, use AI as a first-pass filter and assistant:

- **Automate Hiding/Deleting of Obvious Spam:** For clear-cut spam with no redeeming value, automation can be very effective and save a lot of time.
- **Flag Potentially Problematic Comments for Human Review:** For anything ambiguous, potentially harmful, or negative, AI should flag it for a human moderator to make the final decision on whether to hide, delete, respond, or ignore.
- **Never Auto-Delete Based on Sentiment Alone:** Negative feedback, even if critical, can be valuable. It offers insights into customer dissatisfaction and opportunities to improve or publicly address concerns. Deleting it automatically can damage trust and make your brand appear as though it's hiding something.
- **Develop Clear Moderation Guidelines:** Your human moderators should have clear guidelines on how to handle different types of comments, ensuring consistency and fairness.

Practical Example: The Gaming Community Manager

A popular online gaming company uses AI to help moderate comments on its busy Facebook page and Discord server. The AI automatically filters out and deletes comments containing known spam links and racial slurs. It flags comments with excessive profanity or personal attacks for review by human community managers. This allows the human team to focus on responding to genuine player feedback, answering questions about game updates, and fostering positive interactions, rather than constantly battling spam and overt toxicity. They also use the AI to identify frequently asked questions in comments, which then informs their FAQ chatbot and future content creation.

Automating engagement with AI is about finding the right balance. Use AI to handle the high-volume, low-complexity interactions and to filter out the noise, but always ensure that genuine human interaction, empathy, and strategic oversight remain at the heart of your community management strategy. This approach allows you to be responsive and maintain a positive online environment efficiently, without sacrificing the authenticity that builds lasting relationships and brand loyalty.

References for Chapter 3

AI Tools and Platforms:

- **Aspire (formerly AspireIQ):** Influencer marketing platform.
- **Brandwatch:** Social listening and analytics platform.
- **Buffer:** Social media management and scheduling tool.
- **Chatfuel:** Platform for building AI chatbots, particularly for Facebook.
- **ChatGPT (OpenAI):** Versatile AI language model used for content generation, chatbot responses, etc.
- **CommentGuard:** (Mentioned as a source that notes Smart Moderation).
- **ContentStudio:** Content discovery and curation platform.
- **Copy.ai:** AI-powered copywriting tool (featured in Case Study 1).

- **CreatorIQ:** Influencer marketing platform.
- **Dialogflow (Google):** Platform for building conversational AI.
- **FeedHive:** AI-powered social media scheduling, content creation, and analytics tool.
- **Flick:** AI hashtag generator and analytics tool.
- **Funnel.io:** Marketing data integration and reporting platform.
- **Google Analytics:** Web analytics service that offers insights into website traffic, including referrals from social media.
- **Great Scott Social Media:** (Mentioned as a source that notes Chatfuel).
- **Grin:** Influencer marketing platform.
- **Hootsuite / Hootsuite Impact / Hootsuite Insights:** Social media management, scheduling, analytics, and influencer insights platform.
- **HubSpot:** CRM and marketing automation platform with social media analytics capabilities.
- **HypeAuditor:** AI-powered influencer audit and discovery tool.
- **ManyChat:** Platform for building chatbots, particularly for Facebook Messenger.
- **Metricool:** Social media management and analytics tool.
- **Microsoft Bot Framework:** Platform for building enterprise-grade bots.
- **NetBase Quid:** Consumer and market intelligence platform with social listening and analytics.
- **Pattern89 (now part of Shutterstock.AI):** AI platform for optimizing advertising creative and performance (featured in Case Study 2).
- **Quuu:** Content curation automation tool.
- **SEMrush:** Online visibility management and content marketing platform with social media tracking.

- **Smart Moderation:** AI-powered comment moderation tool.
- **SmarterQueue:** Intelligent social media scheduling tool with content categorization.
- **SocialBee:** Social media management tool with scheduling and content categorization.
- **Socialinsider:** (Mentioned as a source that notes Flick).
- **SocialPilot:** Social media scheduling and marketing tool with curation features.
- **Sprinklr:** Unified customer experience management (CXM) platform with social media listening, moderation, and analytics.
- **Sprout Social:** Social media management, analytics, and listening platform.
- **Supermetrics:** Marketing data integration tool for reporting and analytics.
- **Talkwalker:** Social listening and analytics platform.
- **Tidio:** Live chat and chatbot platform.
- **Tribe.AI:** (Mentioned in the context of AI-powered community moderation).
- **Upfluence:** Influencer marketing platform.
- **Utopia Analytics:** AI content moderation software.
- **Zapier:** Online automation tool that connects apps and services (mentioned as a source for FeedHive and ContentStudio).

Case Study: How A College In the South Charts Their AI Future

Background: I had the opportunity to work with a college in the south with over 5,000 students, who found itself at a crossroads that many educational institutions face today. They knew AI was transforming higher education, but they were unsure where to start. Faculty and staff were experimenting with various AI tools in silos, creating inconsistency and potential risks. Leadership needed a unified vision and a concrete roadmap to harness AI's potential while staying true to their mission and values.

The Challenge: The college faced several interconnected obstacles that were preventing them from moving forward with confidence:

- Scattered Experimentation: Different departments were using AI tools without coordination. Some professors were using ChatGPT for curriculum design, while admissions was exploring chatbots for prospective students. There was no central strategy or governance.

- Fear of the Unknown: Many faculty members were concerned that AI would replace their roles or diminish the personal, faith-centered education that defined the institution.

- Resource Constraints: Like many mid-sized institutions, Mississippi College had limited IT resources and budget. They needed to identify the highest-impact opportunities that wouldn't require massive infrastructure investments.

- Lack of Clarity: Leadership wanted to embrace innovation but didn't know which AI use cases were realistic, which were overhyped, and which aligned with their educational mission.

My Approach: I was invited to facilitate a full-day AI Ideation Workshop with a cross-functional team of 25 stakeholders, including the Provost, IT leadership, faculty representatives, admissions staff, and student services administrators. The goal was not just to educate them about AI, but to collaboratively build a prioritized, actionable 90-day roadmap.

Workshop Facilitation Process:

The workshop was divided into four intensive sessions:

Session 1: AI Foundations & Myth-Busting (90 minutes) I began by demystifying AI. We discussed the difference between Narrow AI (what's available today) and General AI (still science fiction), and I walked through real-world examples of AI in education. Critically, I addressed the elephant in the room: the fear that AI would replace educators. I reframed AI as a "force multiplier" that could handle administrative burdens, allowing faculty to focus on what they do best—mentoring and teaching.

Session 2: Pain Point Mapping (60 minutes) I broke the group into five teams, each representing a different area: Academics, Admissions & Enrollment, Student Services, Operations, and Advancement (fundraising and alumni relations). Each team was tasked with identifying their top three operational pain points—the repetitive, time-consuming tasks that drained resources and prevented them from focusing on strategic work.

The energy in the room shifted. This wasn't a theoretical exercise anymore, but was more personal. Teams surfaced real frustrations: the hours spent manually answering the same prospective student questions, the challenge of personalizing outreach to thousands of alumni, the burden of grading and providing feedback on large class assignments.

Session 3: AI Use Case Ideation (90 minutes) With the pain points identified, we moved into ideation. For each pain point, I guided the teams through a structured brainstorming process: "If you had an AI assistant with no limitations, what would you have it do?" We generated over 40 potential AI use cases.

Then came the critical step: prioritization. Using a simple matrix I've refined over dozens of workshops, we scored each use case on two dimensions: Impact (how much time, cost, or quality improvement it could deliver) and Feasibility (how easy it would be to implement with current resources and data). This exercise surfaced the "quick wins"—high-impact, high-feasibility projects that could be launched in 30-60 days.

Session 4: Roadmap Building & Governance (90 minutes) The final session was about turning ideas into action. We selected the top five use cases and built a 90-day implementation roadmap. For each use case, we defined:

- The specific problem it solved
- The AI tools or approach required
- The owner and team responsible
- The success metrics
- The estimated timeline and budget

We also established a lightweight governance structure: an AI Steering Committee that would meet monthly to review progress, share learnings, and approve new projects.

Specific AI Use Cases Identified:

The five prioritized use cases that made it into the 90-day roadmap were:

1. AI-Powered Admissions Chatbot: Deploy a 24/7 chatbot on the admissions website to answer common questions from prospective students and parents, instantly book campus tours, and capture lead information. This addressed the admissions team's biggest pain point: being overwhelmed with repetitive inquiries during peak season.
2. Personalized Alumni Outreach: Use AI to analyze alumni data (graduation year, major, engagement history, giving patterns) and generate personalized email outreach for fundraising campaigns. The advancement team was spending weeks crafting generic appeals; AI could help them create thousands of personalized messages in hours.
3. Automated Grading Assistant for Writing Assignments: Pilot an AI tool in three large freshman writing courses to provide instant, detailed feedback on grammar, structure, and

argument quality. This would free up professors to focus on higher-order feedback and one-on-one mentoring, while students would get faster turnaround times.

4. Curriculum Content Recommendations: Build an AI system that could analyze course syllabi and recommend relevant, up-to-date articles, videos, and case studies for faculty to integrate into their lessons. This would reduce the time faculty spent on content curation and ensure courses stayed current.
5. Predictive Student Success Analytics: Use AI to analyze early indicators (attendance, assignment completion, engagement in the learning management system) to identify students at risk of falling behind. Student services could then proactively reach out with support before a student was in crisis.

The 90-Day Roadmap:

By the end of the workshop, we had a clear, consensus-driven roadmap:

- Days 1-30: Launch the AI admissions chatbot (Owner: Director of Admissions). Success Metric: Reduce average response time from 24 hours to under 5 minutes.
- Days 30-60: Pilot the AI grading assistant in three courses (Owner: Associate Provost). Success Metric: Reduce faculty grading time by 30% while maintaining or improving feedback quality.
- Days 60-90: Deploy personalized alumni outreach for the fall fundraising campaign (Owner: VP of Advancement). Success Metric: Increase email open rates by 20% and donation conversion by 10%.
- Ongoing: The AI Steering Committee would meet monthly to track progress, troubleshoot issues, and evaluate the next wave of use cases (the curriculum recommendations and predictive analytics).

Key Lessons Learned About AI Adoption in Education:

This workshop reinforced several critical lessons that apply far beyond higher education:

1. Start with Pain, Not Technology: The workshop succeeded because we didn't start by asking, "What can we do with AI?" We started by asking, "What is broken, slow, or frustrating in your daily work?" AI became the solution to real problems, not a solution in search of a problem.
2. Involve the Skeptics: The faculty members who were most resistant at the beginning became some of the strongest advocates by the end. Why? Because they were included in the process. They had a voice in shaping how AI would be used. Inclusion breeds ownership.
3. Quick Wins Build Momentum: By focusing on high-impact, high-feasibility projects first, we were able to generate visible wins within 30 days. Success is contagious. Once people see AI working in one area, they become eager to apply it in theirs.
4. Governance Prevents Chaos: Establishing the AI Steering Committee from day one was crucial. It created a clear process for evaluating new ideas, sharing best practices, and ensuring that AI use remained aligned with the institution's mission and values.

What You Can Apply: Whether you're leading a university, a nonprofit, or a business, the principles are the same. Gather your cross-functional stakeholders, map your pain points, prioritize ruthlessly, and build a roadmap that delivers quick wins. AI adoption is not a technology project, but more like a change management project. Treat it as such, and you will succeed.

AI Prompts: Chapter 3

How to Use These Prompts

Each prompt below is designed to be copied directly into your favorite AI tool (ChatGPT, Claude, Grok, or Gemini). Simply:

1.Copy the entire prompt (including the bracketed placeholders)

2. Replace the [bracketed sections] with your specific information

3.Paste into your AI tool and hit enter

4.Refine the output by asking follow-up questions or requesting revisions

These are battle-tested prompts I use with organizations around the world. They're designed to give you professional-quality outputs that you can use immediately in your business.

Prompt 3.1: Generate Engaging Social Media Posts

Create 10 engaging social media posts for [platform: LinkedIn/Instagram/Twitter/Facebook] for my [type of business].

Business context:

- What we do: [brief description]
- Target audience: [who you serve]
- Main value proposition: [your unique benefit]
- Brand voice: [tone and personality]

For each post, provide:

- The complete post copy
- A compelling hook (first line that stops the scroll)
- Relevant hashtags (3-5 for Instagram, 1-2 for LinkedIn)
- A clear call-to-action
- The content type (educational, inspirational, promotional, behind-the-scenes, etc.)

Mix of content types:

- 3 educational posts (teaching something valuable)
- 3 engagement posts (asking questions, polls, or conversations)
- 2 storytelling posts (personal or customer stories)
- 2 promotional posts (soft sell, value-first)

Keep each post under [150 words for LinkedIn / 100 words for Instagram / 280 characters for Twitter].

Prompt 3.2: Analyze Competitor Social Media Strategy

I want to analyze my competitor's social media strategy to identify opportunities for my business.

My competitor: [competitor name or description]

Their social media handles: [list platforms and handles if known]

My business: [your business type]

My differentiation: [how you're different from this competitor]

Based on common competitive analysis, help me create a framework to evaluate:

1. **Content Analysis**:
   - What types of content do successful competitors typically post?
   - What posting frequency is standard in my industry?
   - What content formats get the most engagement?
2. **Engagement Strategy**:
   - How do top performers in my industry interact with their audience?
   - What questions or topics generate the most discussion?
3. **Gap Analysis**:
   - What topics or content types might my competitors be missing?
   - What unique angles can I take based on my differentiation?
4. **Action Plan**:
   - 5 specific content ideas that would differentiate me from this competitor
   - 3 engagement tactics I should implement immediately
   - A posting schedule that balances consistency with quality

Provide a competitive content strategy that helps me stand out, not just copy what others are doing.

Prompt 3.3: Create a Viral Content Framework

I want to create highly shareable, engaging content for [platform] that has viral potential while staying true to my brand.

My business: [type of business]

Target audience: [who you serve]

Topics I can speak to authentically: [list 3-5 areas of expertise]

Brand personality: [describe your brand's character]

Create a "Viral Content Framework" for me that includes:

1. **5 Proven Content Formulas** that tend to get high engagement in my industry:
   - The format (e.g., "Myth vs. Reality," "Unpopular Opinion," "Here's What Nobody Tells You")
   - Why it works psychologically
   - A specific example I could create
2. **Hook Templates**: 10 opening lines designed to stop the scroll
   - Make them specific to my industry and audience
3. **Storytelling Structure**: A simple 3-part framework for every post
   - Hook → Value → Call-to-Action
4. **Engagement Triggers**: 5 ways to encourage comments and shares
   - Questions to ask
   - Controversial (but professional) takes
   - Interactive elements
5. **Content Calendar**: A 2-week plan using these frameworks
   - Specific post ideas for each day
   - Best times to post for my audience

Make this actionable and authentic to my brand, not gimmicky or clickbait.

For prompts and bonus resources, visit **thejasonfleagle.com/blueprint-resources**. You can copy and paste the prompts from there—no retyping needed.

| 4 |

AI for Email Marketing

Introduction: Email Marketing Reimagined with AI

Email marketing remains a cornerstone of digital communication for businesses of all sizes. It's a direct line to your audience, a powerful tool for nurturing leads, announcing new products, and building lasting customer relationships. However, in a world saturated with digital messages, simply sending out generic email blasts is no longer effective. Your audience craves relevance, personalization, and value. This is where many small business owners and entrepreneurs hit a wall – how do you deliver that personalized touch at scale without spending all your time glued to your email platform? The answer, increasingly, lies in Artificial Intelligence.

If you've ever felt overwhelmed by the thought of segmenting lists endlessly, struggling to write compelling subject lines that actually get opened, or wondering if your emails are even reaching people at the right time, you're not alone. These are common pain points. But imagine if you had an intelligent assistant that could help you understand your subscribers on a deeper level, craft messages that resonate with each individual, automate complex campaign workflows with precision, and tell you exactly what's working and what's not. That's the promise of AI in email marketing.

This chapter is dedicated to demystifying AI for email marketing and revealing the "simple AI secrets" that can transform your email strategy from a chore into a high-performing engine for growth. We'll explore how AI can help you:

- **Deeply personalize emails at scale:** Moving beyond just using a first name to tailoring content, offers, and even send times to individual preferences and behaviors.
- **Intelligently automate email workflows:** Creating sophisticated, adaptive email sequences that nurture leads and engage customers based on their specific actions and needs.
- **Optimize email copy for maximum impact:** Leveraging AI to craft subject lines that demand to be clicked and email content that drives action.
- **Achieve significant improvements in engagement and conversions:** Ultimately turning your email list into a more valuable asset for your business.

AI is not here to replace the human element in your email marketing; rather, it's here to supercharge it. By handling the data-intensive and repetitive tasks, AI frees you up to focus on strategy, creativity, and building genuine connections. So, let's dive into how you can harness the power of AI to make your email marketing smarter, more efficient, and far more effective.

4.1 Personalizing Emails with AI: Crafting Unique Customer Journeys

In the contemporary digital marketing landscape, the one-size-fits-all approach to email communication is rapidly becoming obsolete. Customers today expect interactions that are not only relevant but also deeply personalized, reflecting their individual needs, preferences, and history with a brand. Artificial Intelligence (AI) has emerged as a transformative force in achieving this level of personalization at scale, enabling marketers to move beyond basic name tokenization and delve into creating truly unique customer journeys through email. By leveraging AI, businesses can analyze vast datasets to understand customer behavior, predict future actions, and dynamically tailor email content, subject lines, and send times, thereby significantly enhancing engagement, fostering loyalty, and driving conversions.

The power of AI in email personalization lies in its ability to process and interpret complex customer data from various touchpoints. This includes purchase history, browsing behavior on a website, previous email interactions (opens, clicks, and conversions), demographic information, and even psychographic profiles where available. AI algorithms can identify patterns and correlations within this data that would be imperceptible to human marketers, leading to a much richer understanding of each individual subscriber. This deep insight forms the bedrock of effective personalization strategies.

One of the most immediate applications of AI in email personalization is the crafting of compelling and individualized subject lines. AI tools can analyze past email performance, considering factors such as wording, length, tone, and even the use of emojis, to predict which subject lines are most likely to resonate with specific segments or individual recipients. For instance, platforms like Phrasee and, to some extent, features within broader email marketing suites like ConvertKit or ActiveCampaign, utilize natural language generation (NLG) and machine learning to create and test subject line variations that are optimized for higher open rates. These tools can adapt to evolving customer preferences and market trends, ensuring that subject lines remain fresh and effective over time.

Beyond subject lines, AI excels at hyper-personalizing the actual email content. This goes far beyond simply inserting a recipient's first name. AI can dynamically populate email bodies with product recommendations tailored to past purchases or browsing history, as seen in the capabilities of tools like Omnisend or Optimove, which are particularly adept for eCommerce businesses. For example, if a customer frequently browses hiking gear, AI can ensure that upcoming emails feature new arrivals in that category or highlight promotions on related items. Similarly, AI can tailor articles, blog post snippets, or case studies featured in newsletters based on a subscriber's expressed interests or their engagement with previous content. This level of content customization makes each email feel like a bespoke communication, directly addressing the recipient's current needs or interests.

Optimizing email send times is another critical area where AI delivers significant value. Instead of relying on generic best practices, AI tools like Seventh Sense or features within platforms like GetResponse can analyze individual engagement patterns to determine the optimal moment to send an email to each subscriber. This means that one subscriber might receive an email on a Tuesday morning because that's when they are most active, while another might receive it on a Thursday evening. This individualized send-time optimization dramatically increases the likelihood of an email being seen and acted upon, cutting through the noise of a crowded inbox.

AI also revolutionizes customer segmentation for email marketing. Traditional segmentation often relies on broad demographic or behavioral categories. AI, however, can perform micro-segmentation, identifying nuanced groups of customers with highly specific shared characteristics. This allows for the creation of hyper-targeted email campaigns that speak with unparalleled precision to smaller, more homogenous audience segments. Tools like Drift Email, by integrating with CRM data, can help refine these segments based on ongoing interactions, ensuring that marketing messages are always aligned with the customer's current stage in their journey or their evolving interests.

Furthermore, AI-powered email retargeting takes personalization to a new level. When a customer abandons a cart, browses a specific product category without purchasing, or interacts with a particular piece of content, AI can trigger automated, personalized follow-up emails. These emails can address the specific items left behind, offer assistance, provide additional information, or suggest alternative products, all tailored to the individual's recent activity. This timely and contextually relevant communication significantly increases the chances of re-engaging the customer and guiding them towards conversion.

Several AI email marketing tools facilitate these advanced personalization capabilities. For instance, ConvertKit and ActiveCampaign offer robust automation features that can be enhanced with AI-driven insights for better personalization. Omnisend and Brevo (formerly Sendinblue) provide strong personalization features for e-commerce, including product recommendations and segmentation. Optimove focuses on data-driven personalization by creating customer journeys responsive to individual behaviors. Campaigner offers advanced automation and personalization, while Rasa.io specializes in creating personalized newsletters by aggregating content from various sources based on individual user engagement. Even tools like Jasper AI, primarily known for content generation, can assist in crafting personalized email copy by adapting to different tones and styles suitable for specific audience segments. Mailmodo allows for interactive elements within emails, which can be personalized based on user data to create more engaging experiences.

In essence, AI empowers marketers to treat each subscriber as an individual with unique preferences and needs. By automating the analysis of complex data and the delivery of tailored content, AI not only enhances the effectiveness of email marketing campaigns but also fosters stronger, more meaningful relationships between brands and their customers. The shift towards AI-driven personalization is no longer a futuristic concept but a present-day necessity for businesses aiming to thrive in an increasingly competitive digital environment.

4.2 Automating Email Workflows with AI: Streamlining Engagement and Nurturing Leads

Beyond personalization, Artificial Intelligence is revolutionizing email marketing by enabling sophisticated automation of complex workflows. This automation transcends simple scheduled email blasts, allowing marketers to create dynamic, responsive, and highly efficient communication sequences that adapt to individual customer behaviors and journey stages. AI-driven automation not only saves significant time and resources but also enhances the effectiveness of lead nurturing, customer onboarding, and ongoing engagement efforts by ensuring timely and relevant interactions at every touchpoint.

The core strength of AI in email workflow automation lies in its capacity to analyze real-time data and trigger appropriate actions instantaneously. This means that email sequences are no longer static pathways but rather adaptive systems that can change course based on how a subscriber interacts with previous emails, website content, or other brand communications. This level of responsiveness ensures that subscribers receive the most pertinent information exactly when they need it, significantly improving the chances of conversion and long-term loyalty.

One of the primary ways AI enhances email automation is through the creation of intelligent drip campaigns. Traditional drip campaigns deliver a pre-set sequence of emails at fixed intervals. AI elevates this by allowing for conditional logic based on a multitude of factors. For example, an AI-powered system can adjust the content or timing of the next email in a sequence based on whether a recipient opened the previous email, clicked a specific link, visited a particular page on the website, or even based on their predicted likelihood to convert. Tools like ActiveCampaign, ConvertKit, and HubSpot (often mentioned in broader marketing AI discussions and relevant here for its automation capabilities) offer robust platforms where AI features can be integrated or are natively available to build such intelligent workflows. For instance, if a new subscriber signs up for a newsletter, an AI-driven onboarding sequence can begin, with initial emails providing general information. If the subscriber then clicks on a link related to a specific product category, the AI can automatically shift them to a more targeted drip campaign focusing on that interest, perhaps highlighting benefits, use cases, or customer testimonials related to that product line.

AI also plays a crucial role in automating triggered emails with enhanced precision. Triggered emails, such as welcome messages, abandoned cart reminders, or post-purchase follow-ups, are inherently more effective due to their timeliness and contextual relevance. AI refines these triggers by incorporating more nuanced behavioral data and predictive analytics. For example, an AI system might analyze not just that a cart was abandoned, but also the value of the items in the cart, the customer's past purchase history, and their engagement level to determine the optimal content and timing for the abandoned cart email. Some systems might even decide whether to offer a discount or free shipping based on the AI's assessment of what is most likely to prompt conversion for that specific individual. Platforms like Omnisend and Brevo, with their e-commerce focus, often incorporate such AI-driven trigger optimizations.

Lead scoring and nurturing are significantly improved by AI-powered automation. AI algorithms can analyze a wide array of signals –

email engagement, website activity, social media interactions, and demographic data – to assign a dynamic score to each lead, indicating their sales-readiness. This score is not static; it evolves as the lead interacts further with the brand. Based on these scores, AI can automatically route leads to different nurturing tracks. Highly engaged leads might receive more product-focused content or an invitation for a demo, while less engaged leads might receive more educational content designed to build awareness and interest. This ensures that sales teams focus their efforts on the most promising leads, while others continue to be nurtured automatically until they show greater intent. Many comprehensive marketing automation platforms, which often integrate email marketing, leverage AI for these lead management processes.

Furthermore, AI can automate the process of re-engaging inactive subscribers. Instead of manually identifying and segmenting dormant users, AI can monitor activity levels and automatically trigger re-engagement campaigns when a subscriber's engagement drops below a certain threshold. These campaigns can be personalized based on the subscriber's past interests or behaviors, offering incentives to reconnect or simply reminding them of the value the brand provides. If re-engagement efforts are unsuccessful after a certain period, AI can also assist in list hygiene by recommending or automatically unsubscribing persistently inactive users, which helps maintain deliverability and sender reputation. Tools that focus on email list management and deliverability, like some features within SendGrid or Mailmodo, can be complemented by AI insights for these tasks.

AI-powered automation also extends to optimizing the frequency and timing of ongoing communications. By analyzing individual preferences and engagement patterns, AI can help determine how often to email a particular subscriber without causing fatigue, and as mentioned in personalization, the best times to send those emails. This prevents over-mailing, which can lead to unsubscribes, and under-mailing, which can result in missed opportunities. The goal is to maintain a consistent and welcome presence in the subscriber's inbox.

Several AI email marketing tools contribute to these automation capabilities. ActiveCampaign and ConvertKit are well-regarded for their sophisticated automation builders that can be made more intelligent with AI. Omnisend and Brevo offer strong automation for e-commerce, including abandoned cart sequences and transactional emails. GetResponse provides tools for automated email sequences and incorporates AI for features like Perfect Timing. Campaigner and Optimove allow for the design of complex, behavior-driven automated campaigns. Even tools like Zeta Email and Drift Email, by focusing on data integration and responsive communication, contribute to more effective automation strategies by ensuring that automated workflows are based on rich, real-time customer data.

In summary, AI transforms email automation from a set of rigid, pre-programmed rules into a dynamic, intelligent system that adapts to individual customer needs and behaviors. By automating complex workflows, personalizing communication pathways, and optimizing engagement strategies, AI empowers marketers to nurture leads more effectively, build stronger customer relationships, and drive sustainable growth with greater efficiency.

4.3 Optimizing Email Copy with AI: Enhancing Engagement and Persuasion

In the realm of email marketing, the power of words cannot be overstated. The subject line, the preview text, the body copy, and the call-to-action all play critical roles in capturing attention, conveying value, and compelling subscribers to take the desired next step. Artificial Intelligence offers a sophisticated toolkit for optimizing every textual element of an email, moving beyond guesswork and intuition to data-driven precision. By leveraging AI, marketers can significantly enhance the clarity, persuasiveness, and overall effectiveness of their email copy, leading to higher engagement rates, increased click-throughs, and ultimately, better conversion outcomes.

AI's contribution to email copy optimization spans several key areas, from generating initial drafts to refining existing content and predicting its performance. Natural Language Generation (NLG) is a cornerstone technology in this domain. AI tools equipped with NLG, such as Jasper AI, or specialized email copy generators like MailMeteor's AI Email Writer (especially within its Gmail integration), can produce human-like text for various email components. Marketers can provide prompts outlining the email's purpose, target audience, key message, and desired tone, and the AI can generate multiple copy variations. This is particularly useful for overcoming writer's block, quickly drafting routine communications, or exploring different angles for a campaign. While AI-generated copy often requires human review and refinement to ensure brand voice consistency and contextual accuracy, it provides a strong starting point and significantly accelerates the content creation process.

Beyond initial generation, AI excels at enhancing and refining existing email copy. Many AI writing assistants and platforms offer features that analyze text for clarity, conciseness, grammar, spelling, tone, and readability. For instance, tools integrated into broader marketing platforms or standalone AI writing aids can suggest alternative phrasing, identify jargon that might confuse the audience, or highlight sentences that are too complex. Some AI tools can even assess the emotional sentiment of the copy, helping marketers ensure that the intended tone – whether it's urgent, empathetic, or enthusiastic – is effectively conveyed. This iterative refinement process, guided by AI suggestions, helps polish the copy to its most impactful form.

Predictive analytics, powered by machine learning, is another powerful AI application for copy optimization. By analyzing vast datasets of past email performance, including open rates, click-through rates, and conversion rates associated with different copy elements, AI can predict how likely a new piece of copy is to succeed. For example, AI can assess subject lines and predict their open rate potential before they are even sent. Some advanced platforms, like Phrasee, specialize in using AI to generate and predict the performance of marketing language, including email subject lines, body copy, and calls-to-action. This predictive capability allows marketers to make more informed decisions about which copy variations to use, prioritizing those with the highest likelihood of achieving campaign goals.

A/B testing, a staple of marketing optimization, is also supercharged by AI. While traditional A/B testing involves manually creating a few variations and testing them on a segment of the audience, AI can automate and scale this process significantly. AI can generate numerous copy variations for different email elements (e.g., 10 subject lines, 5 calls-to-action) and then intelligently manage the testing process. Some AI tools can even perform multivariate testing, simultaneously testing combinations of different elements to identify the optimal mix. Furthermore, AI can analyze the results of these tests in real-time and automatically allocate more traffic to the winning variations, a concept known as dynamic optimization or adaptive testing. This ensures that the campaign is continuously learning and improving, maximizing its effectiveness over time. Many comprehensive email marketing platforms like ActiveCampaign, GetResponse, or Campaigner offer A/B testing features that can be enhanced by AI-driven insights or by integrating with specialized AI copy optimization tools.

AI can also help tailor copy to specific audience segments with greater precision. While personalization often focuses on dynamic content blocks or product recommendations, AI can also subtly adjust the language, tone, and style of the core message to resonate more effectively with different demographics, psychographics, or behavioral groups. For example, the copy for a younger audience segment might be more informal and use more emojis, while the copy for a professional audience might be more formal and data-driven. AI can assist in identifying these nuances and generating or adapting copy accordingly.

The optimization of calls-to-action (CTAs) is another area where AI provides significant leverage. AI can analyze the wording, placement, and design of CTAs in relation to conversion rates, suggesting improvements to make them more compelling and clear. This might involve testing different action verbs, button colors (though this is more design-related, the copy on the button is key), or creating a greater sense of urgency or benefit in the CTA text.

Tools that contribute to AI-driven copy optimization are diverse. Dedicated AI writing assistants like Jasper AI are invaluable for generating and refining copy. Email marketing platforms such as ConvertKit, Omnisend, Brevo, and Mailchimp are increasingly incorporating AI features to help with subject line generation, content suggestions, and A/B testing. Specialized tools like Phrasee focus entirely on AI-powered language optimization for marketing. Even platforms like beehiiv, focused on newsletters, are integrating AI text tools to help creators produce engaging content more efficiently. The key is to leverage these tools not as a replacement for human creativity and strategic oversight, but as powerful assistants that can augment the copywriter's skills with data-driven insights and automation.

In conclusion, AI is transforming the art and science of email copywriting. By assisting in content generation, refining clarity and tone, predicting performance, automating A/B testing, and tailoring messages to specific segments, AI empowers marketers to create email copy that is not only well-written but also strategically optimized to achieve specific marketing objectives. This leads to more engaging email experiences for subscribers and ultimately, superior results for the business.

4.4 AI in Action: Email Marketing Case Studies and Success Stories

To truly grasp the transformative potential of Artificial Intelligence in email marketing, it's instructive to examine real-world examples and compelling case studies. These instances showcase how businesses across various sectors are leveraging AI to personalize communication, automate complex workflows, optimize copy, and ultimately achieve significant improvements in engagement, conversions, and revenue. While specific, publicly detailed AI-centric email marketing case studies with hard numbers can sometimes be proprietary, the principles and outcomes observed in broader email marketing successes often highlight the underlying power of intelligent automation and personalization that AI amplifies.

Case Study 1: Endy - AI-Powered Personalization Boosts Revenue Per Subscriber

Endy, a leading Canadian mattress-in-a-box company, provides a strong example of how AI-driven personalization can directly impact e-commerce success. As highlighted in discussions around AI in email marketing (Team-GPT, 2024), Endy utilizes AI to track on-site customer activity. This behavioral data, such as products viewed, time spent on specific pages, and cart interactions, is fed into their email marketing system. AI algorithms then analyze this information to send highly tailored product suggestions and follow-up emails. For instance, if a customer browses a particular mattress model but doesn't purchase, AI can trigger a personalized email featuring that mattress, perhaps with additional information, customer reviews, or a time-sensitive offer. This level of granular personalization, driven by AI's ability to understand individual customer intent, leads to more relevant email content, thereby increasing engagement and, crucially, revenue per subscriber. The core AI principle here is the dynamic adaptation of email content based on real-time behavioral triggers, moving far beyond static segmentation.

Case Study 2: Selsey - Doubling Conversions with AI-Optimized Abandoned Cart Emails

Selsey, an online furniture retailer, demonstrates the power of AI in optimizing a critical touchpoint: abandoned cart recovery. According to a case study featured by GetResponse (2025), Selsey achieved a two-fold increase in conversions from their abandoned cart emails. While the case study primarily highlights the effectiveness of GetResponse's automation features, the underlying intelligence required to optimize such sequences often involves AI capabilities, whether native to the platform or integrated. AI can enhance abandoned cart emails by personalizing the product recommendations within the email (showcasing the exact items left or similar alternatives), optimizing the send timing based on when the user is most likely to re-engage, and even A/B testing different subject lines and calls-to-action in real-time to maximize recovery rates. The AI component ensures that these reminder emails are not just generic prompts but are tailored and timed for maximum impact, directly addressing the reasons for abandonment where possible and nudging the customer towards completing their purchase.

Case Study 3: MobileFun - Leveraging Automation and AI-Driven A/B Testing in Ecommerce

MobileFun, an online retailer of mobile accessories, utilized automation and A/B testing, key areas where AI significantly enhances capabilities, to improve their email marketing performance (GetResponse, 2025). AI can take A/B testing to the next level by enabling more complex multivariate testing and by using predictive analytics to determine which email variations are likely to perform best even before a full test is run. For an e-commerce business like MobileFun, AI could be used to test different promotional offers, product descriptions, or email layouts, automatically identifying and prioritizing the versions that lead to higher click-through and conversion rates. AI-driven automation ensures that these optimized emails are then delivered as part of targeted campaigns, such as welcome series for new subscribers or promotional emails for specific customer segments. The ability to continuously test, learn, and adapt email content and strategy at scale, powered by AI, is crucial for staying competitive in the fast-paced e-commerce landscape.

Hypothetical Case Study: "Company Z" - Increasing Open Rates with AI-Generated Subject Lines

Imagine "Company Z," a B2B software provider, struggling with low open rates for their monthly newsletter, which shares industry insights and product updates. They decide to implement an AI-powered email marketing tool that specializes in subject line generation and optimization, similar to capabilities found in platforms like Phrasee or advanced features within broader ESPs. The AI analyzes Company Z's past email data, industry benchmarks, and current trends to generate a variety of subject lines for each newsletter edition. These subject lines are not only grammatically correct and engaging but are also predicted by the AI to have a higher likelihood of being opened by Company Z's target audience. Furthermore, the AI tool facilitates rapid A/B testing of these subject lines on a small segment of their list, then automatically uses the winning subject line for the main send. Within three months, Company Z sees their average newsletter open rate increase by 35%. This success is attributed to the AI's ability to craft more compelling, data-driven subject lines that resonate with their specific audience, moving beyond human intuition and generic best practices.

Key Learnings from AI Email Marketing Case Studies:

These examples, both real and illustrative, underscore several key benefits of integrating AI into email marketing strategies:

1. **Deep Personalization:** AI enables a level of personalization that goes beyond simple name tokens, tailoring content, product recommendations, and offers to individual user behavior and preferences.
2. **Enhanced Automation:** AI makes automation smarter, allowing for dynamic workflows that adapt to customer interactions in real-time, ensuring timely and relevant communication.
3. **Optimized Copy and Timing:** AI tools can generate, refine, and A/B test email copy (especially subject lines) and predict optimal send times to maximize engagement.
4. **Improved Conversion Rates:** By delivering more relevant and timely messages, AI helps nurture leads more effectively and recover potentially lost sales, directly impacting conversion rates and revenue.

While the specific tools and implementations may vary, the overarching theme is that AI empowers marketers to be more data-driven, efficient, and customer-centric in their email marketing efforts, leading to demonstrably better results.

References:

- Team-GPT. (2024). *AI in Email Marketing: 5 Use Cases, Statistics, Examples and Software.* Retrieved from https://team-gpt.com/blog/

ai-in-email-marketing-5-use-cases-statistics-examples-and-software/

- GetResponse. (2025). *10 Email Marketing Case Studies to Inspire Your Success.* Retrieved from https://www.getresponse.com/blog/email-marketing-case-studies

4.5 Simple AI Secrets for Email Marketing Success: Practical Tips and Tricks

Beyond the broad strategic applications of AI in personalization, automation, and copy optimization, there lies a wealth of practical, actionable "secrets" or tips that marketers can employ to elevate their email campaigns. These aren't necessarily complex undertakings but rather smart, often subtle ways to leverage AI's capabilities for immediate gains. Mastering these simple AI secrets can lead to more efficient workflows, deeper audience engagement, and ultimately, a stronger return on investment from email marketing efforts.

1. AI for Hyper-Specific Subject Line Emojis and Tone Matching: Many AI tools, as discussed by experts (Kickbox, 2024), can go beyond just suggesting subject line text. A simple AI secret is to use these tools specifically for emoji recommendations that align with the subject's sentiment and are known to perform well with your target audience. Some AI can also help fine-tune the *tone* of a subject line (e.g., urgent, playful, inquisitive) with subtle word changes that might not be immediately obvious to a human writer but can significantly impact open rates. For example, instead of just asking an AI to "write a subject line for a sale," prompt it with: "Write 5 subject lines for a 24-hour flash sale on summer dresses, using emojis that convey excitement and urgency, and adopt a friendly, enthusiastic tone suitable for young female shoppers."

2. Leverage AI for Smart Audience Re-segmentation Based on Micro-Engagements: While AI-driven segmentation is a known benefit, a "secret" lies in using AI to identify and act on *micro-engagements.* This means going beyond opens and clicks. AI can help track if a user hovered over a particular image in an email (if tracking capabilities allow), how far they scrolled in a long-form email, or if they re-opened an email multiple times. Based on these subtle cues, AI can dynamically re-segment users into highly specific interest groups for follow-up communication. For instance, a user repeatedly hovering over a specific product image in a promotional email, even without clicking, could be flagged by an AI for a targeted follow-up featuring that product or similar items.

3. Use AI to Predict and Mitigate Churn with Proactive, Personalized Outreach: Many email platforms with AI capabilities can predict which subscribers are at risk of churning (becoming inactive or unsubscribing) based on declining engagement patterns. The simple secret is to not just identify these users but to use AI to craft highly personalized, proactive re-engagement emails *before* they go completely cold. AI can suggest specific content or offers that have previously resonated with that user or similar users, making the re-engagement attempt far more effective than a generic "We miss you!" campaign. This might involve an AI-generated subject line like, "[Subscriber Name], remember that [product category] you loved? We have something new for you!"

4. AI-Powered Content Curation for Hyper-Relevant Newsletters: For businesses that send out newsletters with curated content, AI can be a massive time-saver and relevance-booster. A simple trick is to use AI tools (some are specialized for this, like Rasa.io, or it can be achieved with broader AI content tools) to scan various sources (blogs, news sites, internal content repositories) and automatically select articles or snippets that align with individual subscriber preferences, as indicated by their past reading behavior. This ensures each subscriber receives a newsletter that feels uniquely tailored to their interests, significantly increasing engagement with the curated content.

5. Employ AI for "Second-Chance" Subject Lines on Unopened Emails: Some advanced email marketing platforms, or custom AI setups, allow for an intelligent resend to non-openers with a *different,* AI-optimized subject line. The secret here is to let the AI analyze why the first subject line might not have resonated (perhaps based on A/B testing data or predictive analytics) and generate a completely fresh alternative. This isn't just a simple resend; it's an AI-driven second attempt to capture attention, often with a different angle or emotional appeal, significantly boosting overall reach without simply annoying subscribers with the same message.

6. AI for Optimizing Email Preview Text as a Subject Line Extension: While subject lines get a lot of attention, the preview text (the short snippet visible after the subject line in many email clients) is prime real estate. A simple AI secret is to use AI writing assistants to specifically craft preview text that complements and enhances the subject line, rather than just being the first few words of the email. AI can help generate concise, compelling preview text that provides additional context or a stronger hook, effectively extending the persuasive power of the subject line and increasing open rates. Prompt your AI with: "Given the subject line '[Your Subject Line]', write three compelling preview text options under 100 characters that create curiosity and highlight the key benefit."

7. Use AI to Analyze Competitor Emails for Actionable Insights (Ethically): If you subscribe to competitor newsletters (a common marketing practice), AI tools can help analyze their email strategies. While direct data access isn't possible, AI can analyze the language, frequency, calls-to-action, and types of promotions used in publicly available competitor emails you've received. This can provide insights into their targeting and messaging, which can then inform your own AI-driven A/B tests and content strategies. The secret is to use AI to look for patterns and successful elements that you can adapt and test within your own campaigns, always ensuring ethical data handling and avoiding direct copying.

8. AI-Assisted Image Alt-Text Generation for Accessibility and SEO: Accessibility is crucial, and image alt-text is a key component. A simple AI secret is to use AI image recognition and generation tools (like those from Jasper Art, DALL-E, or integrated within some platforms) to automatically suggest or generate descriptive alt-text for images in your emails. This not only improves accessibility for visually impaired subscribers but can also have minor benefits for email client rendering and even how images are perceived by spam filters. While human review is still important, AI can significantly speed up this often-overlooked task.

By incorporating these "simple AI secrets" into their email marketing practices, marketers can unlock new levels of efficiency and effectiveness. The key is to think creatively about how AI's analytical and generative capabilities can be applied to solve specific challenges and enhance every touchpoint of the email journey, often with minimal additional investment beyond existing AI-enabled tools.

References:

- Kickbox. (2024). *Email Marketing & Artificial Intelligence: AI Tips & Tricks.* Retrieved from https://blog.kickbox.com/email-marketing-artificial-intelligence-ai-tips-tricks/
- GetResponse. (2024). *AI in Email Marketing: 7+ Ways to Get The Most Out of the Trends.* Retrieved from https://www.getresponse.com/blog/ai-in-email-marketing

4.6 Navigating the Ethical Landscape of AI in Email Marketing

The integration of Artificial Intelligence into email marketing brings forth a new set of ethical considerations that marketers must navigate with diligence and responsibility. While AI offers unprecedented capabilities for personalization, automation, and optimization, its power also necessitates a heightened awareness of data privacy, transparency, the potential for bias, and the overall impact on subscriber trust. Adhering to ethical best practices is not merely a matter of compliance; it is fundamental to building and maintaining strong, respectful relationships with customers in an increasingly AI-driven world.

1. Data Privacy and Consent: The Cornerstone of Ethical AI

AI thrives on data, and the more granular the data, the more personalized and potentially effective the AI-driven campaigns can be. However, this reliance on data places a significant ethical burden on marketers to ensure that all data collection and usage practices are transparent and consensual. Subscribers have a right to know what data is being collected about them, how it is being used to power AI-driven email experiences, and who has access to it. Regulations like GDPR (General Data Protection Regulation) in Europe and CCPA (California Consumer Privacy Act) in the United States provide legal frameworks for data privacy, but ethical practice often requires going beyond mere legal compliance. This includes:

- **Clear and Explicit Consent:** Ensuring that subscribers have explicitly opted-in to receive emails and are aware that AI may be used to personalize their experience. Vague or pre-checked consent boxes are ethically questionable.
- **Data Minimization:** Collecting only the data that is strictly necessary for the intended AI application. Hoarding excessive amounts of data increases privacy risks.

- **Secure Data Storage and Handling:** Implementing robust security measures to protect subscriber data from breaches and unauthorized access, especially when this data is being fed into AI models.
- **Easy Opt-Out and Data Access:** Providing clear and straightforward ways for subscribers to opt-out of AI-driven personalization or to request access to, or deletion of, their data.

2. Transparency in Automation and Personalization: Avoiding the "Creepy" Factor

AI can create email experiences that are so personalized they might feel intrusive or "creepy" if subscribers are unaware of the underlying mechanisms. While the goal is relevance, there's a fine line between helpful personalization and surveillance. Ethical AI email marketing involves a degree of transparency about how automation and personalization are being used. This doesn't necessarily mean detailing the specific algorithms, but rather being open about the fact that customer data informs the emails they receive. For example, a disclaimer in the email footer or privacy policy stating that emails may be tailored based on browsing history or past purchases can help manage expectations. The key is to ensure that personalization efforts are perceived as valuable and helpful, not as an invasion of privacy.

3. Algorithmic Bias and Fairness: Ensuring Equitable Treatment

AI models are trained on data, and if that data reflects existing societal biases, the AI can inadvertently perpetuate or even amplify those biases. In email marketing, this could manifest in certain demographic groups being unfairly targeted or excluded from offers, or receiving stereotyped content. Ethical marketers must be vigilant about potential biases in their AI tools and data sets. This involves:

- **Auditing AI Tools:** Where possible, understanding how AI tools make decisions and looking for potential sources of bias.
- **Diverse Data Sets:** Ensuring that the data used to train AI models is representative and diverse, to avoid skewing outcomes.
- **Regular Review of AI-Driven Campaigns:** Monitoring the outcomes of AI-personalized campaigns to ensure they are not disproportionately or unfairly impacting specific subscriber segments.
- **Human Oversight:** Maintaining human oversight over AI-driven decisions, especially those that could have significant implications for subscribers.

4. Responsible Use of AI-Generated Content: Authenticity and Accuracy

AI tools can generate email copy, subject lines, and even suggest imagery. While this can be a significant time-saver, ethical considerations arise around authenticity and accuracy. Marketers have a responsibility to ensure that AI-generated content is truthful, not misleading, and aligns with the brand's voice and values. Over-reliance on AI without human review can lead to generic, impersonal, or even factually incorrect emails. The ethical approach involves using AI as an assistant, not a replacement for human judgment and creativity. All AI-generated content should be carefully reviewed, edited, and approved by a human marketer before being sent to subscribers.

5. Avoiding Spam and Maintaining Deliverability Through Ethical AI Practices

AI can optimize send times and personalize content, which can improve engagement and, consequently, deliverability. However, if AI is used irresponsibly – for example, to aggressively re-target disengaged users or to send an excessive volume of emails – it can quickly lead to spam complaints and damage sender reputation. Ethical AI use in this context means respecting subscriber preferences, honoring unsubscribe requests promptly (which AI can help automate efficiently), and using AI insights to send *more relevant* emails, not just *more* emails. Maintaining a clean and engaged list, a principle that AI can support through predictive churn modeling, is crucial for both ethical practice and long-term deliverability.

6. Compliance with Evolving Regulations

The legal landscape around AI and data privacy is constantly evolving. Ethical email marketers must stay informed about new regulations and industry best practices. This includes understanding the implications of AI-specific legislation that may emerge, as well as adhering to existing email marketing laws like CAN-SPAM in the US. Proactively adopting ethical principles often positions businesses well for future regulatory changes.

In conclusion, while AI offers powerful tools to enhance email marketing, its use must be guided by a strong ethical framework centered on respect for subscriber privacy, transparency, fairness, and accountability. By prioritizing these ethical considerations, marketers can harness the full potential of AI to build trust, foster genuine engagement, and create email experiences that are both effective and respectful.

Case Study: The Growth OS for a B2B Consulting Firm

Background: I had the opportunity to work with a mid-sized B2B consulting firm specializing in leadership training that was struggling with lead generation. They were spending $20,000/month on LinkedIn ads, but their process was manual and leaky. Leads would fill out a form, wait 24-48 hours for a response, and often go cold before a sales call could even be booked.

The Challenge:

- Lead Response Lag: The average time to first contact was 36 hours, killing conversion momentum.
- Manual Overload: A junior salesperson was spending 50% of their time on manual follow-up and scheduling.
- High Cost Per Meeting: Due to the leaky funnel, their effective cost to get one qualified meeting on the calendar was over $1,500.

My Approach: This was a classic case for an AI-powered Growth OS system. The goal was to build an automated, 24/7 engine that could capture, qualify, nurture, and book leads instantly, freeing up the sales team to focus on closing, not chasing.

Implementation:

1. 24/7 AI Chatbot: We trained an AI chatbot on the firm's entire library of case studies, service descriptions, and FAQs. We deployed it on their website and connected it to their LinkedIn lead gen forms via an API.
2. Instant Qualification & Booking: The chatbot was programmed to ask three key qualifying questions. If a lead met the

criteria, it would immediately offer access to the sales team's calendar and book a meeting on the spot.

3. CRM Integration: Every interaction was automatically logged in their CRM (we moved them to GoHighLevel for its robust automation). Leads that weren't ready to book were automatically placed into a 5-day, AI-powered email nurture sequence.
4. AI-Optimized Ads: We used the chatbot interaction data to refine the ad targeting, focusing on the specific pain points that the highest-quality leads were mentioning.

Results:

- Lead response time went from 36 hours to 5 seconds.
- The cost per booked meeting dropped from $1,500 to $450 within 90 days (a 70% reduction).
- The junior salesperson was freed up to handle qualified demos, contributing to a 25% increase in sales pipeline in the first quarter.
- The AI chatbot handled over 80% of initial inquiries, including those coming in at 11 PM on a Saturday.

Key Lesson: Speed is the ultimate competitive advantage in sales. By using AI to close the gap between expressed interest and human conversation, you can dramatically increase conversion rates. The Growth OS doesn't just make the process more efficient; it creates a fundamentally better experience for the buyer.

AI Prompts: Chapter 4

How to Use These Prompts

Each prompt below is designed to be copied directly into your favorite AI tool (ChatGPT, Claude, Grok, or Gemini). Simply:

1.Copy the entire prompt (including the bracketed placeholders)

2. Replace the [bracketed sections] with your specific information

3.Paste into your AI tool and hit enter

4.Refine the output by asking follow-up questions or requesting revisions

These are battle-tested prompts I use with organizations around the world. They're designed to give you professional-quality outputs that you can use immediately in your business.

Prompt 4.1: Create a High-Converting Email Sequence

Create a [5/7/10]-email welcome sequence for new subscribers to my [type of business].

Business details:
- What we sell: [product/service]
- Target audience: [who they are]
- Main benefit: [the transformation you provide]
- Price point: [free, under $100, $100-$1000, $1000+]
- Desired action: [what you want them to do - buy, book a call, download, etc.]

For each email in the sequence, provide:

1. **Subject Line** (3 options for each email)
2. **Preview Text** (the first line that shows in inbox)
3. **Email Body** (200-300 words)

4. **Primary Call-to-Action** (the button or link text)

5. **Send Timing** (e.g., "immediately after signup," "2 days after email 1")

6. **Goal of This Email** (what it's designed to accomplish)

Email sequence structure:
- Email 1: Welcome and set expectations
- Email 2: Deliver immediate value (free resource, tip, or insight)
- Email 3: Share your story or build credibility
- Email 4: Address the main pain point
- Email 5: Present the offer with social proof
- [Continue for longer sequences]

Tone: [warm and personal / professional and authoritative / casual and friendly]

Make each email feel personal, valuable, and lead naturally to the next.

Prompt 4.2: Write Subject Lines That Get Opened

I need 30 high-performing email subject lines for my [type of business] email list.

Context:
- My audience: [describe subscribers]
- Topics I email about: [main themes]
- Current average open rate: [X%] (if known)
- Brand voice: [personality]

Create 30 subject lines across these categories:

Curiosity-Driven (10 subject lines):
- Create intrigue without being clickbait
- Make them want to know more

Benefit-Focused (10 subject lines):
- Lead with the value or outcome
- Answer "what's in it for me?"

Urgency/Scarcity (5 subject lines):
- Create FOMO without being manipulative
- Time-sensitive or limited offers

Personalization/Direct (5 subject lines):
- Feel like a 1-on-1 conversation
- Use "you" language

For each subject line, also provide:
- The type of email content it would introduce
- Why it would work for my audience
- A recommended preview text to pair with it

Keep all subject lines under 50 characters when possible for mobile optimization.

Prompt 4.3: Segment Your Email List for Personalization

I have an email list of [approximate size] subscribers for my [type of business]. I want to segment this list to send more personalized, relevant emails.

Current list information:
- What I know about subscribers: [e.g., purchase history, engagement level, signup source]
- Types of products/services I offer: [list offerings]
- Current email frequency: [how often you email]

Help me create an email segmentation strategy:

1. **Recommended Segments** (5-7 segments based on my business):
   - How to define each segment
   - Why this segment matters
   - What makes them different from other segments

2. **Content Strategy Per Segment**:
   - What topics/offers to send to each segment
   - How often to email each segment
   - Different calls-to-action for each

3. **Segmentation Implementation**:
   - What data I need to collect (and how to collect it)
   - Simple ways to tag or categorize subscribers
   - Automated rules for moving people between segments

4. **3 Specific Email Campaigns** I can run using segmentation:
   - The segment to target
   - The message/offer
   - Expected improvement over non-segmented emails

Make this practical for someone without complex email marketing software - focus on segments I can actually action.

For prompts and bonus resources, visit **thejasonfleagle.com/blueprint-resources**. You can copy and paste the prompts from there—no retyping needed.

| 5 |

AI for Paid Advertising

Introduction: The AI Revolution in Paid Campaigns

The landscape of paid advertising is undergoing a seismic shift, driven by the relentless advancements in artificial intelligence. What was once a field heavily reliant on manual A/B testing, intuition-based targeting, and painstaking bid adjustments is now being revolutionized by AI algorithms capable of processing vast datasets, predicting consumer behavior with remarkable accuracy, and automating complex campaign management tasks in real-time. This AI revolution is not merely about incremental improvements; it represents a fundamental change in how advertisers strategize, create, target, optimize, and measure their paid campaigns across search engines, social media platforms, and display networks.

From generating compelling ad copy and eye-catching visuals at scale to identifying hyper-niche audience segments and dynamically adjusting bids for millions of auctions per second, AI is empowering marketers to achieve unprecedented levels of efficiency, precision, and performance. The ability to leverage AI effectively is rapidly becoming a key differentiator between campaigns that thrive and those that merely survive in the increasingly competitive digital advertising ecosystem.

This chapter delves into the multifaceted role of AI in modern paid advertising. We will explore how AI is transforming ad creative and copy optimization, enabling far more precise and predictive audience targeting, and automating the intricate dance of bid management. Furthermore, we will examine real-world case studies that showcase tangible results achieved through AI adoption, uncover practical "Simple AI Secrets" that marketers can implement to enhance their campaigns, and critically address the crucial ethical considerations that must accompany the deployment of these powerful technologies. As we navigate through these topics, the overarching theme will be clear: AI is no longer a futuristic concept in paid advertising but a present-day reality that offers immense opportunities for those equipped to harness its potential responsibly and strategically. Understanding and embracing this AI revolution is essential for any marketer aiming to maximize their return on investment and achieve sustainable success in the dynamic world of paid campaigns.

5.1 Using AI to Optimize Ad Copy and Creative

Artificial intelligence is fundamentally reshaping how advertisers approach the creation and optimization of ad copy and creative elements. In the highly competitive landscape of paid advertising, the ability to rapidly generate, test, and refine compelling ad materials is paramount. AI-powered tools offer a significant advantage by automating and enhancing these critical processes, leading to more effective campaigns and better return on investment.

One of the primary ways AI assists in this domain is through **automated content generation**. Tools like ChatGPT and Claude, as highlighted in research from Search Engine Land, can produce a wide array of ad copy variations at scale based on user-defined prompts. Marketers can provide these AI systems with core messaging points, target audience characteristics, desired tone, and specific platform requirements (e.g., character limits for Google Ads headlines or a more conversational style for social media ads). The AI then generates multiple options for headlines, body text, calls-to-action, and even entire ad scripts. This capability not only saves considerable time but also helps overcome creative blocks by providing a diverse set of starting points for ad copy. For instance, Optmyzr is a specialized tool that offers ad copy suggestions tailored for PPC campaigns, further streamlining this process.

Beyond text, AI is also making significant strides in **visual creative generation**. Platforms such as Canva, Runway, and Microsoft Copilot enable marketers to create imagery and even video content from textual prompts. This means that advertisers can describe a desired visual concept—perhaps a specific scene, product placement, or emotional tone—and the AI will generate corresponding images or video clips. Synthesia takes this a step further by generating video content from scripts, potentially including AI-generated avatars, which can drastically reduce the costs and complexities associated with traditional video production. Innovations like TikTok's Symphony Creative Studio also point towards a future where advertising platforms themselves offer sophisticated AI-driven creative tools.

The power of AI extends to the **optimization of existing ad copy and creatives**. AI algorithms can analyze vast datasets of past campaign performance, identifying patterns and correlations that humans might miss. This allows them to predict which ad variations are most likely to resonate with specific audience segments. By A/B testing different headlines, images, and calls-to-action, AI can continuously refine ad elements to maximize engagement and conversion rates. For example, AI can analyze which emotional cues in an image lead to higher click-through rates or which turns of phrase in ad copy result in more conversions for a particular demographic.

Furthermore, AI tools can assist in **ensuring brand consistency and adherence to platform guidelines**. They can be trained to recognize brand voice and style, helping to maintain a cohesive message across all ad creatives. They can also flag potential issues with ad copy or visuals that might violate advertising platform policies, reducing the risk of ad disapprovals.

To effectively leverage AI for ad copy and creative optimization, **prompt engineering** is crucial. As noted by Search Engine Land, the quality of the output is directly dependent on the quality of the input.

Marketers need to provide clear, detailed, and context-rich prompts that specify the desired output format, the specific request (e.g., "generate five ad headlines for a new running shoe targeting young professionals"), the intended recipient or platform, relevant context about the product or service, and the target audience. Iterative prompting, where initial outputs are reviewed and prompts are refined, is often necessary to achieve the best results.

In summary, AI offers a powerful suite of tools for optimizing ad copy and creative in paid advertising. From generating diverse text and visual options at scale to continuously testing and refining ad elements based on performance data, AI empowers advertisers to create more impactful and efficient campaigns. By embracing these technologies and mastering the art of prompting, marketers can unlock new levels of creativity and effectiveness in their paid advertising efforts.

Reference:

- Search Engine Land. "Top AI tools and tactics you should be using in PPC." (https://searchengineland.com/top-ai-tools-tactics-ppc-452938)

5.2 Leveraging AI for More Precise Ad Targeting

In the realm of paid advertising, reaching the right audience with the right message is the cornerstone of success. Artificial intelligence offers unprecedented capabilities to move beyond broad demographic targeting and achieve highly precise audience segmentation and engagement. By analyzing vast datasets and identifying subtle patterns in user behavior, AI empowers advertisers to deliver their messages to individuals most likely to convert, thereby maximizing ad spend efficiency and campaign effectiveness.

One of the core strengths of AI in ad targeting lies in its ability to conduct **advanced audience research and persona development**. As noted in research from Search Engine Land, AI tools like Chat-

GPT and Claude can process extensive information about a brand, its website, existing customer data, and broader market trends to generate detailed and nuanced audience personas. These personas go far beyond basic demographics, incorporating psychographics, online behaviors, interests, motivations, and even potential pain points. This deep understanding allows advertisers to tailor their messaging and creative elements to resonate more profoundly with specific segments.

AI excels at **analyzing large and complex datasets** to uncover valuable targeting insights. This includes data from various sources such as website analytics, CRM systems, social media interactions, third-party data providers, and the advertising platforms themselves (e.g., Google, Meta, LinkedIn, YouTube). AI algorithms can identify correlations and predictive indicators of purchasing intent that would be nearly impossible for human analysts to discern. For example, AI might identify that users who exhibit a specific sequence of online behaviors, such as visiting certain types of websites, engaging with particular content, and then searching for related keywords, are highly likely to be in the market for a specific product or service. Tools like Optmyzr, while also used for copy suggestions and performance recommendations, contribute to this by analyzing data that can inform targeting strategies.

This analytical power translates into several key AI-driven targeting tactics:

1. **Predictive Targeting:** AI models can predict future customer behavior based on historical data. This allows advertisers to target users who are likely to convert in the future, even if they haven't explicitly shown interest yet. This is particularly powerful for identifying new customer segments and expanding market reach.
2. **Lookalike Audiences:** AI can analyze the characteristics of an advertiser's best existing customers and then find other users across advertising networks who share similar traits and behav-

iors. This is a highly effective way to scale campaigns by reaching new, relevant audiences.

3. **Dynamic Audience Segmentation:** Instead of relying on static audience lists, AI can dynamically segment audiences in real-time based on their current behavior and context. This means that ad targeting can adapt on the fly, ensuring that users are always receiving the most relevant ads based on their immediate needs and interests.
4. **Contextual Targeting Refinement:** While traditional contextual targeting places ads on websites with relevant content, AI enhances this by understanding the nuance and sentiment of the content. This ensures that ads are not only placed in relevant environments but also in contexts that are brand-safe and conducive to positive engagement.
5. **Cross-Channel Targeting Optimization:** AI can track user journeys across multiple devices and channels, enabling more cohesive and effective cross-channel targeting strategies. This ensures that messaging is consistent and that ad spend is allocated to the channels where it will have the greatest impact for specific audience segments.

Furthermore, AI helps in **understanding user intent** with greater accuracy. By analyzing search queries, browsing history, and content consumption patterns, AI can infer the underlying intent of a user—whether they are in an initial research phase, comparing options, or ready to make a purchase. This allows advertisers to tailor their ad copy, offers, and landing pages to match the user's specific stage in the customer journey, significantly increasing the likelihood of conversion.

In essence, AI transforms ad targeting from a relatively broad-stroke approach to a highly granular and adaptive process. By leveraging the analytical power of AI, advertisers can identify and reach their ideal customers with unparalleled precision, leading to more efficient use of advertising budgets, higher engagement rates, and ultimately, improved campaign performance.

Reference:

- Search Engine Land. "Top AI tools and tactics you should be using in PPC." (https://searchengineland.com/top-ai-tools-tactics-ppc-452938)

5.3 Automating Bid Management with AI

Effective bid management is a critical lever for success in paid advertising, directly impacting campaign visibility, cost-per-acquisition (CPA), and overall return on ad spend (ROAS). Traditionally a manual and time-intensive process, bid management has been revolutionized by artificial intelligence, which brings speed, precision, and predictive capabilities to the forefront. AI-powered bid management strategies enable advertisers to optimize their bids in real-time, allocate budgets more effectively, and adapt to the ever-changing dynamics of ad auctions.

One of the most significant contributions of AI to bid management is the advent of **automated and smart bidding strategies**. As highlighted in research from Search Engine Land, AI has been an integral part of PPC platforms for years through features like smart bidding. These systems leverage machine learning algorithms to analyze a multitude of signals in real-time—far more than a human could process—to determine the optimal bid for each individual ad auction. These signals can include device type, time of day, user location, browsing history, ad creative, and the specific conversion goal of the campaign.

Key aspects of AI-driven bid automation include:

1. **Real-Time Bidding (RTB) Adjustments:** AI algorithms can adjust bids dynamically for every impression. If the AI predicts a high likelihood of conversion based on the available sig-

nals for a particular user and auction, it can increase the bid to improve the chances of winning that impression at an optimal price. Conversely, it can lower bids for less promising auctions, conserving budget.

2. **Goal-Oriented Bidding:** Advertisers can set specific campaign goals, such as maximizing conversions, achieving a target CPA, maximizing click volume, or attaining a certain ROAS. The AI then works to optimize bids to meet these predefined objectives. For example, if the goal is a target CPA of $20, the AI will adjust bids to try and acquire conversions at or below that cost.
3. **Predictive Bid Optimization:** AI doesn't just react to current conditions; it also predicts future trends and performance. By analyzing historical data and market dynamics, AI can anticipate changes in competition, user behavior, or conversion rates, and proactively adjust bidding strategies to capitalize on opportunities or mitigate risks.
4. **Budget Allocation and Pacing:** AI can assist in optimizing how the overall campaign budget is allocated across different ad groups, keywords, or targeting segments. It can also manage budget pacing throughout the day or campaign duration to ensure that the budget is spent efficiently and opportunities are not missed due to premature budget depletion.
5. **Portfolio Bid Strategies:** Many advertising platforms offer portfolio bid strategies where AI optimizes bids across multiple campaigns simultaneously. This allows the AI to learn from a larger dataset and make more informed decisions, shifting budget and adjusting bids between campaigns to achieve the best overall performance for the advertiser's portfolio.

Tools and platforms that facilitate AI-powered bid management are often integrated directly into major advertising networks like Google Ads and Meta Ads. These platforms continuously refine their AI bidding algorithms. Additionally, third-party tools like Optmyzr, while known for ad copy and data analysis, also offer functionalities that support or complement AI bidding strategies by providing insights and recommendations that can inform bidding decisions or help in managing automated bidding more effectively.

The benefits of automating bid management with AI are substantial. It frees up advertisers from the tedious task of manual bid adjustments, allowing them to focus on higher-level strategy, creative development, and audience insights. More importantly, AI-driven bidding typically leads to improved campaign performance, as the algorithms can process more data and make faster, more nuanced decisions than humanly possible. This often results in lower CPAs, higher conversion volumes, and better ROAS.

However, it's important to note that while AI automates much of the process, human oversight remains crucial. Advertisers need to provide the AI with accurate conversion tracking data, set clear and realistic goals, and monitor performance to ensure the AI is working effectively. Understanding the principles behind AI bidding and how to guide the algorithms is key to unlocking the full potential of automated bid management.

In conclusion, AI has transformed bid management from a manual chore into a sophisticated, data-driven, and automated process. By leveraging AI's ability to analyze vast datasets, predict outcomes, and make real-time adjustments, advertisers can significantly enhance the efficiency and effectiveness of their paid advertising campaigns.

Reference:

- Search Engine Land. "Top AI tools and tactics you should be using in PPC." (https://searchengineland.com/top-ai-tools-tactics-ppc-452938)

5.4 Case Study: Audi Taiwan Reduces Cost Per Click by 42.6% Using AI for Paid Ads

Introduction: In the competitive automotive market, effectively reaching potential customers while managing advertising costs is a significant challenge. Audi Taiwan, during the launch of their e-tron electric vehicle in December 2020, faced a difficult environment characterized by the COVID-19 pandemic, which led to reduced interest in test drives and simultaneously high social media ad costs, particularly on Meta platforms. To navigate these challenges and optimize their campaign performance, Audi Taiwan partnered with SoMin.ai to leverage their AI-driven advertising solutions.

The Challenge: Audi Taiwan needed to generate leads and drive interest for the new Audi e-tron amidst a pandemic-induced market slowdown and escalating advertising costs. The primary objectives were to improve lead generation, enhance campaign efficiency, and achieve a better return on their advertising spend, with a key focus on reducing the Cost Per Click (CPC).

AI-Powered Solution by SoMin.ai: SoMin.ai implemented a multifaceted AI strategy to address Audi Taiwan's challenges. The core components of their solution included:

1. **Omni-Sourced User Profiling:** AI algorithms were used to gather and analyze data from diverse sources to create comprehensive profiles of potential e-tron buyers. This went beyond basic demographics to include online behaviors, interests, and psychographic attributes.
2. **AI Audience Analysis:** Advanced AI-driven analysis was performed on the gathered user data to identify the most promising audience segments. This involved pinpointing specific characteristics and online signals that indicated a higher propensity to be interested in an electric luxury vehicle like the Audi e-tron.
3. **Long-Tail Targeting:** Instead of focusing only on broad, highly competitive keywords and audience segments, the AI

identified and targeted more specific, niche (long-tail) interests and user groups that showed strong potential but were often overlooked by traditional targeting methods. This allowed Audi to reach relevant users with less direct competition.

4. **Automated Campaign Management and Optimization:** The AI platform automated various aspects of campaign management, including real-time bid adjustments and dynamic ad creative optimization based on performance data. The system continuously learned and adapted to maximize engagement and minimize costs.

Results and Outcomes: The implementation of SoMin.ai's AI-driven solutions yielded significant positive results for Audi Taiwan's e-tron launch campaign:

- **Cost Per Click (CPC) Reduction:** The most striking outcome was a **42.6% reduction in CPC**. This demonstrated the AI's effectiveness in identifying and targeting the right audiences more efficiently and optimizing bids in real-time.
- **Ad Cost Savings:** Alongside the CPC reduction, Audi Taiwan achieved a **45% saving in their overall advertising budget** while still meeting or exceeding their campaign goals. This highlighted the AI's ability to eliminate wasteful spending on underperforming segments and ad placements.
- **Improved Lead Generation and Campaign Efficiency:** The significant cost savings and improved targeting precision led to a notable improvement in lead generation quality and overall campaign efficiency.

Lessons Learned and Key Takeaways:

- **The Power of Granular Audience Insights:** AI's ability to perform deep audience analysis and identify nuanced user profiles is crucial for effective targeting in competitive markets.

- **Long-Tail Strategy Pays Off:** Targeting niche, long-tail segments can uncover high-potential audiences with lower competition, leading to better CPC and ROI.
- **Automation Drives Efficiency:** AI-driven automation in campaign management and bid optimization allows for rapid adjustments and continuous improvement, which is difficult to achieve manually at scale.
- **Data-Driven Adaptation is Key:** In dynamic market conditions, such as those experienced during the pandemic, the ability of AI to quickly adapt strategies based on real-time data is invaluable.

The success of the Audi Taiwan campaign led to an expanded partnership with SoMin.ai, with Audi integrating more advanced social media and competitor analysis tools into their broader marketing strategy. This case study serves as a compelling example of how leveraging AI in paid advertising can lead to substantial cost savings, improved targeting precision, and enhanced overall campaign performance, even in challenging market conditions.

Reference:

- SoMin.ai. "AI Driven Ad Performance Boosting Tool | Achieve 38% Better Results (Audi e-Tron Case Study)." (https://www.somin.ai/soads-case-study/)

5.5 Simple AI Secrets for Paid Advertising Success

Beyond the complex algorithms and sophisticated platforms, there are several straightforward "Simple AI Secrets" that marketers can leverage to significantly enhance their paid advertising efforts. These are practical tips and approaches that, when consistently applied, can unlock greater efficiency, better targeting, and improved campaign performance without requiring deep technical expertise in AI development.

1. Master the Art of Prompt Engineering (Even for Simple Tasks): This might sound advanced, but at its core, it's about clear communication with AI tools. Whether you're using an AI to brainstorm ad headlines, suggest keywords, or even analyze a small dataset, the quality of your input (the prompt) directly dictates the quality of the output.

- **Secret:** Be specific. Instead of asking an AI like ChatGPT to "write ad copy," try "Write five compelling Facebook ad headlines (under 40 characters each) for a new vegan protein powder targeting fitness enthusiasts aged 25-40, highlighting its organic ingredients and great taste." The more context and constraints you provide, the more relevant and useful the AI's suggestions will be. This applies to generating creative ideas, refining targeting parameters, or even asking for explanations of performance data.

2. Let AI Handle Repetitive Analysis, So You Can Strategize: Paid advertising involves a lot of data sifting – analyzing keyword performance, ad creative click-through rates, and audience segment responses. AI is exceptionally good at this.

- **Secret:** Use AI tools (even basic features within ad platforms or tools like ChatGPT with data analysis capabilities) to perform initial data cuts and identify outliers or trends. For example, ask it to "Identify the top 3 underperforming keywords in this campaign based on CPC and conversion rate from the provided data." This frees you up to focus on the *why* behind the data and develop strategic responses, rather than getting bogged down in manual spreadsheet analysis.

3. Leverage AI for Hyper-Niche Audience Discovery: AI can uncover audience segments you might never have thought of.

- **Secret:** Feed your AI tools (like those mentioned in the Search Engine Land article, or even the audience insights tools within platforms like Meta or Google) with data about your best existing customers. Then, ask the AI to identify less obvious shared characteristics or interests. This can lead to discovering "long-tail" audience segments that are highly relevant but less competitive, often resulting in lower CPCs and higher engagement, as seen in the Audi Taiwan case study with SoMin.ai.

4. Use AI as a Creative Brainstorming Partner, Not Just a Generator: Stuck for ad ideas? AI can be an inexhaustible source of inspiration.

- **Secret:** Don't just ask AI to *create* ads. Ask it to brainstorm *concepts.* For example: "Suggest three unconventional ad campaign themes for a sustainable fashion brand targeting Gen Z." Or, "What are some visual metaphors we could use to represent speed and efficiency for our new software?" Use these as starting points for your own creative development.

5. Continuously Feed the AI Learning Loop (Especially with Bidding): AI-powered bidding systems, like Google's Smart Bidding, learn and improve over time. The more relevant data they have, the better they perform.

- **Secret:** Ensure your conversion tracking is impeccably accurate and that you're feeding as much relevant conversion data (including offline conversions if applicable) back into the ad platforms. For proprietary AI bidding, as highlighted by Eight by Eight, focus on one primary goal initially (e.g., maximize conversions at a target CPA) to help the AI optimize effectively. Don't set too many conflicting goals at once, especially in the early stages of an AI-driven bidding strategy.

6. Stress-Test Your Assumptions with AI: Sometimes, you need an objective second opinion on why campaign performance is changing.

- **Secret:** Present your performance data and your theories to an AI (like ChatGPT or Claude) and ask it to play devil's advocate or suggest alternative explanations. For example: "Our CPC has increased by 20% this month. We think it's due to increased competition. What are other potential factors AI might consider based on this data?" This can help uncover blind spots or validate your hypotheses.

7. Don't Set It and Forget It – Monitor and Tweak AI Outputs: While AI automates many tasks, human oversight is still critical. AI is a tool, not a replacement for a skilled marketer.

- **Secret:** Regularly review the performance of AI-generated ad copy, AI-selected audiences, and AI-managed bids. As Eight by Eight advises, after implementing something AI-powered, thoroughly analyze results before adding more. Be prepared to tweak AI settings, refine prompts, or even pause AI-driven elements if they aren't performing as expected. The interaction between your AI and the ad platforms' AI can sometimes produce unexpected results, so vigilance is key.

8. Start Small and Scale: If you're new to using more advanced AI tools in your paid advertising, don't try to overhaul everything at once.

- **Secret:** Pick one area where AI can provide a quick win – perhaps generating ad copy variations for a single campaign or using an AI tool to analyze the performance of one ad group. Learn from that experience, demonstrate value, and then gradually expand your use of AI to other areas.

By incorporating these simple AI secrets into their daily workflows, paid advertising professionals can harness the power of artificial intelligence to work smarter, achieve better results, and stay ahead in an increasingly complex digital landscape.

References:

- Search Engine Land. "Top AI tools and tactics you should be using in PPC." (https://searchengineland.com/top-ai-tools-tactics-ppc-452938)
- SoMin.ai. "AI Driven Ad Performance Boosting Tool | Achieve 38% Better Results (Audi e-Tron Case Study)." (https://www.somin.ai/soads-case-study/)
- Eight by Eight. "11 Proven Ways Marketing Artificial Intelligence Will Improve Your Paid Advertising Program." (https://www.eightbyeight.com/11-proven-ways-marketing-artificial-intelligence-will-improve-your-paid-advertising-program/)

5.6 Ethical Considerations in AI for Paid Advertising

As artificial intelligence becomes increasingly integrated into paid advertising, it brings forth a range of ethical considerations that marketers must navigate responsibly. While AI offers powerful tools for optimizing campaigns and reaching target audiences with unprecedented precision, its misuse can lead to privacy violations, discriminatory practices, a lack of transparency, and the manipulation of consumer behavior. Adhering to ethical principles is not only a matter of compliance but also crucial for building and maintaining consumer trust.

1. Data Privacy and Consumer Consent: AI-driven advertising heavily relies on the collection and analysis of vast amounts of consumer data, including browsing history, purchase patterns, location data, and social media interactions. This raises significant privacy concerns.

- **Ethical Imperative:** Advertisers must be transparent about the data they collect and how it is used for advertising purposes. Obtaining explicit and informed consent from users before collecting and processing their personal information is paramount. As highlighted by Dragonfly Digital Marketing, compliance with data privacy regulations like GDPR (General Data Protection Regulation) and CCPA (California Consumer Privacy Act) is a baseline, not a ceiling. Robust data protection measures must be in place to prevent unauthorized access or breaches.
- **Best Practices:** Clearly articulate data usage policies in easily understandable language. Provide users with granular control over their data, including the ability to access, rectify, and delete their information, and to opt-out of data collection for advertising purposes. Anonymizing data where possible and implementing strong encryption methods are also key, as suggested by Silverback Strategies.

2. Algorithmic Bias and Fairness: AI algorithms learn from historical data, which can inadvertently perpetuate and even amplify existing societal biases related to race, gender, age, socioeconomic status, or other characteristics. This can lead to discriminatory ad targeting, where certain groups are unfairly excluded from opportunities or targeted with predatory offers.

- **Ethical Imperative:** Marketers have a responsibility to ensure their AI-driven campaigns are fair and do not discriminate. This involves actively working to identify and mitigate biases within their AI models and datasets.
- **Best Practices:** Regularly audit AI models and targeting parameters for biased outcomes, as recommended by both Dragonfly Digital Marketing and Silverback Strategies. Utilize diverse and representative datasets for training AI algorithms. Incorporate human oversight in AI decision-making processes

to catch and correct biases. Promoting diversity within AI development teams can also help in creating fairer and more inclusive algorithms.

3. Transparency and Explainability: Many AI systems used in advertising operate as "black boxes," making it difficult to understand how they arrive at certain decisions regarding ad targeting or content personalization. This lack of transparency can erode consumer trust and make it challenging to identify and rectify errors or biases.

- **Ethical Imperative:** Strive for transparency in how AI is used to make advertising decisions. Consumers have a right to understand why they are seeing particular ads.
- **Best Practices:** Clearly label AI-generated content and AI-driven interactions (e.g., chatbots), as suggested by Dragonfly Digital Marketing. While full algorithmic transparency might be complex, provide users with clear explanations about why they were targeted by an ad or why certain product recommendations are being made. Silverback Strategies emphasizes that many consumers (63%) want to know when content is AI-generated.

4. Consumer Autonomy and Manipulative Practices: AI's ability to predict consumer behavior and deliver hyper-personalized messages can be powerful, but it also carries the risk of manipulative marketing. This includes using AI to exploit psychological vulnerabilities, create undue urgency, or employ deceptive "dark patterns" that trick users into actions they wouldn't otherwise take.

- **Ethical Imperative:** AI should be used to empower consumer choice, not to manipulate or coerce. Respect for consumer autonomy is paramount.
- **Best Practices:** Avoid deceptive tactics such as false scarcity or pressure-driven countdowns. Provide consumers with clear

opt-out mechanisms from hyper-personalized advertising. Ensure that AI-driven recommendations are genuinely helpful and do not exploit vulnerabilities. Focus on providing value rather than simply driving conversions through potentially unethical means.

5. Accountability and Governance: Establishing clear lines of responsibility and robust governance frameworks for the ethical use of AI in advertising is essential.

- **Ethical Imperative:** Companies must be accountable for the actions of their AI systems and the impact of their AI-driven advertising campaigns.
- **Best Practices:** Develop and implement company-wide ethical AI guidelines, as advocated by both Dragonfly Digital Marketing and Silverback Strategies. This may involve setting up an ethics committee or defining specific roles and responsibilities for AI governance. Establish feedback loops and reporting systems to address any AI-related ethical issues promptly and transparently.

Navigating the ethical landscape of AI in paid advertising requires a proactive and principled approach. By prioritizing data privacy, fairness, transparency, consumer autonomy, and accountability, marketers can harness the power of AI responsibly, build lasting consumer trust, and contribute to a more ethical digital advertising ecosystem.

References:

- Dragonfly Digital Marketing. "Ethical Considerations in AI Marketing: Fairness and Transparency." (https://dragonflydm.com/ethical-considerations-in-ai-marketing-ensuring-fairness-and-transparency/)

- Silverback Strategies. "Ethics Considerations in AI Marketing." (https://www.silverbackstrategies.com/blog/ai-marketing-ethics/)

My Personal Take on AI for Paid Advertising (From Jason's Desk):

I once took over a campaign for a coaching company spending $15,000 a month on Facebook ads with a dismal 1.5x ROAS. They were manually creating a handful of ad variations and guessing at what would work. We immediately implemented an AI-assisted creative generation tool and turned on value-based bidding.

What Actually Happened: For the first two weeks, performance got worse. The AI was in its learning phase, and the client panicked. They were ready to pull the plug.

What I Learned: AI optimization is not a magic switch, but more like a learning process. You have to be willing to pay the "data tax." Most platforms need 50-100 conversions within a learning period before the algorithm can effectively optimize. Trying to judge performance on day three is a recipe for failure.

What You Should Do: When implementing AI for paid ads, budget for a 2-4 week learning phase. Communicate this timeline clearly to all stakeholders and resist the urge to make drastic changes. Let the machine learn, and you will be rewarded.

Have questions about optimizing PPC or paid ads? Feel free to reach out to me and my team to help out.

AI Prompts: Chapter 5

How to Use These Prompts

Each prompt below is designed to be copied directly into your favorite AI tool (ChatGPT, Claude, Grok, or Gemini). Simply:

1.Copy the entire prompt (including the bracketed placeholders)

2. Replace the [bracketed sections] with your specific information

3.Paste into your AI tool and hit enter

4.Refine the output by asking follow-up questions or requesting revisions

These are battle-tested prompts I use with organizations around the world. They're designed to give you professional-quality outputs that you can use immediately in your business.

Prompt 5.1: Generate Ad Copy Variations for Testing

Create 20 ad copy variations for a [Facebook/Google/LinkedIn] ad campaign promoting my [product/service].

Campaign details:

- Product/Service: [what you're selling]
- Target audience: [demographics and psychographics]
- Main benefit: [the #1 reason someone should buy]
- Key differentiator: [what makes you different from competitors]
- Offer: [discount, free trial, limited time, etc.]
- Ad objective: [awareness, consideration, conversion]

For each ad variation, provide:

1. **Headline** (under 40 characters for Facebook, 30 for Google)
2. **Primary Text** (125 words max for Facebook, 90 for Google)
3. **Call-to-Action** (the button text)
4. **Why This Angle Works** (the psychological trigger it uses)

Vary the approaches across these frameworks:

- Problem-Solution (5 variations)
- Social Proof/Testimonial (5 variations)
- Benefit-Driven (5 variations)
- Curiosity/Intrigue (5 variations)

Make each variation distinct enough to test different messaging angles, not just minor word changes.

Prompt 5.2: Audience Targeting Strategy

Help me build a comprehensive audience targeting strategy for my [platform: Facebook/Google/LinkedIn] ad campaign.

My business:

- What we sell: [product/service]
- Ideal customer: [detailed description]
- Average customer value: [LTV or purchase amount]
- Current customers come from: [where you find them now]
- Geographic target: [locations]

Create a targeting strategy that includes:

1. **Core Audiences** (3-5 audience segments):
   - Demographic targeting (age, location, job title, income, etc.)
   - Interest targeting (what they care about, follow, or engage with)
   - Behavior targeting (purchase behavior, device usage, etc.)
   - Estimated audience size for each
2. **Custom Audiences** (based on my existing data):
   - Website visitors (what pages to target)
   - Email list segments
   - Past customers (for upsell/cross-sell)
   - Engaged social media users
3. **Lookalike Audiences**:
   - Which source audience to use (e.g., past purchasers, high-value customers)
   - Recommended lookalike percentage (1%, 5%, 10%)
4. **Exclusion Strategy**:
   - Who to exclude from seeing ads (to avoid wasted spend)
5. **Testing Plan**:
   - Which audiences to test first
   - How to measure performance
   - When to scale winners

Prioritize audiences most likely to convert, not just largest reach.

Prompt 5.3: Ad Performance Analysis and Optimization

I'm running a [Facebook/Google/LinkedIn] ad campaign and need help analyzing performance and optimizing for better results.

Current campaign data:

- Campaign objective: [awareness/traffic/leads/sales]

- Budget: [daily or total budget]
- Running for: [number of days]
- Impressions: [number]
- Clicks: [number]
- Click-through rate (CTR): [percentage]
- Conversions: [number]
- Cost per conversion: [amount]
- Target cost per conversion: [your goal]

Based on these metrics, provide:

1. **Performance Diagnosis**:
   - What's working well
   - What's underperforming
   - The biggest bottleneck in the funnel
2. **Optimization Recommendations** (prioritized):
   - If CTR is low: [specific creative/copy improvements]
   - If conversion rate is low: [landing page or offer improvements]
   - If cost is too high: [bidding or targeting adjustments]
3. **A/B Testing Plan**:
   - The #1 element to test first
   - Specific variations to try
   - How long to run the test
   - What success looks like
4. **Scaling Strategy** (if performance is good):
   - How to increase budget without killing performance
   - New audiences to expand into
   - Creative refresh timeline
5. **When to Kill It**:
   - Clear criteria for when to pause and pivot

Give me specific, actionable next steps I can implement today.

For prompts and bonus resources, visit **thejasonfleagle.com/blueprint-resources**. You can copy and paste the prompts from there—no retyping needed.

| 6 |

AI for Search Engine Optimization (SEO)

Search Engine Optimization (SEO) stands as a cornerstone of digital marketing, the art and science of making websites more visible and attractive to search engines like Google, Bing, and others. The ultimate goal is to achieve higher rankings in search results for relevant queries, thereby driving organic (non-paid) traffic to a website. In an increasingly competitive digital landscape, the ability to appear prominently in search results can be the difference between thriving and obscurity. As search algorithms become more sophisticated, relying on hundreds of ranking factors, the strategies required to succeed in SEO have grown more complex. This is where Artificial Intelligence (AI) has emerged as a transformative force, offering powerful new ways to analyze data, generate insights, optimize content, and automate tasks that were previously labor-intensive or beyond human scale.

This chapter, "AI for Search Engine Optimization (SEO): Unlocking Organic Growth," will explore the multifaceted role of AI in modern SEO. We will delve into how AI is revolutionizing key aspects of SEO, from the creation of highly relevant and engaging content to the meticulous optimization of web pages for both search engines and users. We will examine how AI-powered tools are enabling marketers to conduct more profound keyword research, uncovering hidden opportunities and understanding user intent with unprecedented accuracy. Furthermore, we will look at practical applications through a real-world case study demonstrating tangible results achieved with AI SEO strategies. The chapter will also uncover "Simple AI Secrets" – practical tips and tricks that can be readily applied to enhance SEO efforts. Finally, and crucially, we will address the ethical considerations inherent in using AI for SEO, ensuring that these powerful technologies are wielded responsibly and sustainably. By understanding and leveraging AI, businesses and marketers can unlock new levels of organic growth and establish a more resilient and effective online presence.

6.1 Generating SEO Content with AI

Artificial Intelligence has fundamentally reshaped the landscape of Search Engine Optimization (SEO), particularly in the realm of content generation. The ability of AI to process vast amounts of data, understand user intent, and mimic human-like writing styles has made it an invaluable asset for marketers and content creators aiming to produce high-quality, SEO-friendly content at scale. This section will delve into how AI can be effectively utilized for generating various forms of SEO content, highlighting some of the prominent tools that facilitate this process.

One of the primary applications of AI in SEO content generation is the creation of initial drafts for articles, blog posts, product descriptions, and other web copy. AI tools can take a given topic or a set of keywords and produce a structured piece of content that serves as a strong foundation for further refinement. For instance, tools like **Jasper** (formerly Jarvis) and **Copy.ai** are renowned for their ability to generate creative and engaging text across different formats and tones. Jasper, with its extensive library of templates and its capacity to understand brand voice, can quickly produce outlines and even full-length articles that are optimized for specific keywords. Similarly, **Writesonic** offers features to generate blog intros, outlines, and full articles, significantly reducing the time and effort required in the initial stages of content creation. These tools often leverage sophisticated natural language processing (NLP) models, such as GPT-3 and its successors, to ensure the generated content is coherent, grammatically correct, and contextually relevant.

Beyond full article generation, AI excels at creating specific content elements crucial for SEO. This includes crafting compelling meta descriptions and title tags that are optimized for click-through rates (CTRs) and search engine visibility. Tools like **Ahrefs** provide free AI-powered generators for these elements, allowing users to input their target keywords and receive optimized suggestions. **Semrush**, another comprehensive SEO platform, incorporates AI into its Content Marketing Toolkit, offering features like the SEO Writing Assistant which provides real-time feedback on content readability, SEO, originality, and tone of voice, helping to refine AI-generated or human-written text. **Surfer SEO** is particularly adept at creating data-driven content briefs by analyzing top-ranking pages for target keywords. These briefs guide content creation by outlining optimal word count, keyword density, topics to cover, and even common questions to answer, ensuring the content is highly relevant and competitive. Surfer SEO can also assist in writing and optimizing content based on these briefs.

AI can also be instrumental in brainstorming content ideas and identifying content gaps. By analyzing search trends, competitor content, and user queries, AI tools can suggest relevant topics that are likely to attract organic traffic. **ChatGPT**, a versatile conversational AI model, can be prompted to generate lists of blog post ideas, frequently asked questions (FAQs) related to a specific keyword, or even different angles to approach a topic. **TeamAI**, which integrates various AI models including ChatGPT, Claude, and Gemini, offers a collaborative platform where users can leverage these capabilities for content ideation and brief creation. Its ability to use custom training data and build custom workflows further enhances its utility in generating tailored SEO content.

Furthermore, AI tools are increasingly being used for content repurposing and rewriting. Existing articles can be transformed into different formats, such as social media posts, video scripts, or email newsletters, with the help of AI. This not only extends the reach of the content but also caters to different audience preferences. Tools like **Jasper** and **Ahrefs** offer rewriting and summarization features that can help refresh old content or adapt it for new channels while maintaining its SEO value. The ability to generate content in multiple languages, as offered by Ahrefs, also opens up opportunities for global SEO strategies.

In summary, AI offers a powerful suite of capabilities for generating SEO content. From drafting entire articles and optimizing meta descriptions to brainstorming ideas and repurposing existing material, AI tools like Jasper, Surfer SEO, Ahrefs, Semrush, ChatGPT, and TeamAI are empowering marketers to create more effective and engaging content more efficiently. However, it is crucial to remember that while AI can significantly augment the content creation process, human oversight and editing remain essential to ensure accuracy, originality, and a genuine connection with the target audience. The best results are typically achieved when AI-generated content is used as a starting point or a supportive tool, rather than a complete replacement for human creativity and expertise.

Reference: The information on AI tools mentioned in this section is based on research from sources including seo.com/tools/ai/ (Accessed May 13, 2025).

6.2 Optimizing Pages for SEO with AI

Beyond content generation, Artificial Intelligence plays a pivotal role in the intricate process of on-page SEO optimization. AI algorithms can analyze web pages with a level of granularity and speed that surpasses human capabilities, identifying areas for improvement and providing actionable recommendations to enhance search engine rankings. This section explores how AI is leveraged to optimize various on-page elements, ensuring that content is not only well-written but also perfectly structured and technically sound for search engines.

One of the core strengths of AI in on-page optimization lies in its ability to perform comprehensive content audits and provide data-driven suggestions. Tools like **Surfer SEO** excel in this domain by analyzing the top-ranking pages for a target keyword and comparing them against the user's content. Surfer SEO's audit feature examines over 500 on-page signals, including keyword density, content structure (headings, paragraphs), image alt text, meta tags, and even page speed factors. It then provides a clear, actionable list of recommendations to align the page more closely with what search engines like Google evidently prefer for that specific query. This ensures that optimization efforts are based on empirical data rather than guesswork. **Semrush**, through its On-Page SEO Checker and SEO Writing Assistant, also offers robust AI-powered recommendations. It can identify opportunities for semantic keyword inclusion, suggest improvements for readability, and flag technical SEO issues that might be hindering performance.

AI is also transforming how technical on-page elements are managed. **Alli AI** is a notable platform that focuses on automating on-page SEO changes. It integrates with popular Content Management Systems (CMS) and can automatically implement optimizations such as generating and deploying schema markup, optimizing title tags and meta descriptions based on performance data, and even making code-level changes to improve site speed and mobile-friendliness. Alli AI allows users to approve recommendations before they go live, providing a balance between automation and control. This capability to push SEO updates live faster is a significant advantage in the dynamic digital landscape.

Keyword optimization, a cornerstone of on-page SEO, is significantly enhanced by AI. While keyword research identifies the terms to target (covered in the next section), AI helps ensure these keywords are used effectively within the content. This goes beyond simple keyword stuffing, which is now penalized by search engines. Modern AI tools understand context and semantics, helping to incorporate relevant LSI (Latent Semantic Indexing) keywords and entities naturally within the text. For example, **Surfer SEO**'s Content Editor provides real-time feedback on keyword usage as content is being written or edited, suggesting terms and phrases that are contextually related and prevalent in top-ranking content. **Outranking** also offers an AI writing assistant that helps weave keywords into the content naturally and provides guidance on optimizing for topical authority.

Furthermore, AI tools can analyze user engagement signals, which are increasingly important for SEO. By understanding how users interact with a page (e.g., bounce rate, time on page, click-through rates from SERPs), AI can help identify content or design elements that may be causing users to leave prematurely. While direct optimization based on these signals is complex, AI-driven A/B testing tools, sometimes integrated within broader SEO platforms, can help experiment with different page layouts, calls-to-action, or content structures to improve user experience and, consequently, SEO performance. **Alli AI**, for instance, includes A/B SEO testing capabilities, allowing marketers to test the impact of different on-page changes.

AI also assists in optimizing for other critical on-page factors such as internal linking and image optimization. Tools like **Surfer SEO** and **Outranking** provide suggestions for relevant internal links, helping to distribute link equity throughout the site and improve navigation for both users and search engine crawlers. For image optimization, while not always a primary feature of mainstream SEO tools, AI can be used to generate descriptive alt text (important for accessibility and image search) or compress images without significant loss of quality, contributing to faster page load times.

In conclusion, AI-powered tools have become indispensable for effective on-page SEO optimization. Platforms like Surfer SEO, Semrush, Alli AI, and Outranking offer sophisticated capabilities to audit content, optimize technical elements, refine keyword usage, and improve user engagement signals. By leveraging these AI-driven insights and automation features, marketers can ensure their web pages are not only discoverable but also provide a superior experience for users, ultimately leading to higher search engine rankings and increased organic traffic. As with content generation, the most successful strategies involve a synergistic approach where AI tools augment human expertise, allowing SEO professionals to focus on strategy and complex problem-solving while AI handles the data-intensive analysis and routine optimization tasks.

Reference: The information on AI tools mentioned in this section is based on research from sources including seo.com/tools/ai/ (Accessed May 13, 2025).

6.3 Analyzing Keyword Opportunities with AI

Identifying the right keywords is a foundational element of any successful SEO strategy. Artificial Intelligence has significantly advanced the methodologies for keyword research and opportunity analysis, enabling marketers to uncover valuable insights with greater precision and efficiency than ever before. AI-powered tools can sift through massive datasets of search queries, competitor rankings, and user behavior to pinpoint keyword opportunities that align with business goals and user intent. This section will explore how AI is revolutionizing the process of analyzing keyword opportunities.

Traditional keyword research often involves manual brainstorming and sifting through long lists of potential terms. AI streamlines this by automating the discovery of relevant keywords, including long-tail variations and semantic relatives that humans might overlook. Platforms like **Ahrefs** and **Semrush** are leaders in this space, offering sophisticated AI-driven keyword research tools. Ahrefs' Keywords Explorer, for example, not only provides standard metrics like search volume and keyword difficulty but also uses AI to generate extensive lists of keyword ideas categorized by parent topics, questions, and newly discovered terms. It can also analyze the SERP (Search Engine Results Page) landscape for any keyword, revealing the top-ranking content and the features present (e.g., featured snippets, People Also Ask boxes), which AI can help target.

Semrush offers a comprehensive suite of tools for keyword analysis, including its Keyword Magic Tool and Topic Research tool. These leverage AI to help users discover millions of keywords, group them into topic clusters, and identify question-based queries that indicate user intent. The AI algorithms can also assess keyword intent (informational, navigational, transactional, commercial) with a higher degree of accuracy, allowing marketers to tailor their content more effectively. **Outranking** is another platform that incorporates AI into its keyword research process, helping users find high-potential keywords and build out content strategies around them. It focuses on creating topical authority by identifying clusters of related keywords that should be covered to demonstrate expertise in a particular niche.

AI is particularly effective at uncovering long-tail keywords, which are longer, more specific phrases that often have lower search volume but higher conversion rates. Because they are more specific, they can indicate a user who is further along in the buying cycle or looking for very particular information. AI algorithms can identify these long-tail opportunities by analyzing user search patterns and natural language queries. **ChatGPT** and **TeamAI** can be prompted to generate long-tail keyword variations based on a seed keyword or topic, providing a rich source of ideas for targeted content creation. TeamAI, with its ability to integrate multiple AI models and custom data, can be particularly powerful for niche keyword discovery.

Competitive keyword analysis is another area where AI provides a significant advantage. AI tools can automatically track the keywords for which competitors are ranking, identify their top-performing content, and uncover keyword gaps – terms that competitors are ranking for but the user's site is not. **Ahrefs**' Site Explorer and **Semrush**'s Competitive Research Toolkit offer deep insights into competitor strategies, powered by AI-driven data analysis. This allows businesses to understand the competitive landscape better and identify opportunities to outperform rivals by targeting underserved keywords or creating superior content for existing ones.

Furthermore, AI helps in prioritizing keyword opportunities. Not all keywords are created equal; some offer a better return on investment than others. AI tools can assess various factors, such as search volume, keyword difficulty, click-through rate potential, and business relevance, to score and prioritize keywords. This helps marketers focus their efforts on the terms that are most likely to drive meaningful organic traffic and conversions. Some advanced platforms are also beginning to use predictive analytics, powered by AI, to forecast the potential traffic and revenue impact of ranking for specific keywords.

AI also assists in understanding the nuances of user intent behind search queries. Search engines are increasingly focused on satisfying user intent, and AI helps marketers align their content accordingly. By analyzing the language used in search queries and the type of content that ranks for those queries, AI tools can help determine whether users are looking for information, a specific website, a product to buy, or a comparison of options. This understanding is crucial for creating content that truly meets user needs and therefore ranks well.

In summary, AI has transformed keyword opportunity analysis from a labor-intensive task into a more strategic and data-driven process. Tools like Ahrefs, Semrush, Outranking, ChatGPT, and TeamAI empower SEO professionals to discover a wider range of relevant keywords, understand user intent more deeply, analyze competitor strategies effectively, and prioritize their efforts for maximum impact. By harnessing the power of AI, businesses can uncover untapped keyword opportunities and build a more robust and effective SEO strategy that drives sustained organic growth.

Reference: The information on AI tools mentioned in this section is based on research from sources including seo.com/tools/ai/ (Accessed May 13, 2025).

6.4 Case Study: Rocky Brands Boosts Search Revenue by 30% with AI SEO Tools

To illustrate the tangible impact of Artificial Intelligence on Search Engine Optimization, let's examine the success story of Rocky Brands, a prominent footwear retail company. Facing the challenge of enhancing its online visibility and organic search revenue, Rocky Brands turned to AI-powered SEO strategies to revamp its content and optimization efforts. This case study, detailed by ResultFirst, highlights how strategic implementation of AI tools can lead to significant and measurable improvements in SEO performance.

The core of Rocky Brands' strategy involved leveraging the BrightEdge platform, an AI-driven SEO and content performance marketing solution. The primary objectives were to identify and target relevant, high-value keywords, optimize crucial on-page elements like page titles and meta descriptions, and meticulously track the impact of these optimizations on both brand equity and, critically, revenue generation.

Using BrightEdge's Data Cube and Recommendations features, Rocky Brands was able to conduct in-depth keyword research, uncovering terms that their target audience was actively searching for. The AI capabilities of the platform allowed them to move beyond simple keyword matching to understand user intent and semantic relationships between topics. This informed the creation and optimization of their content, ensuring it was highly relevant to user search queries. The Storybuilder feature within BrightEdge likely assisted in structuring and presenting this optimized content effectively.

The results of this AI-driven approach were compelling. Rocky Brands experienced a substantial **30% increase in search revenue** directly attributable to these SEO enhancements. This demonstrates a clear return on investment from their AI SEO initiatives. Beyond this direct revenue impact, the company also saw an impressive **74% year-over-year growth in overall revenue**, indicating the broader positive effects of a strengthened online presence. Furthermore, the optimized content and improved search visibility led to a **13% in-**

crease in new users visiting their website, expanding their customer base.

The success of Rocky Brands underscores several key aspects of leveraging AI in SEO. Firstly, the strategic use of AI tools for comprehensive keyword research and data-driven content optimization is crucial. By aligning their content more precisely with user search queries and intent, Rocky Brands was able to attract more qualified organic traffic. Secondly, the ability to track and measure the impact of SEO changes on tangible business outcomes, such as revenue, is vital for demonstrating value and refining strategies. AI platforms often provide sophisticated analytics that make this tracking more effective.

This case study serves as a powerful example of how AI is not just a theoretical concept in SEO but a practical set of tools that can deliver significant business results. By embracing AI-powered platforms, companies like Rocky Brands can gain a competitive edge, enhance their online visibility, and drive substantial growth in organic search revenue.

Reference: This case study is based on information reported by ResultFirst in "5 AI SEO Case Studies to Scale Your Organic Traffic" (Accessed May 13, 2025 from https://www.resultfirst.com/blog/ai-seo/5-ai-seo-case-studies-to-scale-your-organic-traffic/).

6.5 Simple AI Secrets for SEO Success

Leveraging Artificial Intelligence for Search Engine Optimization doesn't always require complex strategies or expensive, enterprise-level tools. Many "Simple AI Secrets" can be implemented by marketers of all levels to significantly enhance their SEO efforts. These secrets often involve using readily available AI functionalities in creative ways to gain an edge. This section unveils some practical, actionable AI tips and tricks that can be integrated into your daily SEO workflow for improved rankings and visibility.

One of the simplest yet most powerful AI secrets is to **use AI for supercharged keyword research and intent analysis**. While comprehensive tools like Ahrefs and Semrush offer deep AI capabilities, even free or freemium AI tools like Google's Keyword Planner (which incorporates AI in its forecasting) or the AI-powered suggestions within ChatGPT can uncover valuable long-tail keywords and question-based queries. The secret lies in prompting the AI effectively. For instance, instead of just asking for keywords related to "sustainable gardening," you could ask ChatGPT to "Generate a list of informational long-tail keywords a beginner interested in sustainable urban gardening might search for, categorized by user intent (e.g., learning, troubleshooting, buying guides)." This level of specificity, guided by AI's understanding of natural language, can yield highly targeted keyword lists. The Writesonic blog on AI for SEO emphasizes that AI excels at search intent classification and predictive keyword analysis, helping prioritize high-converting keywords even with simpler AI interactions.

Another secret is to **employ AI for rapid content ideation and outline creation**. Marketers often face writer's block or struggle to find fresh angles for their content. AI tools, including free versions of content generators or even ChatGPT, can be prompted to brainstorm blog post titles, subheadings, and core arguments based on a target keyword or topic. The trick is to use these AI-generated ideas as a springboard, not a final product. For example, you can ask an AI tool to "Suggest five unique blog post angles for the keyword 'AI in small business marketing,' focusing on practical benefits for non-technical owners." This can quickly provide a diverse set of ideas that can then be fleshed out with human expertise and unique insights. This aligns with the idea that AI can help analyze top-ranking pages to suggest topics and optimizations, as noted by Writesonic.

Leveraging AI for meta description and title tag optimization is a widely accessible secret. Many SEO plugins and platforms now incorporate AI to suggest optimized meta tags. Even without specialized tools, you can use a model like ChatGPT to draft compelling meta descriptions. Provide it with the primary keyword, a brief summary of the page content, and ask it to generate a meta description under 160 characters that is engaging and includes a call to action. The secret is to iterate: generate a few options and then refine them. This is a simple way to ensure these crucial on-page elements are always well-crafted for click-through rates.

An often-overlooked AI secret is **using AI for basic competitor content analysis.** While full-fledged competitor analysis requires dedicated tools, you can use AI in simpler ways. For example, you can take the text from a top-ranking competitor's article, feed it into an AI summarization tool (many free ones exist, or use ChatGPT), and quickly grasp the main topics they cover and their core arguments. This can inform your own content strategy, helping you identify gaps or areas where you can provide more value. Writesonic's guide points out AI's capability in competitor gap analysis, and this is a simplified application of that principle.

Automating parts of your technical SEO audit with AI is another practical tip. While a full technical SEO audit is complex, AI can help with specific tasks. For instance, you can use AI-powered tools (some free or with free trials) to quickly check for broken links on your site or to analyze page speed and get basic recommendations. Some AI writing assistants can also help generate schema markup for common elements like FAQs or articles, which can enhance your SERP visibility. The key is to identify repetitive or data-intensive micro-tasks within technical SEO that AI can handle efficiently.

Finally, a crucial "secret" is to **always combine AI with human oversight and E-E-A-T (Experience, Expertise, Authoritativeness, Trustworthiness).** Google's algorithms, as highlighted by Writesonic, increasingly prioritize content that demonstrates E-E-A-T. AI-generated content, while often a good starting point, typically lacks genuine experience and deep expertise. The secret to successful AI SEO is to use AI as an assistant – to generate ideas, draft initial content, analyze data – but then to have human experts review, edit, and infuse the content with unique insights, real-world examples, and authoritative perspectives. This human touch is what ultimately builds trust with both users and search engines.

By incorporating these simple AI secrets into your SEO practices, you can harness the power of artificial intelligence to work smarter, gain deeper insights, and ultimately achieve better search engine rankings without necessarily investing in the most complex or expensive solutions. The key is creative application and a commitment to quality.

Reference: Insights for this section were drawn from practical AI SEO strategies discussed in sources like Writesonic's "How to Use AI for SEO: A 10-Step Practical Guide" (Accessed May 13, 2025 from https://writesonic.com/blog/ai-seo/).

6.6 Ethical Considerations in AI for SEO

The rapid integration of Artificial Intelligence into Search Engine Optimization practices brings forth a spectrum of ethical considerations that marketers and businesses must navigate responsibly. While AI offers unprecedented capabilities for enhancing online visibility and efficiency, its power also necessitates a mindful approach to ensure fairness, transparency, user trust, and adherence to ethical guidelines. This section delves into the key ethical challenges and best practices associated with using AI in SEO.

One of the foremost ethical concerns revolves around **transparency and honesty in AI-generated content**. AI tools like ChatGPT, Jasper, and Copy.ai can produce vast quantities of content quickly. However, as highlighted by ProfileTree in their article "Ethical Considerations for Using AI in SEO," the authenticity of this content can be a significant issue. AI-generated text, if not carefully reviewed and imbued with human insight, can feel impersonal, generic, or even misleading. There's also the risk of AI inadvertently generating factually incorrect information, plagiarized material, or biased perspectives, which can severely damage a brand's reputation and erode audience trust. Best practices dictate disclosing when content is substantially AI-generated, always fact-checking and supplementing AI content with human expertise, and using AI as an assistant to human creativity rather than a complete replacement.

Data privacy and compliance represent another critical ethical dimension. AI-driven SEO tools rely heavily on data, from analyzing search trends to tracking user behavior. The collection, storage, and use of this data must be handled ethically and in compliance with regulations like GDPR. ProfileTree emphasizes that collecting data without explicit user consent is unethical and illegal. Businesses must implement robust data protection policies, ensure transparency in their data collection practices, use anonymization techniques where appropriate, and provide users with clear information and opt-out mechanisms. Excessive or non-consensual data collection can lead to significant legal penalties and a loss of user trust.

The potential for **manipulative practices using AI** is a serious concern. AI's automation capabilities can be misused to implement black-hat SEO tactics at scale, such as creating spammy backlinks, generating low-quality keyword-stuffed content, or using cloaking techniques to deceive search engines. These practices, as ProfileTree notes, harm user experience and undermine the integrity of search results. While they might offer short-term gains, they inevitably lead to penalties from search engines like Google, which continuously update their algorithms to detect and penalize such manipulative behaviors. Ethical AI use in SEO focuses on providing genuine value to users and improving website content and structure in alignment with search engine guidelines, rather than attempting to exploit algorithmic loopholes.

Bias in AI algorithms is an insidious ethical challenge. AI systems are trained on datasets, and if these datasets contain inherent biases (e.g., related to demographics, gender, or cultural perspectives), the AI's outputs will reflect and potentially amplify these biases. In SEO, this could manifest as AI tools prioritizing certain keywords or demographics, leading to unintentional exclusion or misrepresentation. ProfileTree suggests that mitigating this requires regularly reviewing training datasets for diversity, auditing AI outputs for bias, and combining AI-generated insights with human judgment to ensure balanced and inclusive content strategies.

Concerns about the **impact on human employment** also arise with the increasing automation capabilities of AI in SEO. While AI can automate tasks like content creation, keyword research, and data analysis, it's crucial to view AI as a tool that augments human capabilities rather than entirely replacing human roles. Ethical approaches involve using AI to handle repetitive tasks, freeing up human SEO professionals to focus on higher-level strategy, creativity, and complex problem-solving. Providing training to upskill employees in AI-driven workflows and emphasizing human oversight are key to fostering a collaborative human-AI environment.

Furthermore, **accountability in AI decision-making** is essential. AI systems can sometimes operate as "black boxes," making it difficult to understand their reasoning or identify the cause of errors or unethical outcomes. Ethical practice demands transparency from AI providers and the establishment of clear accountability frameworks within organizations using AI for SEO. Regular monitoring and auditing of AI systems are necessary to ensure they align with ethical principles and business objectives.

Lastly, though not always at the forefront of SEO ethics discussions, **environmental considerations** are becoming increasingly relevant. Training and running large AI models are computationally intensive and consume significant energy, contributing to carbon emissions. Businesses committed to sustainability should consider the environmental footprint of their AI usage, opting for energy-efficient AI tools and providers who prioritize renewable energy sources where possible.

In conclusion, while AI offers transformative potential for SEO, its deployment must be guided by strong ethical principles. Prioritizing transparency, data privacy, user value over manipulation, fairness, and accountability will not only ensure compliance with guidelines and regulations but also build long-term trust with users and contribute to a healthier, more reliable digital ecosystem.

Reference: This section draws upon insights from "Ethical Considerations for Using AI in SEO" by ProfileTree (Accessed May 13, 2025 from https://profiletree.com/using-ai-in-seo/).

AI Prompts: Chapter 6

How to Use These Prompts

Each prompt below is designed to be copied directly into your favorite AI tool (ChatGPT, Claude, Grok, or Gemini). Simply:

1.Copy the entire prompt (including the bracketed placeholders)

2. Replace the [bracketed sections] with your specific information

3.Paste into your AI tool and hit enter

4.Refine the output by asking follow-up questions or requesting revisions

These are battle-tested prompts I use with organizations around the world. They're designed to give you professional-quality outputs that you can use immediately in your business.

Prompt 6.1: Keyword Research and Content Strategy

I want to rank for keywords related to [your main topic/industry] for my [type of business].

Business context:

- What we offer: [products/services]
- Target audience: [who searches for this]
- Geographic focus: [local, national, global]
- Current website authority: [new site / established site / domain authority if known]

Create a comprehensive keyword strategy:

1. **Primary Keywords** (3-5 main terms):
   - The keyword phrase
   - Estimated search volume
   - Difficulty level (high/medium/low)
   - Why it matters for my business
2. **Long-Tail Keywords** (10-15 specific phrases):

- Lower competition, higher intent keywords
- Question-based keywords (what people actually ask)
- "Near me" or local variations (if applicable)

3. **Content Cluster Strategy**:
- A pillar page topic (comprehensive guide)
- 8-10 supporting blog post topics that link to the pillar
- How they interconnect for SEO value

4. **Quick Win Keywords** (5 keywords):
- Lower competition terms I can rank for in 30-60 days
- Specific content to create for each

5. **Search Intent Mapping**:
- Informational keywords (top of funnel)
- Consideration keywords (middle of funnel)
- Transactional keywords (bottom of funnel)

Prioritize keywords that balance search volume with realistic ranking potential for my site.

Prompt 6.2: Optimize Existing Content for SEO

I have an existing blog post/page that I want to optimize for better search rankings.

Current content URL: [URL if available]

Target keyword: [main keyword]

Current ranking: [position if known, or "not ranking"]

Content summary:

[Paste a brief summary or the first few paragraphs of your content]

Provide a detailed SEO optimization checklist:

1. **Title Tag Optimization**:
- Current title: [your current title]
- 3 improved title options (include keyword, under 60 characters, compelling)

2. **Meta Description**:
- Write a compelling meta description (155 characters, includes keyword and CTA)

3. **Header Structure** (H1, H2, H3):

- Recommended header hierarchy
- Where to naturally include target keyword and related terms

4. **Content Improvements**:
- Missing topics or questions to add
- Recommended word count (based on top-ranking competitors)
- LSI keywords (related terms) to include naturally
- Internal linking opportunities (what other pages to link to)

5. **On-Page SEO Elements**:
- Image alt text recommendations
- URL structure (if it needs changing)
- Schema markup to add (FAQ, How-To, Article, etc.)

6. **User Experience Enhancements**:
- Readability improvements
- Visual elements to add (images, videos, infographics)
- Call-to-action placement

7. **Content Refresh Priority**:
- What to update first for biggest impact
- Estimated time to see ranking improvements

Make recommendations specific and actionable, not generic SEO advice.

Prompt 6.3: Create SEO-Optimized Content Briefs

Create a detailed content brief for an SEO-optimized blog post on: [your topic]

Target keyword: [primary keyword]

Secondary keywords: [2-3 related keywords]

Target audience: [who will read this]

Business goal: [what you want this content to achieve]

The content brief should include:

1. **Recommended Title** (3 options):
- Include target keyword
- Under 60 characters
- Compelling and click-worthy

2. **Content Outline** (detailed structure):
   - H1 (main title)
   - 6-8 H2 sections with brief descriptions of what to cover
   - 2-3 H3 subsections under each H2 where appropriate
   - Natural keyword placement throughout
3. **Search Intent Analysis**:
   - What is the searcher actually looking for?
   - What questions must this content answer?
   - What format do top-ranking pages use? (listicle, how-to, guide, comparison)
4. **Competitive Content Gap**:
   - What do top 3 ranking pages cover?
   - What are they missing that I can include?
   - My unique angle or perspective
5. **Content Requirements**:
   - Recommended word count
   - Images/visuals needed (and what they should show)
   - Examples or case studies to include
   - Data or statistics to reference
   - Internal and external links to include
6. **Engagement Elements**:
   - Key takeaways or summary box
   - FAQ section (5 questions)
   - Clear call-to-action
7. **SEO Checklist**:
   - Meta description
   - URL slug
   - Image alt text examples
   - Schema markup type

This brief should be detailed enough that a writer can create the content without additional research.

For prompts and bonus resources, visit **thejasonfleagle.com/blue-print-resources**. You can copy and paste the prompts from there—no retyping needed.

| 7 |

AI for Competitive Analysis

In today's fiercely competitive business environment, understanding your competitors is not just an advantage—it's a necessity. Traditional methods of competitive analysis, often manual and time-consuming, struggle to keep pace with the dynamic nature of modern markets. Artificial Intelligence (AI) is revolutionizing this critical business function, offering unprecedented capabilities to monitor competitors, identify their weaknesses, predict their actions, and ultimately, gain a significant strategic edge.

This chapter delves into how AI is transforming competitive analysis, exploring the tools and techniques that empower businesses to make more informed, proactive, and data-driven decisions. We will examine how AI automates the collection and processing of vast amounts of competitor data, uncovers subtle patterns and insights that human analysis might miss, and provides the foresight needed to navigate complex market dynamics.

From real-time monitoring of competitor activities to sophisticated predictive analytics, AI is equipping organizations with the intelligence to not only react to competitive pressures but to anticipate and shape them. We will also explore practical case studies, simple AI secrets for everyday application, and the crucial ethical considerations that must guide the use of these powerful technologies.

7.1 Monitoring Competitors with AI

In the hyper-competitive modern business landscape, staying ahead requires not just a deep understanding of your own operations but also a vigilant eye on the actions and strategies of your competitors. Traditional methods of competitive monitoring, often manual and sporadic, are no longer sufficient to keep pace with the rapid changes in the market. Artificial Intelligence (AI) has emerged as a transformative force in this domain, offering businesses the ability to monitor their competitors with unprecedented breadth, depth, and timeliness. AI-powered tools can sift through vast oceans of data from diverse sources, identify relevant signals, and provide actionable insights, enabling organizations to proactively adapt their strategies and maintain a competitive edge.

The core strength of AI in competitor monitoring lies in its capacity to automate and scale the process of information gathering and analysis. These systems can continuously scan the digital landscape, including competitor websites, social media channels, news articles, press releases, industry reports, patent filings, job postings, customer reviews, and even regulatory documents. This relentless, 24/7 vigilance ensures that no significant competitor activity goes unnoticed, from subtle shifts in marketing messaging to major product launches or strategic partnerships.

Several AI-powered platforms excel in providing comprehensive competitor monitoring capabilities. For instance, tools like **AlphaSense** leverage sophisticated AI to aggregate and analyze information from an extensive range of sources, including broker research, earnings call transcripts, and patent databases. This allows businesses to track not only publicly announced competitor activities but also to glean insights from more nuanced data points that might indicate future strategic directions. Similarly, platforms such as **Crayon** and **Klue** specialize in tracking competitors' digital footprints in real-time. Crayon, for example, monitors changes across competitor websites, content marketing efforts, product updates, and news mentions, providing timely alerts and AI-driven summaries to distill vast amounts of data into actionable intelligence. Klue focuses on collecting and curating competitive intelligence from both external and internal sources, helping teams stay informed about competitor movements and market changes.

AI's role extends beyond simple data collection. Natural Language Processing (NLP), a key AI technology, enables these tools to understand the context and sentiment behind the information gathered. This means that AI can not only tell you *what* your competitors are saying but also *how* it's being received by the market. For example, AI can analyze customer reviews and social media conversations related to a competitor's new product, identifying common themes, positive feedback, and pain points. This sentiment analysis provides a qualitative layer to competitor monitoring, offering insights into public perception and potential vulnerabilities.

Furthermore, AI tools can help monitor competitor activities across various marketing channels. Platforms like **Semrush** and **Ahrefs**, while primarily known for SEO and content marketing, offer robust features for tracking competitor performance in organic search, paid advertising, and content strategies. They can identify the keywords competitors are targeting, the backlinks they are acquiring, the content formats that are performing well for them, and their share of voice in specific market segments. **SpyFu** provides deep insights into competitors' PPC campaigns and organic rankings, revealing their ad spend, keyword choices, and ad copy variations over time. **Similarweb** offers extensive analysis of competitor website and app traffic, engagement metrics, and digital marketing campaigns, allowing businesses to benchmark their performance against rivals.

AI-driven monitoring also helps in identifying emerging competitors or disruptive technologies that might not yet be on the radar. By analyzing patterns in patent filings, startup funding announcements (via tools like **Crunchbase Pro** and **CB Insights**), and industry news, AI can flag potential future threats, giving businesses valuable time to prepare and adapt. **Contify**, for instance, gathers data from a massive array of sources and uses AI to generate insights, helping companies track not just established players but also up-and-coming challengers.

In essence, AI-powered competitor monitoring provides a dynamic, comprehensive, and insightful view of the competitive landscape. It automates the laborious task of data collection, enhances the depth of analysis through NLP and machine learning, and delivers timely alerts that enable businesses to react swiftly and strategically. By understanding what competitors are doing, how their actions are perceived, and where they are focusing their efforts, organizations can make more informed decisions, identify new opportunities, and proactively defend their market position. This continuous stream of intelligence is no longer a luxury but a necessity for thriving in today's fast-paced business environment.

7.2 Identifying Competitor Weaknesses with AI

Understanding where competitors are vulnerable is as crucial as knowing their strengths. Artificial Intelligence provides powerful capabilities to dissect competitor strategies, products, and customer perceptions, thereby pinpointing weaknesses that can be leveraged for strategic advantage. AI tools go beyond surface-level observations, delving into vast datasets to uncover subtle yet significant vulnerabilities that might be missed by manual analysis.

One of the primary ways AI helps in identifying competitor weaknesses is through advanced **sentiment analysis and customer feedback processing**. Platforms like **AlphaSense** and **Crayon** can analyze millions of customer reviews, social media comments, forum discussions, and survey responses related to competitors. By applying Natural Language Processing (NLP), these tools can identify recurring negative themes, pain points, and areas of dissatisfaction among a competitor's customer base. For example, AI might detect a consistent pattern of complaints about a competitor's customer service, a specific product flaw, or confusing pricing structures. This provides a clear indication of a weakness that a business can highlight in its own marketing or address with a superior offering.

AI also excels at **analyzing competitor content and messaging**. Tools such as **Crayon** and **Klue** can deconstruct a competitor's marketing materials, website copy, and sales collateral to identify inconsistencies, outdated information, or messaging that fails to resonate with target audiences. AI can compare this content against industry best practices or even against a company's own successful content to highlight gaps. For instance, if a competitor's website has a high bounce rate on key product pages, or if their blog content receives low engagement, AI can help pinpoint the reasons, such as poor readability, lack of relevant keywords, or a disconnect with user intent. **Semrush** and **Ahrefs**, while primarily SEO tools, can reveal weaknesses in a competitor's content strategy by identifying content gaps for important keywords or topics where the competitor is underperforming or not present.

Product and service gap analysis is another area where AI provides significant value. By analyzing competitor product descriptions, feature lists, user manuals, and customer reviews, AI can identify features that are lacking, poorly implemented, or frequently criticized. Tools like **AlphaSense** can scan patent databases and R&D publications to understand a competitor's innovation pipeline, potentially revealing areas where they are lagging or where their future products might have inherent limitations. This allows a business to position its own products or services as superior alternatives that address these specific shortcomings.

Furthermore, AI can identify operational weaknesses by analyzing data related to a competitor's **hiring patterns, financial performance (where publicly available), and supply chain**. For example, a sudden increase in job postings for customer support roles might indicate existing service issues. Financial reports, analyzed by AI, can reveal declining profitability in certain segments or over-reliance on a narrow product line. While direct access to a competitor's internal operational data is rare, AI can piece together publicly available information to infer potential vulnerabilities.

Competitive benchmarking powered by AI offers a structured way to identify weaknesses. Tools like **Similarweb** allow businesses to benchmark their website traffic, engagement metrics, and audience demographics against competitors. Significant underperformance in key areas can highlight weaknesses in a competitor's digital strategy or user experience. AI can also help in benchmarking product features, pricing models, and customer satisfaction scores, providing a clear, data-driven comparison that exposes areas where competitors are falling short.

Tools like **Contify** and **Kompyte** (by Semrush) continuously monitor a wide array of data sources and use AI to distill this information into actionable insights, often presented in formats like battlecards or competitive intelligence dashboards. These insights frequently highlight competitor weaknesses that sales and marketing teams can use directly in their efforts. For example, if a competitor has recently received negative press regarding a data breach, AI-powered monitoring tools will flag this, and it can be used (ethically) to emphasize a company's own robust security measures.

In summary, AI transforms the process of identifying competitor weaknesses from a reactive, often anecdotal exercise into a proactive, data-driven strategic function. By leveraging AI's ability to process and analyze vast amounts of diverse data, businesses can gain a much clearer and more objective understanding of where their competitors are vulnerable. This allows for the development of targeted strategies to exploit those weaknesses, differentiate their offerings, and ultimately gain a stronger position in the market.

7.3 Predicting Competitor Actions with AI

Anticipating a competitor's next move is a significant strategic advantage, allowing businesses to prepare, counteract, or even preempt competitive threats. While perfect prediction remains elusive, Artificial Intelligence is increasingly empowering organizations to forecast competitor actions with greater accuracy than ever before. By analyzing historical data, market trends, and subtle behavioral signals, AI can identify patterns and probabilities that suggest future competitor strategies, product launches, market entries, or pricing changes.

AI's predictive capabilities in competitive intelligence stem from its power to process and interpret vast and complex datasets. Machine learning algorithms, particularly those focused on **trend analysis and pattern recognition**, are at the heart of this. Tools like **AlphaSense** excel in this area by not only monitoring current activities but also by identifying emerging trends and market shifts through the analysis of diverse data sources, including broker reports, earnings calls, and patent filings. For instance, a sudden increase in a competitor's patent filings in a specific technology area, coupled with targeted hiring in related R&D roles (information potentially gleaned from job posting aggregators analyzed by AI), could be a strong indicator of an upcoming product launch or a strategic pivot in that direction.

CB Insights is another platform that leverages AI for predictive intelligence, particularly in the technology and startup landscape. By tracking funding rounds, investments, partnerships, and technology adoption trends, it can help predict which emerging companies might become significant competitors or which technologies are likely to disrupt the market. Their AI-powered "Instant Insights" aim to transform complex data into actionable intelligence that can inform predictions about market dynamics and competitor trajectories.

Predictive analytics in this context often involves identifying leading indicators of competitor behavior. For example, AI can monitor a competitor's digital marketing spend, changes in their website architecture, or shifts in their social media messaging. A significant ramp-up in advertising spend in a new geographical region, detected by tools like **Semrush** or **SpyFu**, might predict an imminent market entry. Similarly, AI can analyze the language used in competitor communications (e.g., CEO statements, press releases) for subtle cues that signal strategic intent. Sentiment analysis, as discussed earlier, can also play a role; a sharp decline in customer sentiment towards a competitor's flagship product might predict a forthcoming product update or a price reduction to regain market share.

Platforms like **Contify** contribute to predictive capabilities by offering customizable dashboards that visualize data and trends over time. By tracking competitor movements and market dynamics, businesses can start to see patterns that suggest likely future actions. For example, if a competitor consistently launches new products on a specific annual cycle, or if they typically respond to price drops from rivals within a certain timeframe, AI can help identify and flag these recurring patterns, making their future actions more predictable.

AI can also assist in **scenario planning** by modeling potential competitor responses to a company's own strategic moves. By inputting various actions (e.g., launching a new product, entering a new market, changing pricing), AI can simulate likely competitive reactions based on historical data and game theory principles. While still an evolving area, this provides a more data-driven approach to anticipating the competitive chessboard.

It's important to note that predicting competitor actions with AI is not about crystal-ball gazing. Instead, it's about using data-driven probabilities and identifying early warning signals. The accuracy of these predictions depends heavily on the quality and breadth of the data fed into the AI systems, as well as the sophistication of the algorithms used. AI might not predict the exact date of a competitor's product launch, but it can significantly increase the likelihood of anticipating such a move, providing valuable lead time for strategic planning.

Moreover, AI can help in **identifying anomalies** in competitor behavior that deviate from established patterns. These anomalies can be strong indicators of a significant, unannounced strategic shift. For instance, a sudden halt in marketing activities for a particular product line, or an unexpected acquisition of a smaller company in an unrelated field, could be flagged by AI as deviations requiring closer scrutiny and potentially indicating a major change in direction.

In conclusion, AI offers a powerful toolkit for moving beyond reactive competitor analysis to a more proactive and predictive stance. By continuously learning from data, identifying subtle patterns, and analyzing market trends, AI helps businesses anticipate competitor actions with greater confidence. This foresight enables companies to develop more resilient strategies, mitigate risks, and seize opportunities by being better prepared for the competitive moves that lie ahead.

7.4 Case Study: Company C Outperforms Competitors Using AI Competitive Intelligence

Company C: A Mid-Sized E-commerce Retailer

Background: Company C, a mid-sized e-commerce retailer specializing in consumer electronics, found itself in an increasingly crowded market. Larger competitors with significant resources were constantly adjusting prices, launching new product bundles, and running aggressive marketing campaigns. Company C struggled to keep pace, often reacting too slowly to competitor moves and missing out on key market opportunities. Their existing competitive analysis process was manual, time-consuming, and relied heavily on anecdotal evidence and sporadic website checks.

The Challenge: Staying Agile and Proactive

The primary challenge for Company C was the inability to gather and process competitive intelligence quickly and effectively enough to make timely strategic decisions. They needed a way to:

1. **Monitor competitor pricing and promotions in real-time:** Manually tracking price changes across hundreds of SKUs from multiple competitors was impossible.
2. **Understand competitor product strategies:** They needed insights into new product launches, feature updates, and product discontinuations by competitors.
3. **Analyze competitor marketing campaigns and messaging:** Identifying what resonated with the target audience for their

competitors was crucial for refining their own marketing efforts.

4. **Identify emerging threats and opportunities:** They were often caught off-guard by new market entrants or shifts in competitor focus.

The Solution: Implementing an AI-Powered Competitive Intelligence Platform

Company C decided to invest in an AI-powered competitive intelligence platform. They chose a solution similar to **Kompyte** or **Crayon**, which offered features like automated website tracking, real-time alerts on competitor changes (pricing, product descriptions, new content), AI-driven summarization of competitor activities, and battlecard generation for their sales team.

The AI platform was configured to continuously monitor the websites, social media profiles, press releases, and product pages of their top five competitors. It also tracked industry news sites and forums for mentions of these competitors and relevant market trends.

How AI Transformed Their Competitive Intelligence:

1. **Real-Time Price Monitoring and Dynamic Adjustments:** The AI tool automatically scraped competitor pricing data multiple times a day. This allowed Company C to identify when competitors were running promotions or making price adjustments almost instantly. For example, when a key competitor launched a surprise flash sale on a popular gaming console, Company C received an alert within minutes. Their pricing team, armed with this AI-driven insight, was able to quickly assess the situation and implement a competitive counter-offer on a related accessory bundle, mitigating potential lost sales and even capturing customers looking for a complete package. This was a significant improvement from their previous state, where they might have learned about such a sale days later through customer feedback or a manual check.

2. **Early Detection of Competitor Product Launches:** The AI platform tracked changes in competitor website navigation, new product page additions (even before they were officially announced), and mentions in industry forums. On one occasion, the AI detected subtle changes on a competitor's staging website (inadvertently made public for a short period) that hinted at the imminent launch of a new line of noise-canceling headphones. This early warning allowed Company C to adjust its inventory of similar products, prepare a counter-marketing campaign focusing on their own product's unique selling propositions, and train their sales team on how to position against the new offering. When the competitor product launched, Company C was prepared, not surprised.
3. **Identifying Competitor Messaging Weaknesses:** By analyzing competitor marketing copy and customer reviews using NLP, the AI tool identified that a major competitor, while strong on product features, consistently received negative feedback regarding their complex return process. Company C leveraged this insight by prominently highlighting their own hassle-free returns policy in their marketing campaigns and on their product pages. This resonated with customers and helped differentiate them from the competitor on a key service aspect.
4. **Predicting Competitor Focus Shifts:** The AI tool analyzed the content themes and keywords that competitors were increasingly focusing on in their blogs and social media. It noticed one competitor significantly increasing content around "work from home" solutions and accessories. This insight, identified months before the broader market shift became obvious, allowed Company C to proactively increase its own stock and marketing efforts for relevant products, capturing a significant share of the emerging demand.

Results:

Within six months of implementing the AI-powered competitive intelligence platform, Company C observed significant improvements:

- **Increased Agility:** Their ability to respond to competitor price changes improved from days to hours.
- **Improved Sales:** By proactively countering competitor promotions and identifying product gaps, they saw a 15% increase in sales for targeted product categories.
- **Enhanced Marketing ROI:** Insights into competitor messaging weaknesses allowed them to refine their own campaigns, leading to a 10% improvement in conversion rates for specific ad groups.
- **Better Strategic Planning:** Early warnings about competitor product launches and strategic shifts enabled more proactive and informed long-term planning.

Conclusion: Company C's experience demonstrates how AI can level the playing field for mid-sized businesses. By automating data collection, providing deeper analytical insights, and offering predictive capabilities, AI-powered competitive intelligence transformed Company C from a reactive follower into a proactive and agile competitor, capable of anticipating market changes and strategically outmaneuvering larger rivals.

7.5 Simple AI Secrets for Competitive Analysis

Leveraging Artificial Intelligence for competitive analysis doesn't always require complex, enterprise-level deployments. There are several straightforward "AI secrets" or practical approaches that businesses of any size can adopt to gain a competitive edge. These secrets often involve using readily available AI features within existing tools or applying AI thinking to your competitive intelligence processes.

1. Automate Your Competitor Keyword Monitoring (The "Set It and Forget It" Sentry): Many businesses manually check competitor rankings for key terms. A simple AI secret is to use SEO tools like **Semrush**, **Ahrefs**, or even Google Alerts (with advanced search operators) to automate the tracking of your competitors' keyword performance and content changes. Set up alerts for when competitors rank for new valuable keywords, when their existing rankings change significantly, or when they publish new content around specific topics. This AI-driven monitoring acts as an early warning system for shifts in their SEO and content strategy, saving you countless hours of manual checks.

2. Use AI for Smarter Social Listening (Beyond Mentions): Don't just track mentions of your competitors; use AI-powered social listening tools (many are built into platforms like **Determ**, **Brandwatch**, or even advanced features in social media management tools) to analyze the *sentiment* and *context* around those mentions. A simple secret is to configure these tools to flag not just high volumes of mentions, but specifically spikes in negative sentiment or discussions around particular product features or customer service issues of your competitors. This helps you quickly identify their emerging weaknesses or PR crises.

3. Leverage AI-Powered Content Summarization (The Quick Digest): Competitors are constantly publishing blog posts, white papers, and press releases. Staying on top of all this content is daunting. A simple AI secret is to use AI-powered summarization tools (some are standalone, others integrated into competitive intelligence platforms like **AlphaSense** or even browser extensions) to quickly get the gist of lengthy competitor documents. This allows you to rapidly assess the key takeaways and decide if a deeper dive is necessary, significantly speeding up your content review process.

4. Uncover Hidden Competitor Strategies through Ad Creative Analysis (The Ad Detective): AI tools within platforms like **SpyFu** or social media ad libraries (e.g., Facebook Ad Library) allow you to see the ad creatives your competitors are running. A simple AI secret is to look for patterns and A/B tests in their ad copy, visuals, and calls-to-action. AI can help categorize these ads and identify which messages or offers they are pushing most aggressively or testing frequently. This provides insights into their current marketing focus and target audience segments.

5. Turn Website Change Detection into Strategic Insights (The Digital Watchdog): Tools like **Visualping** or features within platforms like **Crayon** use AI to monitor competitor websites for any changes, from minor text edits to major structural overhauls. The secret is to not just get alerted to *any* change, but to focus on changes to key pages like pricing, product features, or career pages. A sudden update to a pricing page might signal a new pricing strategy, while a flurry of new job postings in a specific department could indicate expansion or a new product focus. AI helps filter the noise and highlight strategically relevant changes.

6. Use AI to Benchmark Your Content Against Competitors (The Performance Grader): Several AI writing assistants and SEO tools (e.g., **Surfer SEO, INK**) allow you to analyze your content against top-ranking competitor content for specific keywords. The secret is to use these tools not just for your own content optimization, but to also run competitor content through them. This can reveal weaknesses in their on-page SEO, content structure, or readability that you can exploit by creating superior content.

7. Predict Competitor Focus with AI-Driven Trend Analysis (The Future Gazer Lite): While full-blown predictive analytics can be complex, a simpler AI secret is to use tools that analyze the topics and keywords your competitors are increasingly focusing on over time. Many competitive intelligence platforms offer trend identification features. If a competitor starts consistently publishing content or running ads around a new technology or market segment, AI can flag this emerging trend in their strategy, giving you a heads-up on their potential future direction.

By incorporating these simple AI secrets into your competitive analysis workflow, you can automate tedious tasks, uncover deeper insights, and react more quickly to the competitive landscape, all without necessarily needing a massive budget or a dedicated data science team. The key is to think strategically about how AI can augment your existing efforts and provide actionable intelligence.

7.6 Ethical Considerations in AI-Powered Competitive Analysis

While Artificial Intelligence offers powerful advantages in competitive analysis, its use also brings forth significant ethical considerations that businesses must navigate responsibly. The ability to gather, analyze, and predict competitor behavior at scale necessitates a strong ethical framework to ensure fairness, transparency, and respect for privacy. Ignoring these ethical dimensions can lead to reputational damage, legal repercussions, and a loss of trust among stakeholders.

1. Data Privacy and Collection Methods: AI-driven competitive intelligence often relies on collecting vast amounts of publicly available data. However, the line between public and private can sometimes blur, especially when dealing with data related to individuals (e.g., competitor employees, customers expressing opinions). Ethical AI practice dictates:

- **Respecting Data Sources:** Only utilizing data that is genuinely in the public domain and obtained through legitimate, ethical means. This means avoiding scraping data from sources that explicitly prohibit it in their terms of service or using methods that could be construed as hacking or unauthorized access.
- **Anonymization and Aggregation:** When analyzing data that might contain personally identifiable information (PII), even if publicly available (like social media profiles), efforts should be made to anonymize or aggregate data to protect individual privacy where appropriate.
- **Compliance with Regulations:** Adhering to data privacy regulations like GDPR, CCPA, and others, even when analyzing

competitor data, as these regulations often have broad applicability regarding the processing of personal data.

2. Transparency and Algorithmic Bias: AI algorithms are trained on data, and if that data reflects existing biases, the AI can perpetuate or even amplify them. In competitive analysis, this could manifest as:

- **Biased Interpretation:** AI tools might misinterpret sentiment or context due to biases in their training data, leading to flawed conclusions about competitor strengths or weaknesses.
- **Overemphasis on Certain Data Points:** Algorithms might be unintentionally weighted to favor certain types of information, leading to a skewed view of the competitive landscape. Ethical practice requires:
- **Algorithmic Transparency (where possible):** Understanding, to the extent possible, how the AI tools arrive at their conclusions. While many commercial AI tools are black boxes, businesses should seek vendors who are transparent about their methodologies and efforts to mitigate bias.
- **Human Oversight and Critical Evaluation:** AI-generated insights should not be taken at face value. Human analysts must critically evaluate the findings, cross-reference them with other sources, and apply their own judgment to avoid acting on biased or incomplete information.
- **Diverse Data Sets for Training (Vendor Responsibility):** While users may not control this, advocating for and choosing vendors who prioritize diverse and representative data sets for training their AI models is crucial.

3. Misinformation and Manipulation: The power of AI to analyze and predict can also be misused. There's a risk of:

- **Spreading Misinformation:** Using AI-generated insights out of context or selectively to create a misleading narrative about competitors.
- **Unfair Competitive Practices:** Employing AI in ways that could be considered manipulative, such as creating fake social media profiles to disparage competitors (which is unethical regardless of AI use, but AI could scale such efforts). Ethical guidelines include:
- **Truthfulness and Accuracy:** Ensuring that any competitive claims made based on AI analysis are accurate, verifiable, and not misleading.
- **Fair Play:** Using competitive intelligence to inform strategy and improve one's own offerings, not to engage in slander or deceptive practices against competitors.

4. **Responsible Use and Intent:** The ultimate ethical litmus test lies in the intent behind using AI for competitive analysis. The goal should be to achieve a legitimate competitive advantage through better understanding of the market and superior strategy, not to harm or unfairly disadvantage competitors through unethical means.

- **Focus on Improvement, Not Sabotage:** Competitive intelligence should drive internal improvements in products, services, and marketing, rather than focusing solely on undermining competitors.
- **Respect for Intellectual Property:** AI tools should not be used to infringe on competitors' copyrights, patents, or trade secrets.
- **Long-Term Reputation:** Businesses should consider the long-term reputational impact of their competitive intelligence practices. Aggressive or ethically questionable tactics can backfire and damage a company's brand.

5. Security of Competitive Intelligence Data: The insights gathered through AI-powered competitive analysis are themselves valuable and sensitive. Businesses must ensure they have robust security measures in place to protect this data from unauthorized access or breaches, just as they would protect their own proprietary information.

In conclusion, AI offers transformative potential for competitive analysis, but this power must be wielded responsibly. By proactively addressing ethical considerations related to data privacy, algorithmic bias, transparency, and fair play, businesses can harness the benefits of AI while maintaining trust and upholding ethical business standards. This involves not only choosing ethical AI tools and vendors but also fostering a culture of ethical decision-making within the organization regarding the collection and use of competitive intelligence.

Case Study: ARI AI Chatbot for Military Veterans Community

ARI AI Chatbot for Military Veterans Community: Building Trust Through Technology

Background: A leading private organization dedicated to supporting military veterans was struggling to keep up with demand for the life coaching and services they were providing to US military veterans. They operated a peer support network where veterans could connect with each other, share resources, and find help navigating the often-complex landscape of VA benefits, mental health services, and career transition programs. The organization had a small staff and a network of volunteer peer mentors, but they were overwhelmed. Veterans reaching out for help often waited days for a response, and many fell through the cracks.

The organization came to me with a question: Could AI help them scale their support without losing the personal, trusted connection that was the foundation of their community? Could an AI-powered chatbot serve as a companion for the members in their online community and help them get the information they need?

Understanding the Unique Needs of Veterans:

Before we designed anything, I spent two-three weeks in deep discovery. I interviewed staff, volunteer mentors, and most importantly, veterans themselves. I needed to understand not just what they needed, but how they communicated, what they valued, and what they feared.

How We Trained the Chatbot on Sensitive Topics:

Training an AI to handle sensitive, high-stakes conversations required a fundamentally different approach than training a customer service bot.

Step 1: Building the Knowledge Base We compiled a comprehensive knowledge base that included:

- FAQs about VA benefits, healthcare, education programs, and career services
- A directory of vetted resources (crisis hotlines, legal aid, job placement programs)
- Transcripts of past peer mentor conversations (anonymized and with consent)
- Guidance on how to recognize signs of crisis (suicidal ideation, severe distress) and escalate immediately
- Online course content & other recommended resources

Step 2: Fine-Tuning for Tone and Empathy We fine-tuned the language model (using GPT-3.5 at the time, with custom training data) to adopt a specific tone:

- Peer-to-Peer, Not Professional-to-Client: ARI spoke like a fellow veteran—direct, respectful, with a touch of humor when appropriate.
- Empathetic, Not Patronizing: ARI was trained to acknowledge emotions ("That sounds incredibly frustrating") without being condescending.

- Humble About Limitations: ARI was programmed to be upfront when it didn't know something or when a question required human judgment. It would say, "This is beyond my expertise. Let me connect you with one of our peer mentors who can help."

Step 3: Building in Safeguards Given the sensitive nature of the community, we built multiple layers of safeguards:

- Crisis Detection: ARI was trained to recognize keywords and phrases associated with crisis situations (mentions of self-harm, hopelessness, immediate danger). When detected, ARI would immediately provide crisis hotline numbers and offer to connect the veteran to a human mentor or emergency services.
- Human-in-the-Loop Escalation: Any conversation that ARI flagged as high-risk was automatically routed to a staff member for review. We also gave veterans an easy "talk to a human" button at any point in the conversation.
- Continuous Monitoring: We reviewed a sample of conversations weekly to identify gaps in ARI's knowledge or tone issues, and we retrained the model accordingly.

Usage Statistics and Impact Stories:

ARI launched six months after the initial discovery phase. The impact was immediate and measurable:

- 24/7 Availability: In the first 90 days, ARI handled over 500 conversations. 40% of these interactions happened outside of business hours (evenings, weekends, and late at night), times when human support was previously unavailable.
- Reduced Wait Times: The average time for a veteran to get an initial response dropped from 18 hours to under 30 seconds. For many, this immediate acknowledgment was itself a form of support.

- High Satisfaction: We surveyed users after their interactions. 78% rated ARI as "helpful" or "very helpful." Many appreciated the anonymity and the non-judgmental nature of the interaction.
- Effective Triage: ARI successfully handled approximately 60% of inquiries end-to-end, providing the information or resources the veteran needed without requiring human escalation. For the remaining 40%, ARI gathered context and background information before connecting the veteran to a peer mentor, making those human conversations far more efficient and focused.
- Crisis Interventions: ARI's crisis detection system flagged 23 high-risk conversations in the first six months. In each case, a staff member was able to intervene immediately, connecting the veteran to appropriate crisis support. In at least two documented cases, this rapid response was potentially life-saving.

Lessons on AI for Underserved Communities:

This project taught me several profound lessons that apply to any effort to use AI to serve marginalized or vulnerable populations:

1. Start with Deep Empathy, Not Technology: We didn't start by asking, "What can AI do?" We started by asking, "What do veterans need, and what are the barriers preventing them from getting it?" The technology was secondary to the human need.

2. Co-Design with the Community: The veterans we served were not passive recipients of our solution; they were active co-creators. Their input was invaluable, and their endorsement was essential for trust.

3. Transparency Builds Trust: Being honest about ARI's capabilities and limitations didn't undermine trust; it built it. People appreciate honesty, especially when they've been let down by overpromises before.

4. AI is a Bridge, Not a Replacement: ARI's success was not measured by how many conversations it handled without human involve-

ment. It was measured by how effectively it connected veterans to the right support at the right time—whether that was an article, a hotline, or a human mentor.

What You Can Apply: If your business serves customers who are in vulnerable situations, facing complex problems, or who have been underserved by traditional systems, AI can be a powerful tool—but only if it's built with empathy, transparency, and a commitment to human dignity. Use AI to lower barriers, provide immediate support, and ensure no one falls through the cracks. But never lose sight of the fact that, at the end of the day, people need people.

You can watch a video demo of this AI platform clicking here.

AI Prompts: Chapter 7

How to Use These Prompts

Each prompt below is designed to be copied directly into your favorite AI tool (ChatGPT, Claude, Grok, or Gemini). Simply:

1.Copy the entire prompt (including the bracketed placeholders)

2. Replace the [bracketed sections] with your specific information

3.Paste into your AI tool and hit enter

4.Refine the output by asking follow-up questions or requesting revisions

These are battle-tested prompts I use with organizations around the world. They're designed to give you professional-quality outputs that you can use immediately in your business.

Prompt 7.1: Comprehensive Competitor Analysis

I want to conduct a thorough competitive analysis for my [type of business].

My business: [brief description]

My main competitors: [list 2-3 competitor names or descriptions]

My differentiation: [what makes you unique]

Create a comprehensive competitive analysis framework:

1. **Product/Service Comparison**:

- What they offer vs. what I offer
- Pricing comparison
- Features and benefits comparison
- Quality or value perception

2. **Marketing Strategy Analysis**:
- Their messaging and positioning
- Marketing channels they use
- Content strategy (topics, frequency, format)
- Advertising approach (if visible)

3. **Customer Experience**:
- Their website user experience
- Sales process (if known)
- Customer service approach
- Reviews and reputation (what customers say)

4. **Strengths and Weaknesses**:
- What they do better than me
- Where they're vulnerable
- Gaps in their offering

5. **Opportunity Identification**:
- Underserved customer segments they're missing
- Content topics they're not covering
- Channels they're not using effectively
- Messaging angles they're not taking

6. **Differentiation Strategy**:
- How I can position against them
- My unique value proposition
- Messaging that sets me apart

7. **Action Plan**:
- 3 immediate moves to gain competitive advantage
- What to copy (best practices)
- What to avoid (their mistakes)

Be specific and actionable, not just descriptive.

Prompt 7.2: Market Positioning and Messaging Strategy

Help me develop a clear market positioning and messaging strategy that differentiates me from competitors.

My business:

- What we do: [product/service]
- Who we serve: [target audience]
- Current positioning: [how you currently describe yourself]

My main competitors:

- Competitor 1: [name and their positioning]
- Competitor 2: [name and their positioning]
- Competitor 3: [name and their positioning]

What makes us different:

- [List 3-5 unique attributes, capabilities, or approaches]

Create a positioning strategy that includes:

1. **Positioning Statement**:

- A clear, one-sentence statement of who we are and why we matter
- Format: "For [target audience] who [need/want], [our brand] is the [category] that [unique benefit] because [reason to believe]."

2. **Value Proposition**:

- The core promise we make
- The transformation we deliver
- Why customers should choose us over alternatives

3. **Messaging Pillars** (3-4 main themes):

- Key messages that support our positioning
- Proof points for each pillar
- How this differentiates from competitors

4. **Messaging by Audience Segment**:

- How to adapt messaging for different customer types
- Pain points each segment cares about most
- Language and tone for each

5. **Competitive Messaging**:

- How to talk about competitors (if asked)
- Comparison talking points

- What NOT to say
6. **Tagline Options** (5 options):
- Memorable, differentiated taglines
- Each under 10 words
7. **Elevator Pitch** (3 versions):
- 30-second version
- 60-second version
- 2-minute version

Make this clear, compelling, and ownable - not generic business speak.

Prompt 7.3: Identify Market Trends and Opportunities

I want to identify emerging trends and opportunities in [your industry] that I can capitalize on before my competitors.

My industry: [specific industry or niche]

My business: [what you do]

My current focus: [main products/services/markets]

Analyze the market and provide:

1. **Emerging Trends** (5-7 trends):
- What's changing in the industry
- Why this trend matters
- Timeline (happening now, 6 months, 12+ months)
- Opportunity or threat for my business
2. **Customer Behavior Shifts**:
- How customer expectations are evolving
- New pain points emerging
- Changing buying patterns
- Technology adoption trends
3. **Competitive Landscape Changes**:
- New types of competitors entering the market
- Business models that are disrupting the industry
- What's becoming commoditized
4. **Technology Opportunities**:
- New tools or platforms I should explore

- Automation opportunities
- AI applications specific to my industry
5. **Untapped Market Segments**:
- Customer groups that are underserved
- Geographic markets with potential
- Adjacent industries I could serve
6. **Strategic Opportunities** (prioritized):
- Top 3 opportunities to pursue in the next 12 months
- What I need to do to capitalize on each
- Estimated investment and potential return
7. **Threats to Watch**:
- What could disrupt my current business model
- How to prepare or pivot

Focus on actionable insights I can use to make strategic decisions, not just general industry commentary.

For prompts and bonus resources, visit **thejasonfleagle.com/blueprint-resources**. You can copy and paste the prompts from there—no retyping needed.

| 8 |

AI for Customer Understanding

Introduction: The Imperative of Deep Customer Understanding in the AI Era

In the hyper-competitive and increasingly personalized modern marketplace, the ability to truly understand customers – their needs, preferences, behaviors, and aspirations – has transcended from a strategic advantage to an absolute business imperative. Customers today expect more than just products or services; they seek tailored experiences, empathetic engagement, and proactive solutions that resonate with their individual contexts. As businesses strive to meet these escalating expectations, the sheer volume and complexity of customer data generated across myriad digital and physical touchpoints present both an unprecedented opportunity and a formidable challenge. This is where Artificial Intelligence (AI) emerges not merely as a technological novelty, but as a transformative catalyst, fundamentally reshaping how organizations approach customer understanding.

This chapter, "AI for Customer Understanding: Unlocking Deeper Insights and Stronger Relationships," delves into the multifaceted ways AI is empowering businesses to move beyond superficial demographic segmentations and achieve a profound, nuanced, and actionable comprehension of their clientele. We will explore how AI-driven analytics can dissect vast datasets to reveal hidden patterns in customer behavior, how machine learning can construct dynamic and accurate customer personas, and how predictive models can forecast future customer value and potential churn with remarkable accuracy. Furthermore, we will uncover practical AI strategies and tools, particularly those accessible to small and medium-sized businesses, and examine a real-world case study demonstrating the tangible benefits of AI-powered personalization in enhancing customer retention.

From analyzing diverse data streams – including transactional records, behavioral patterns on websites and apps, and social media interactions – to leveraging sophisticated techniques like Natural Language Processing (NLP) for sentiment analysis and machine learning for predictive modeling, AI offers a powerful toolkit. This toolkit enables businesses to not only listen to the explicit voice of the customer but also to infer their implicit needs and anticipate future desires. The goal is to foster a level of customer intimacy that translates into more relevant product development, more effective marketing campaigns, more responsive customer service, and ultimately, more enduring and profitable customer relationships.

However, the journey into AI-driven customer understanding is not without its ethical considerations. As we harness the power of AI to glean deeper insights, we must also navigate critical issues of data privacy, algorithmic bias, transparency, and the responsible use of these potent technologies. This chapter will therefore also address the ethical imperatives that accompany the use of AI in understanding customers, emphasizing the importance of building trust and ensuring fairness in an increasingly AI-mediated world.

Join us as we explore how AI is revolutionizing customer understanding, providing businesses of all sizes with the tools to connect with their customers on a more meaningful level, anticipate their needs with greater precision, and cultivate loyalty that stands the test of time.

8.2 Building Customer Personas with AI

Understanding the customer, as explored in the previous section, lays the groundwork for a more targeted and empathetic approach to business strategy. A crucial tool in operationalizing this understanding is the development of customer personas. Traditionally, creating these semi-fictional representations of ideal customers has been a labor-intensive process, often relying on manual data collection, surveys, interviews, and subjective interpretation. However, the advent of Artificial Intelligence (AI) has revolutionized persona creation, offering pathways to automate, enhance, and inject a greater degree of data-driven objectivity into this vital marketing and product development exercise.

Customer personas are detailed archetypes representing specific segments of a target audience. They typically encompass demographic information (age, gender, income, location), psychographic details (interests, values, lifestyle, personality traits), behavioral patterns (purchasing history, online engagement, product usage), and pain points or needs that a product or service aims to address. Well-crafted personas enable businesses to step into their customers' shoes, fostering a deeper understanding that informs product design, marketing messaging, content creation, and overall customer experience strategies. The challenge has always been to create personas that are not only representative but also dynamic and actionable.

AI steps in to address these challenges by leveraging its capacity to analyze vast and diverse datasets far more efficiently and comprehensively than human analysts alone. AI can automate and significantly enhance the creation of detailed customer personas by identifying subtle patterns, correlations, and common characteristics within customer data that might otherwise go unnoticed. This leads to personas that are not only richer in detail but also more accurately reflect the multifaceted nature of modern consumers.

One of the primary ways AI enhances persona creation is through **automated data collection and synthesis**. AI algorithms can tap into a multitude of data sources simultaneously, including CRM systems, website analytics, social media platforms, customer support logs, and third-party data providers. For instance, an AI tool might analyze website clickstream data to understand user navigation patterns, social media listening data to gauge sentiment and identify trending topics among a customer base, and transactional data to pinpoint purchasing habits. By synthesizing these disparate data points, AI can construct a foundational layer for personas that is grounded in empirical evidence (Source: Allsopp Media, "How AI Can Create Customer Personas: a Guide for Modern Marketing"). UXPressia, for example, highlights how AI can generate initial persona content and even a representative photo based on user input, providing a rapid starting point for marketers (Source: UXPressia, "AI User Persona Generator").

Beyond simple data aggregation, AI excels at **advanced segmentation and pattern identification**. Machine learning algorithms, particularly unsupervised learning techniques like clustering (e.g., k-means, hierarchical clustering), can sift through large datasets to automatically group customers with similar attributes and behaviors. These clusters form the basis of distinct personas. AI can identify non-obvious correlations; for example, it might find that customers who purchase a specific product are also highly active on a particular social media platform and tend to respond positively to a certain type of marketing imagery. This level of granularity allows for the creation of nuanced personas that go beyond broad generalizations. AI can process demographic data (age, gender, income), psychographic data (interests, values), and behavioral data (purchase history, engagement habits) to define these segments with remarkable precision (Source: Allsopp Media).

The process often involves AI identifying patterns in how different customer segments interact with a brand across various touchpoints. For example, AI might analyze the language used in customer reviews or support chats (using NLP) to understand common pain points or desired features for different user groups. It can also track how different segments respond to marketing campaigns, content types, or product features, allowing for the continuous refinement of persona definitions.

Once initial personas are drafted, often with AI assistance, the role of human insight remains crucial. Marketers and researchers must then **adapt and validate these AI-generated personas** to their specific business context. While AI provides a powerful, data-driven foundation, human expertise is needed to interpret the nuances, add qualitative depth (perhaps from direct customer interviews that AI can help analyze), and ensure the personas align with strategic business goals. UXPressia emphasizes that the AI-generated persona is a starting point that needs to be adapted, with necessary adjustments and supplementation with additional research to validate and ensure accuracy (Source: UXPressia).

The **benefits of AI-driven personas for targeted marketing** are substantial. Firstly, they lead to **enhanced accuracy and deeper insights**. By minimizing human bias and processing data at scale, AI helps create personas that are more representative of the actual customer base, leading to more effective marketing strategies. As noted by Allsopp Media, AI can create detailed and realistic persona descriptions free from human bias, and these personas can evolve with new data, keeping them relevant.

Secondly, AI-driven personas enable **increased personalization at scale**. With a clearer understanding of different customer segments' specific needs, preferences, and pain points, businesses can tailor their marketing messages, content, product recommendations, and even user interfaces to resonate more effectively with each persona. This hyper-personalization fosters stronger customer relationships, improves engagement, and ultimately drives higher conversion rates. For example, understanding that one persona values sustainability while another prioritizes convenience allows a company to craft distinct messaging for each, even when promoting the same product.

Thirdly, AI contributes to **significant time savings and operational efficiency**. The traditional persona creation process can take weeks or even months. AI can generate initial, data-rich persona drafts in a fraction of that time, allowing marketing teams to move more quickly from research to strategy implementation (Source: Allsopp Media). This agility is critical in today's fast-paced market environment.

Furthermore, AI-driven personas are not static. They can be **dynamically updated** as new customer data flows in. This ensures that personas remain relevant and reflective of evolving customer behaviors and market trends, preventing marketing strategies from becoming outdated. This continuous learning and adaptation capability is a key advantage over traditionally created personas, which can quickly become obsolete.

Several best practices should be followed when implementing AI-driven personas. **Ensuring data quality** is paramount, as the accuracy of AI output is directly dependent on the quality of the input data. It's also crucial to **combine AI with human insight**; AI handles the heavy lifting of data analysis, but human expertise is invaluable for interpreting emotional nuances and strategic implications. Finally, **frequent persona updates**, facilitated by AI, are necessary to keep them current and effective (Source: Allsopp Media).

Real-world examples illustrate the power of AI in persona development. Super Butcher, an Australian retailer, utilized AI-driven personas to enhance customer experiences across both physical stores and their online platform. By analyzing customer data, they created personas that helped refine in-store layout, online navigation, and targeted marketing efforts, leading to increased customer satisfaction and engagement. Similarly, Bask Suncare, with the help of Delve AI, implemented AI-generated personas to segment their audience effectively, tailoring brand messaging to resonate with specific audiences and strengthening brand loyalty (Source: Allsopp Media).

In conclusion, AI is transforming the art and science of building customer personas. By automating data analysis, identifying complex patterns, and enabling dynamic updates, AI empowers businesses to create more accurate, detailed, and actionable personas. These AI-driven personas, in turn, fuel more effective targeted marketing, enhance personalization efforts, and ultimately contribute to a deeper, more empathetic, and more profitable relationship with customers.

References:

- Allsopp Media. (n.d.). *How AI Can Create Customer Personas: a Guide for Modern Marketing.* Retrieved from https://allsoppmedia.com/how-ai-can-create-customer-personas
- UXPressia. (n.d.). *AI User Persona Generator.* Retrieved from https://uxpressia.com/ai-persona-generator

8.3 Predicting Customer Lifetime Value (CLV) with AI

Following the analysis of customer data and the creation of detailed personas, a critical next step in deepening customer understanding is the prediction of Customer Lifetime Value (CLV). CLV represents the total net profit a business can expect to generate from a single customer over the entire duration of their relationship. It is a forward-looking metric that shifts the focus from short-term transactional gains to long-term customer relationship value. Traditionally, CLV calculations were often based on historical averages and relatively simple formulas. However, Artificial Intelligence (AI), particularly machine learning, has introduced far more sophisticated and accurate methods for predicting CLV, enabling businesses to make more strategic decisions regarding resource allocation, customer retention, and personalization efforts.

Understanding CLV is vital for several reasons. It helps businesses identify their most valuable customers, allowing them to prioritize resources and efforts towards nurturing these relationships. It informs marketing budget allocation, as companies can determine how much they can afford to spend to acquire customers with a high predicted CLV. Furthermore, CLV insights are crucial for developing effective customer retention strategies, as it is often more cost-effective to retain existing high-value customers than to acquire new ones. According to Comarch, CLV is a key metric for assessing customer profitability, guiding strategic marketing initiatives, and informing customer segmentation (Source: Comarch, "Predicting Customer Lifetime Value with AI").

Traditional methods for calculating CLV often involve formulas such as: CLV = Average basket value * Purchase frequency * Customer lifespan. While useful for a basic understanding, these historical-average-based models may not accurately capture the nuances of individual customer behavior or adapt to changing market dynamics. They often fail to account for the heterogeneity within customer bases and the non-linear progression of customer value over time.

AI revolutionizes CLV prediction by employing machine learning models that can analyze vast and complex datasets to identify subtle patterns and predict future behavior with greater precision. These models go beyond simple averages, incorporating a wide array of data inputs to build a more holistic view of each customer. Key **data inputs** for AI-driven CLV models typically include:

1. **Transactional Data:** Purchase history (frequency, recency, monetary value – RFM metrics), average order value, products purchased, returns, and discount usage.
2. **Demographic Data:** Age, gender, location, income level, education, and other demographic attributes that might correlate with spending habits.
3. **Behavioral Data:** Website engagement (pages visited, time on site, click-through rates), app usage (features used, session duration), email engagement (open rates, click rates), and social media interactions.
4. **Customer Service Interactions:** Frequency and nature of support requests, sentiment expressed during interactions, and resolution times.
5. **Engagement Data:** Participation in loyalty programs, response to marketing campaigns, and overall interaction frequency with the brand.

Various **AI algorithms and machine learning models** are employed for CLV prediction, each with its strengths:

- **Regression Models:** Simpler models like Linear Regression can be used as a baseline, but more advanced regression techniques are often preferred. Logistic Regression is commonly used for predicting binary outcomes like churn, which is a key component of CLV.
- **Probabilistic Models:** Models like the Beta Geometric/Negative Binomial Distribution (BG/NBD) model and the Pareto/NBD model are specifically designed to model customer purchase frequency and dropout probability based on historical transaction data.
- **Machine Learning Models:**
    - **Decision Trees, Random Forests, and Gradient Boosting Machines (GBM):** These ensemble methods are powerful for capturing complex, non-linear relationships in the data and are widely used for their accuracy in prediction tasks. They can handle a mix of numerical and categorical features effectively.
    - **Neural Networks (Deep Learning):** For very large and complex datasets, neural networks can uncover intricate patterns and achieve high predictive accuracy. Recurrent Neural Networks (RNNs) or Long Short-Term Memory (LSTM) networks can be particularly useful for modeling sequential behavioral data.
    - **Survival Analysis Models:** Techniques like the Cox Proportional Hazards model can predict the "survival" time of a customer (i.e., how long they will remain active) and identify factors influencing churn. This is directly applicable to estimating customer lifespan for CLV.

AI-powered CLV prediction offers significant benefits for **resource allocation and customer retention strategies**. By accurately forecasting the future worth of individual customers or segments, businesses can:

1. **Optimize Marketing Spend:** Allocate marketing budgets more effectively by focusing acquisition efforts on customer profiles with high predicted CLV and tailoring retention spend based on the value at stake. For instance, a company might invest more in retaining a customer predicted to have a high future value, even if their current spending is moderate.
2. **Personalize Customer Experiences and Offers:** Use CLV predictions to segment customers and deliver highly personalized experiences. High-CLV customers might receive exclusive offers, early access to new products, or dedicated customer support. Conversely, customers with a lower predicted CLV but potential for growth could be nurtured with targeted campaigns designed to increase their engagement and spending.
3. **Proactively Manage Churn:** AI models can identify customers at high risk of churning or significantly reducing their spending. This early warning allows businesses to implement proactive retention strategies, such as personalized outreach, special incentives, or addressing specific pain points before the customer disengages. Comarch notes that AI can predict which customers are likely to decrease their spending or cease interactions, enabling businesses to intervene (Source: Comarch).
4. **Inform Product Development:** Understanding the characteristics and behaviors of high-CLV customers can provide valuable insights for product development and service enhancements, ensuring that offerings are aligned with the needs of the most profitable customer segments.
5. **Enhance Loyalty Programs:** CLV segmentation allows for the creation of more effective and personalized loyalty programs. Instead of a one-size-fits-all approach, rewards and ben-

efits can be tiered and tailored to different CLV segments, maximizing engagement and perceived value (Source: Comarch).

Despite the power of AI in CLV prediction, certain **challenges** exist. **Data quality and completeness** are paramount; inaccurate or insufficient data will lead to unreliable predictions. The **predictive power can be limited** by unforeseen external events, rapid shifts in market dynamics, or changes in customer preferences that are not captured in historical data. Furthermore, CLV models often rely on certain **assumptions and simplifications** that may not perfectly reflect real-world complexities. Traditional CLV models might also have a **limited scope**, focusing primarily on monetary value and potentially overlooking other valuable contributions like referrals or brand advocacy, although more advanced AI models are beginning to incorporate such factors.

In conclusion, AI-driven CLV prediction marks a significant advancement over traditional methods. By leveraging sophisticated machine learning algorithms and diverse data sources, businesses can gain a much more accurate and actionable understanding of the long-term value of their customers. This, in turn, empowers them to make smarter decisions about resource allocation, personalize customer interactions more effectively, and implement proactive retention strategies, ultimately fostering stronger customer loyalty and maximizing profitability.

References:

- Comarch. (n.d.). *Predicting Customer Lifetime Value with AI.* Retrieved from https://www.comarch.com/trade-and-services/loyalty-marketing/blog/predicting-customer-lifetime-value-with-ai/

8.4 Case Study: Financial Institution Increases Retention 20% with AI-Powered Personalization and CLV Optimization

To illustrate the tangible impact of AI in enhancing customer understanding and driving business outcomes, let us examine a real-world case involving a major financial institution. This institution, while possessing a vast customer base, faced significant challenges in retaining customers and maximizing profitability. Their core issues stemmed from an inability to deeply understand customer behaviors and preferences, which in turn led to suboptimal resource allocation and lower-than-desired retention rates. This case study, based on the work by Data Sentinels, demonstrates how AI-driven predictive analytics and personalization can lead to substantial improvements in customer retention and profitability (Source: Data Sentinels, "Enhancing Customer Retention through Predictive Analytics").

The Challenge: Low Retention and Unclear Customer Value

The financial institution grappled with a common yet critical problem: a disconnect between the data they held and the actionable insights needed to foster customer loyalty. Despite accumulating extensive customer data, they struggled to translate this information into effective strategies for keeping customers engaged and understanding their long-term value. This resulted in generic customer interactions, missed opportunities for targeted engagement, and ultimately, a customer churn rate that impacted their bottom line. The institution recognized the need for a more sophisticated approach to segment its customers, predict their future value, and personalize interactions to prevent attrition.

The Solution: AI-Driven Predictive Analytics and CLV-Based Segmentation

To address these challenges, the institution partnered with Data Sentinels to implement a comprehensive AI-driven predictive analytics solution. The core of this solution was the strategic use of AI to analyze extensive customer data, encompassing transactional history, interaction patterns, demographic information, and other relevant touchpoints. The primary goals were to accurately predict Customer

Lifetime Value (CLV) and to segment customers dynamically based on this predicted value and their evolving behaviors.

Several key AI-powered components were deployed:

1. **Dynamic Customer Segmentation:** The AI system moved beyond static segmentation models. It continuously analyzed incoming customer data to group customers based not only on their historical behavior but also on their predicted CLV. This segmentation was dynamic, meaning that as a customer's interactions and transaction patterns changed, their segment and associated CLV prediction could be updated in real-time. This allowed for a much more fluid and accurate understanding of the customer base.
2. **Predictive Behavioral Analysis:** Utilizing advanced machine learning algorithms, the AI tool was designed to predict future buying behaviors, engagement levels, and potential churn risk for individual customers and segments. These predictive insights were crucial for anticipating customer needs and proactively addressing potential issues.
3. **CLV Calculation and Optimization:** The AI system calculated the CLV for each customer segment. This enabled the institution to clearly identify high-value customers, understand their characteristics, and tailor specific strategies to nurture these profitable relationships. It also allowed for a more strategic allocation of resources, focusing retention efforts where they would yield the highest return.
4. **Personalized Interactions:** Armed with predictive insights and a clear understanding of CLV, the institution could move towards more personalized and relevant customer interactions. This included tailoring communication, offering relevant financial products or advice at the right time, and customizing service approaches based on the predicted needs and value of each customer segment.

The Results: Significant Uplift in Retention and Profitability

The adoption of this AI-driven predictive analytics solution yielded remarkable and measurable results for the financial institution:

- **20% Increase in Customer Retention Rates:** This was a primary success metric. The ability to predict potential churn and engage customers with more personalized and relevant interactions based on predictive insights directly contributed to a significant reduction in customer attrition. By understanding who was likely to leave and why, the institution could implement targeted interventions to keep them engaged.
- **15% Increase in Profitability Per Customer:** The focus on high-CLV segments and the more efficient use of resources led to a notable increase in the profitability derived from each customer. By investing wisely in retaining and growing the value of their most profitable customers, the institution saw a direct positive impact on its overall financial performance.

Key Learnings from the Case:

This case study underscores several important aspects of leveraging AI for customer understanding:

- **The Power of Predictive CLV:** Moving beyond historical CLV calculations to AI-driven predictive CLV provides a much more powerful tool for strategic decision-making.
- **Dynamic Segmentation is Crucial:** Customer behavior is not static. AI's ability to dynamically segment customers ensures that strategies remain relevant and effective over time.
- **Personalization Drives Retention:** Generic approaches are no longer sufficient. AI enables the level of personalization required to make customers feel understood and valued, which is a key driver of loyalty and retention.

- **Measurable ROI:** Implementing AI for customer understanding is not just a technological upgrade; it is a strategic investment that can deliver clear and significant returns in terms of increased retention, higher profitability, and more efficient resource allocation.

In conclusion, the experience of this financial institution, as detailed by Data Sentinels, provides compelling evidence that AI-powered personalization, grounded in predictive analytics and a deep understanding of customer lifetime value, is a highly effective strategy for increasing customer retention and maximizing profitability. It highlights how transforming raw customer data into actionable intelligence through AI can create a significant competitive advantage.

References:

- Data Sentinels. (n.d.). *Enhancing Customer Retention through Predictive Analytics: Maximizing Customer Lifetime Value with AI.* Retrieved from https://www.data-sentinels.com/case-studies/enhancing-customer-retention-through-predictive-analytics%3A-maximizing-customer-lifetime-value-with-ai-

8.5 Simple AI Secrets for Customer Understanding

While the previous sections have delved into sophisticated AI applications for customer understanding, many small to medium-sized businesses (SMBs) might feel that such advanced capabilities are beyond their reach. However, the landscape of AI tools is rapidly evolving, and numerous accessible and affordable solutions can empower SMBs to gain valuable customer insights without requiring extensive technical expertise or massive budgets. This section unveils some "Simple AI Secrets" – practical, actionable tips and tools that SMBs can leverage to enhance their customer understanding.

1. Embrace AI-Powered Chatbots for Instant Feedback and Insights:

- **The Secret:** Chatbots are no longer just for large enterprises. Many user-friendly platforms allow SMBs to deploy AI-powered chatbots on their websites or social media channels. These bots can handle common customer inquiries 24/7, freeing up human agents for more complex issues. More importantly, the interactions chatbots have with customers are a goldmine of data.
- **Actionable Tip:** Implement a chatbot (e.g., using tools like Tidio, HubSpot Free Chatbot Builder, or Drift for more advanced features) and regularly review chat transcripts. AI features within these platforms can often automatically categorize inquiries, identify frequently asked questions, and even perform sentiment analysis on customer messages. This provides direct insight into customer pain points, common queries, and overall satisfaction levels. This aligns with findings from the U.S. Chamber of Commerce, which notes that AI-powered chatbots can automate simple inquiries, helping SMBs scale customer service (Source: U.S. Chamber of Commerce, "A Small Business Guide to AI").

2. Utilize AI-Enhanced CRM Systems for a Unified Customer View:

- **The Secret:** Modern Customer Relationship Management (CRM) systems, even those with free or entry-level tiers, are increasingly incorporating AI features. These features can help consolidate customer data from various touchpoints (email, social media, website interactions, sales calls) into a single, unified profile.
- **Actionable Tip:** Opt for a CRM that offers AI capabilities, such as HubSpot CRM (which has free tools and AI features like Breeze), Zoho CRM (with its Zia AI assistant), or Salesforce Essentials (with Einstein AI). These tools can automatically enrich customer profiles, score leads based on their likelihood to

convert, segment customers based on behavior, and suggest optimal times for outreach. By having AI organize and analyze customer data within the CRM, SMBs can gain a clearer understanding of customer journeys and preferences without manual data sifting.

3. Leverage AI-Powered Email Marketing Tools for Engagement Insights:

- **The Secret:** AI is revolutionizing email marketing by providing insights into what resonates with different customer segments. This goes beyond simple open and click-through rates.
- **Actionable Tip:** Use email marketing platforms with AI features (e.g., Mailchimp's AI-powered content optimizer, Constant Contact's AI tools). These tools can help optimize subject lines for better open rates, suggest the best times to send emails based on past engagement, personalize email content at scale, and even predict which subscribers are likely to churn. Analyzing these AI-driven recommendations and performance data provides valuable clues about customer content preferences and engagement patterns.

4. Tap into AI for Social Listening and Sentiment Analysis:

- **The Secret:** Understanding what customers are saying about your brand, competitors, and industry on social media is crucial. AI-powered social listening tools can automate this process, scanning vast amounts of social data for relevant mentions and sentiment.
- **Actionable Tip:** Explore social listening tools with AI capabilities (e.g., Hootsuite Insights, Sprout Social, or more budget-friendly options like Mention). These tools can track brand mentions, identify key influencers, analyze the sentiment (pos-

itive, negative, neutral) around specific topics or your brand, and highlight emerging trends. This provides SMBs with a real-time pulse on customer opinions and market perceptions, enabling them to respond proactively.

5. Use AI-Driven Survey Tools for Deeper Qualitative Insights:

- **The Secret:** While quantitative data is important, qualitative feedback provides the "why" behind customer actions. AI can enhance survey tools by helping to analyze open-ended responses more efficiently.
- **Actionable Tip:** Employ survey tools (like SurveyMonkey, Typeform, or Google Forms) and look for integrations or AI features that assist in analyzing textual responses. Some AI tools can perform thematic analysis on open-ended feedback, identifying common themes, keywords, and sentiment. This allows SMBs to extract rich insights from qualitative data without manually reading through hundreds or thousands of responses, helping to understand customer needs and frustrations in their own words.

6. Experiment with AI Content Generation Tools (with a Human Touch):

- **The Secret:** AI content generators (like ChatGPT, Jasper, or HubSpot's Breeze) can help brainstorm ideas, draft initial content, and even suggest ways to repurpose existing content to appeal to different customer segments. While not a replacement for human creativity, they can be powerful assistants.
- **Actionable Tip:** Use AI content tools to generate ideas for blog posts, social media updates, or email campaigns based on topics your customers care about (identified through other AI tools like social listening or chatbot analytics). Always review,

edit, and personalize AI-generated content to ensure it aligns with your brand voice and provides genuine value. The key is to use AI as a starting point to understand what kind of content might resonate, rather than a final solution.

7. Start Small and Iterate:

- **The Secret:** You don't need to implement every AI tool at once. The most effective approach for SMBs is to start with one or two tools that address their most pressing customer understanding challenges.
- **Actionable Tip:** Identify a key area where customer insight is lacking (e.g., understanding website visitor behavior, improving email engagement). Choose an accessible AI tool that targets this area, learn how to use it effectively, and measure the results. As you gain confidence and see benefits, you can gradually explore other AI solutions.

By demystifying AI and focusing on these practical applications, SMBs can unlock powerful secrets to better understand their customers, leading to more effective marketing, improved customer service, and ultimately, sustainable business growth. The key is to leverage AI as an intelligent assistant that augments human intuition and expertise, not replaces it.

References:

- HubSpot. (2024, April 18). *The 19 Best AI Tools for Small Businesses and How to Use Them.* Retrieved from https://blog.hubspot.com/sales/small-business-ai-tools
- U.S. Chamber of Commerce. (2024, August 28). *A Small Business Guide to AI.* Retrieved from https://www.uschamber.com/co/run/technology/small-business-ai-guide

- Neurond. (n.d.). *AI For Small Business: How Artificial Intelligence Transforms Them.* Retrieved from https://www.neurond.com/blog/ai-for-small-business

8.6 Ethical Considerations in AI for Customer Understanding

The increasing sophistication of AI in analyzing customer data and predicting behavior offers unprecedented opportunities for businesses to personalize experiences and optimize strategies. However, this power comes with significant ethical responsibilities. As organizations delve deeper into leveraging AI for customer understanding, it is paramount to navigate the complex ethical landscape concerning data privacy, algorithmic bias, transparency, accountability, and the overall impact on individuals. Responsible AI use is not just a matter of compliance but a cornerstone of building and maintaining customer trust.

1. Data Privacy and Consent: The Foundation of Trust

- **The Challenge:** AI systems thrive on data, often vast amounts of personal and behavioral information. The collection, storage, and analysis of this data raise fundamental privacy concerns. Customers have a right to know what data is being collected, how it is being used, and who has access to it. The line between personalized service and intrusive surveillance can be thin.
- **Ethical Imperative:** Organizations must prioritize data privacy by design and by default. This involves:

    - **Explicit Consent:** Obtaining clear, informed, and unambiguous consent from customers before collecting and processing their data for AI-driven analysis. This means avoiding jargon-laden privacy policies and providing easy-to-understand explanations of data usage

(Source: LinkedIn, "Ethical Considerations in AI-Driven Customer Data Analysis").

- **Data Minimization:** Collecting only the data that is strictly necessary for the intended purpose of customer understanding. Avoid amassing data speculatively.
- **Anonymization and Pseudonymization:** Wherever possible, anonymize or pseudonymize data to protect individual identities while still allowing for aggregate analysis.
- **Secure Data Handling:** Implementing robust security measures to protect customer data from breaches, unauthorized access, and cyberattacks, as highlighted by HBS Online (Source: HBS Online, "5 Ethical Considerations of AI in Business").
- **Right to Access and Erasure:** Providing customers with mechanisms to access their data, understand how it's used, and request its deletion (in line with regulations like GDPR).

2. Bias and Fairness: Guarding Against Discrimination

- **The Challenge:** AI algorithms learn from the data they are trained on. If this historical data reflects existing societal biases (e.g., related to race, gender, age, or socioeconomic status), the AI models can inadvertently perpetuate and even amplify these biases. This can lead to discriminatory outcomes in customer segmentation, product recommendations, credit scoring, or even in the way customer service inquiries are prioritized.
- **Ethical Imperative:** Actively work to identify and mitigate bias in AI systems:

  - **Diverse and Representative Data:** Strive to use training datasets that are diverse and representative of the entire customer population to avoid skewed outcomes (Source: ScienceDirect, "Ethical and Bias Considerations in Artificial Intelligence/Machine Learning").

- **Regular Audits for Bias:** Implement processes to regularly audit AI models and their outputs for potential biases. This involves testing for fairness across different demographic groups.
- **Fairness Metrics:** Utilize fairness-aware machine learning techniques and metrics during model development and deployment to ensure equitable treatment.
- **Diverse Development Teams:** Encourage diversity within AI development teams to bring varied perspectives that can help identify and address potential biases early on.

3. Transparency and Explainability: Opening the Black Box

- **The Challenge:** Many advanced AI models, particularly deep learning algorithms, operate as "black boxes," making it difficult to understand precisely how they arrive at a particular decision or prediction. This lack of transparency can erode trust, especially when AI-driven decisions significantly impact customers (e.g., loan applications, insurance premiums).
- **Ethical Imperative:** Strive for greater transparency and explainability in AI systems:

  - **Explainable AI (XAI):** Invest in and utilize XAI techniques that can provide insights into the reasoning behind AI model predictions. This helps in debugging models, ensuring they are working as intended, and providing customers with understandable explanations for decisions that affect them (Source: IBM, "What is AI Ethics?").
  - **Clear Communication:** Be transparent with customers about when and how AI is being used to make de-

cisions or personalize their experiences. Avoid deceptive practices.

- **Accountability Frameworks:** Establish clear lines of accountability for the outcomes of AI systems. If an AI makes an erroneous or unfair decision, there should be a mechanism for redress and correction (Source: CloudThat, "The Ethics of AI Addressing Bias, Privacy, and Accountability in Machine Learning").

4. Security and Cybersecurity: Protecting Sensitive Insights

- **The Challenge:** AI systems that analyze customer data become valuable targets for cyberattacks. A breach could expose highly sensitive personal information and predictive insights, leading to identity theft, financial loss, and severe reputational damage.
- **Ethical Imperative:** Implement robust cybersecurity measures tailored to the risks associated with AI systems:

  - **End-to-End Encryption:** Ensure data is encrypted both in transit and at rest.
  - **Access Controls:** Implement strict access controls to limit who can access sensitive customer data and AI models.
  - **Regular Security Audits and Penetration Testing:** Proactively identify and address vulnerabilities in AI systems and data storage.
  - **Incident Response Plan:** Have a clear plan in place to respond to and mitigate the impact of any data breaches.

5. Unintended Consequences and Human Oversight

- **The Challenge:** The complexity of AI systems and their interactions with dynamic customer data can sometimes lead to unintended or unexpected consequences. Over-reliance on automated decision-making without adequate human oversight can result in errors or outcomes that are misaligned with ethical principles or business objectives.
- **Ethical Imperative:** Maintain a balance between AI automation and human judgment:

    - **Human-in-the-Loop:** For critical decisions, especially those with significant ethical implications or potential for harm, ensure there is meaningful human oversight and the ability to intervene or override AI-driven recommendations (Source: LinkedIn, "Ethical Considerations in AI-Driven Customer Data Analysis").
    - **Continuous Monitoring:** Regularly monitor the performance and impact of AI systems to detect and rectify any unintended negative consequences promptly.
    - **Ethical Review Boards:** Consider establishing internal ethical review boards or consulting with external ethics experts to assess the potential impact of new AI applications for customer understanding.

6. Responsible AI Use and Corporate Social Responsibility

- **The Challenge:** Beyond specific technical considerations, there is a broader responsibility for businesses to use AI in a way that benefits customers and society, rather than exploiting vulnerabilities or contributing to negative societal trends.
- **Ethical Imperative:** Embed responsible AI principles into the core of the business strategy:

    - **Value Alignment:** Ensure that the use of AI for customer understanding aligns with the company's core values and its commitment to corporate social responsibility.

- **Avoidance of Manipulation:** Refrain from using AI-driven insights to manipulate customer behavior in ways that are detrimental to their well-being (e.g., exploiting psychological biases to drive impulsive purchases of harmful products).
- **Promoting Digital Literacy:** Help customers understand how their data is being used and empower them to make informed choices.

Navigating the ethical landscape of AI in customer understanding requires a proactive, ongoing commitment from businesses. It involves establishing strong governance frameworks, fostering a culture of ethical awareness, and continuously evaluating the impact of AI systems on individuals and society. By prioritizing ethical considerations, businesses can harness the transformative power of AI to build stronger, more trusting relationships with their customers and contribute to a more equitable and responsible digital future.

References:

- LinkedIn. (2023, August 15). *Ethical Considerations in AI-Driven Customer Data Analysis.* Retrieved from https://www.linkedin.com/pulse/ethical-considerations-ai-driven-customer-data-analysis-murali-rohana
- HBS Online. (2024, August 14). *5 Ethical Considerations of AI in Business.* Retrieved from https://online.hbs.edu/blog/post/ethical-considerations-of-ai
- IBM. (n.d.). *What is AI Ethics?.* Retrieved from https://www.ibm.com/think/topics/ai-ethics
- ScienceDirect. (2024). *Ethical and Bias Considerations in Artificial Intelligence/Machine Learning.* Retrieved from https://www.sciencedirect.com/science/article/pii/S0893395224002667

- CloudThat. (2024, February 29). *The Ethics of AI Addressing Bias, Privacy, and Accountability in Machine Learning.* Retrieved from https://www.cloudthat.com/resources/blog/the-ethics-of-ai-addressing-bias-privacy-and-accountability-in-machine-learning
- Alation. (2024, July 15). *Data Ethics in AI: 6 Key Principles for Machine Learning.* Retrieved from https://www.alation.com/blog/data-ethics-in-ai-6-key-principles-for-responsible-machine-learning/
- Lumenalta. (2024, October 13). *Ethical Considerations of AI.* Retrieved from https://lumenalta.com/insights/ethical-considerations-of-ai

Case Study: Voice AI Healthcare Roleplay App

Background: A leading healthcare education organization that trains healthcare professionals was facing a critical challenge. Their students and medical professionals needed to develop not just clinical skills, but also the soft skills required for effective patient communication: empathy, active listening, and the ability to handle difficult conversations. Traditional training methods—lectures and occasional in-person roleplay with instructors—were expensive, time-consuming, and didn't scale. Students often graduated with limited real-world practice in these crucial interactions.

The Training Problem: The organization identified several specific gaps in their training program:

- Limited Practice Opportunities: Students might participate in 3-5 roleplay scenarios during an entire semester. This was not enough repetition to build true confidence and competence.
- Instructor Bottleneck: Roleplay sessions required a trained instructor to play the role of the patient, which was resource-

intensive. Instructors could only work with a handful of students at a time.

- Lack of Personalized Feedback: In group settings, students received general feedback, but there was little opportunity for detailed, personalized coaching on their specific communication weaknesses.
- High-Stakes, Low-Reps Environment: Students' first real practice with difficult conversations (e.g., delivering bad news, calming an anxious patient) often happened during their clinical rotations with actual patients. This was stressful for students and suboptimal for patients.

The organization needed a solution that would allow students to practice patient interactions anytime, anywhere, and receive immediate, constructive feedback—without requiring an army of human instructors.

My Approach: I was brought in to design and build a Voice AI Healthcare Roleplay App—an intelligent, voice-based training system that could simulate realistic patient interactions and provide real-time feedback on communication skills. This was not a simple chatbot; it was a sophisticated, multi-modal AI system designed to understand, respond to, and evaluate human conversation.

Technical Architecture:

Building this system required integrating several cutting-edge AI technologies:

1.Speech-to-Text (STT) Engine: We used a medical-grade STT API (specifically, a HIPAA-compliant version of Google Cloud Speech-to-Text) to convert the student's spoken words into text with high accuracy, even when medical terminology was used.

2. Natural Language Processing (NLP) and Understanding: The core of the system was a fine-tuned large language model (we used a customized version of GPT-4o, trained on a dataset of real patient-caregiver conversations). This model was responsible for:

- Understanding the intent behind the student's words (e.g., "Are they trying to build rapport? Gather information? Provide reassurance?")
- Generating realistic, contextually appropriate patient responses based on the scenario
- Detecting key communication elements like empathy statements, open-ended questions, and active listening cues

3. Text-to-Speech (TTS) Engine: We used a high-quality TTS system (ElevenLabs) to give the AI "patient" a natural, human-like voice. We created multiple voice profiles (different ages, genders, emotional states) to increase realism.

4. Scenario Engine: We built a library of 20 core scenarios, ranging from routine check-ins to high-stress situations like delivering a difficult diagnosis or managing a patient in pain. Each scenario had a defined patient backstory, emotional state, and set of conversational goals.

5. Real-Time Feedback Loop: As the student spoke, the AI analyzed their communication in real-time across several dimensions:

At the end of each 5-10 minute roleplay session, the student received a detailed report card with specific examples of what they did well and concrete suggestions for improvement.

- Empathy Score: Did they acknowledge the patient's feelings?
- Clarity Score: Were their explanations clear and jargon-free?
- Active Listening Score: Did they ask follow-up questions and reflect back what the patient said?
- Professionalism Score: Did they maintain appropriate boundaries and tone?

Challenges We Overcame:

1. **Challenge: Making the AI "Patient" Feel Real:** Early versions of the AI felt robotic and overly polite. Real patients are not always calm and cooperative; they can be anxious, confused, or even frustrated. We had to teach the AI to exhibit a range of emotions and to respond realistically to the student's approach. If a student was dismissive, the AI patient would become more withdrawn. If the student showed empathy, the AI patient would open up. This dynamic responsiveness was key to creating a valuable learning experience.
2. **Challenge: Balancing Automation with Human Oversight:** We didn't want the AI to be the sole judge of a student's performance, especially in a high-stakes educational context. We built in a "human-in-the-loop" review process. Instructors could review flagged sessions (e.g., where a student received a very low score or where the AI detected a potential safety issue) and provide additional coaching. The AI was a tool to augment, not replace, human judgment.

User Adoption and Training Effectiveness Metrics:

The pilot results exceeded our expectations and validated the investment:

- High Engagement: Students used the app an average of 8 times per month, far exceeding the 3-5 traditional roleplay sessions they would have participated in during an entire semester. The app was available 24/7, so students practiced at their convenience—often late at night before exams.
- Skill Improvement: We measured communication skills using a standardized rubric at the beginning and end of the semester. Students who used the app regularly (6+ sessions) showed a 35% improvement in their empathy and active listening scores, compared to a 12% improvement in the control group that only participated in traditional roleplay.

- Confidence Boost: In post-pilot surveys, 89% of students reported feeling "more confident" in their ability to handle difficult patient conversations. Many noted that the ability to practice privately, without fear of judgment from peers, was a game-changer.
- Instructor Efficiency: Instructors reported that they could now focus their in-person time on the most complex, nuanced scenarios, rather than spending hours on basic communication drills. The AI handled the foundational practice, freeing up human expertise for higher-value coaching.

How This Differs from Generic Chatbots:

It's important to understand that this was not a simple FAQ chatbot. Generic chatbots are rule-based and can only handle scripted interactions. This Voice AI system was fundamentally different:

- Conversational, Not Transactional: It engaged in open-ended, multi-turn conversations that could go in unpredictable directions based on what the student said.
- Emotionally Intelligent: It detected and responded to emotional cues, adjusting its tone and responses based on the student's approach.
- Evaluative: It didn't just respond; it analyzed the quality of the student's communication and provided coaching.
- Voice-First: It operated entirely through natural speech, mimicking real-world patient interactions far more closely than text-based chat.

Key Lesson: AI's most powerful application is not in replacing human connection, but in creating more opportunities for humans to practice and perfect the skills that make connection possible. This app didn't replace instructors; it multiplied their impact. It gave every student access to a tireless, patient, and insightful practice partner, available whenever they needed it.

What You Can Apply: If your business involves training, coaching, or skill development, consider how AI could create low-stakes, high-repetition practice environments. Whether it's sales roleplay, customer service training, or leadership coaching, the same principles apply: use AI to scale practice, provide immediate feedback, and free up human experts to focus on the most complex, high-value interactions.

You can watch a video demo of this app in action clicking here.

AI Prompts: Chapter 8

How to Use These Prompts

Each prompt below is designed to be copied directly into your favorite AI tool (ChatGPT, Claude, Grok, or Gemini). Simply:

1.Copy the entire prompt (including the bracketed placeholders)

2. Replace the [bracketed sections] with your specific information

3.Paste into your AI tool and hit enter

4.Refine the output by asking follow-up questions or requesting revisions

These are battle-tested prompts I use with organizations around the world. They're designed to give you professional-quality outputs that you can use immediately in your business.

Prompt 8.1: Customer Interview Analysis and Insights

I've conducted customer interviews and want to extract actionable insights from the conversations.

[Paste interview transcripts, customer feedback, or survey responses here - or describe the key themes if you don't have transcripts]

Number of customers interviewed: [number]

Interview focus: [what you asked about]

Analyze this feedback and provide:

1. **Key Themes** (5-7 recurring themes):

- What customers consistently mentioned

   - Direct quotes that illustrate each theme
   - How many customers mentioned this
2. **Pain Points Identified**:
   - The top 5 problems customers are trying to solve
   - The emotional impact of each pain point
   - How urgent/important each is
3. **Desired Outcomes**:
   - What success looks like to customers
   - The transformation they're seeking
   - Metrics they use to measure success
4. **Language and Phrases**:
   - Exact words customers use to describe their problems
   - Metaphors or analogies they use
   - Language to use in marketing (their words, not ours)
5. **Objections and Concerns**:
   - Hesitations about buying
   - Misconceptions about our solution
   - Comparison to alternatives
6. **Buying Journey Insights**:
   - How they discovered us
   - What convinced them to buy (or not buy)
   - Decision-making process and timeline
7. **Product/Service Improvements**:
   - Features or services they wish we had
   - What they love most (to double down on)
   - What's confusing or frustrating
8. **Marketing Action Items**:
   - 5 specific changes to make to messaging
   - Content topics to create based on their questions
   - Testimonial angles to highlight

Turn this qualitative data into quantified insights and clear action steps.

Prompt 8.2: Create Customer Journey Map

Help me create a detailed customer journey map for my [type of business].

Business context:

- What we sell: [product/service]
- Target customer: [description]
- Sales cycle length: [typical time from awareness to purchase]
- Price point: [range]

Create a customer journey map across these stages:

Stage 1: Awareness

- How they first become aware of their problem
- Where they go for information
- What they're thinking and feeling
- Our opportunity to reach them
- Content/messaging for this stage

Stage 2: Consideration

- Questions they're asking
- Alternatives they're evaluating
- Information they need
- Common objections or concerns
- Content/messaging for this stage

Stage 3: Decision

- Final decision criteria
- Who else is involved in the decision
- What tips them toward "yes"
- Last-minute hesitations
- Content/messaging for this stage

Stage 4: Purchase

- The buying experience
- Potential friction points
- What would make this smoother
- First impression opportunities

Stage 5: Onboarding/First Use

- Initial experience with product/service

- Success metrics they're watching
- Support they need
- Risk of buyer's remorse

Stage 6: Retention/Loyalty
- Ongoing value delivery
- Reasons they might churn
- Opportunities for upsell/cross-sell
- How to turn them into advocates

For each stage, include:
- Customer emotions and mindset
- Touchpoints with our brand
- Pain points or friction
- Opportunities to add value
- Specific actions we should take

Make this actionable - show me where we're losing customers and how to fix it.

Prompt 8.3: Analyze Customer Feedback and Reviews

I want to analyze customer feedback, reviews, and testimonials to extract insights and improve our business.

Customer feedback data:

[Paste reviews, testimonials, support tickets, survey responses, or social media comments - or summarize the main feedback themes]

Source of feedback: [Google reviews, testimonials, support tickets, surveys, etc.]

Number of feedback items: [approximate number]

Provide a comprehensive analysis:

1. **Sentiment Analysis**:
   - Overall sentiment (% positive, neutral, negative)
   - Most common positive themes
   - Most common negative themes
2. **What Customers Love** (Top 5):
   - Specific features, benefits, or experiences they praise
   - Direct quotes illustrating each

- Why this matters (the underlying value)
3. **What Customers Complain About** (Top 5):
   - Specific pain points or frustrations
   - How frequently each is mentioned
   - Severity (minor annoyance vs. deal-breaker)
4. **Feature Requests and Unmet Needs**:
   - What customers wish we offered
   - Problems we're not solving
   - Comparisons to competitors
5. **Customer Language Analysis**:
   - Words and phrases customers use repeatedly
   - How they describe the transformation
   - Testimonial-worthy quotes to use in marketing
6. **Segmentation Insights**:
   - Do different customer types have different experiences?
   - Patterns by customer segment, product, or use case
7. **Actionable Improvements** (prioritized):
   - Quick wins (easy fixes with high impact)
   - Product/service enhancements
   - Customer experience improvements
   - Marketing message refinements
8. **Testimonial Strategy**:
   - Best quotes to use in marketing
   - Stories to develop into case studies
   - Themes to highlight in social proof

Turn this feedback into a prioritized action plan for improving customer satisfaction and retention.

For prompts and bonus resources, visit **thejasonfleagle.com/blueprint-resources**. You can copy and paste the prompts from there—no retyping needed.

| 9 |

AI for Marketing Automation

In the relentless pursuit of efficiency and effectiveness, modern marketing departments are increasingly turning to automation to manage complex campaigns, nurture leads, and engage customers across a multitude of channels. Marketing automation, at its core, promises to liberate marketers from repetitive, time-consuming tasks, allowing them to focus on strategy, creativity, and building meaningful customer relationships. However, the true transformative potential of marketing automation is now being unlocked by the integration of Artificial Intelligence (AI). As we have explored in previous chapters how AI is reshaping various facets of marketing—from content creation and personalization to paid advertising and customer understanding—this chapter delves into the profound impact of AI on the very engine of marketing operations: automation.

AI is not merely an add-on to existing automation platforms; it is a fundamental catalyst that elevates marketing automation from rule-based execution to intelligent, adaptive, and predictive operations. By infusing automation with the ability to learn from data, identify complex patterns, make nuanced decisions, and personalize interactions at an unprecedented scale, AI is revolutionizing how businesses approach their marketing workflows, lead management, and multichannel campaign orchestration. This chapter will explore the multifaceted role of AI in supercharging marketing automation, examining how it streamlines intricate workflows, implements highly accurate and dynamic lead scoring, and automates the sophisticated orchestration of personalized customer journeys across diverse touchpoints.

We will investigate practical applications, from AI tools that simplify content approval and campaign setup to advanced algorithms that power predictive lead scoring and real-time campaign adjustments. Furthermore, we will present a case study illustrating the tangible benefits, such as significant time savings and efficiency gains, that businesses can achieve by embracing AI-driven automation. Recognizing that the adoption of powerful technologies also brings responsibilities, we will also delve into the critical ethical considerations that marketers must navigate, including data privacy, algorithmic bias, and the evolving role of human marketers in an AI-augmented landscape. Finally, we will uncover simple yet potent "AI secrets" to help businesses, particularly small to medium-sized enterprises, harness the power of AI in their marketing automation efforts effectively and responsibly. Join us as we explore how AI is not just automating marketing tasks, but making marketing automation itself smarter, more strategic, and ultimately, more human-centric in its ability to deliver value.

9.1 Streamlining Marketing Workflows with AI

Marketing, in its essence, is a symphony of interconnected tasks, from conceptualizing campaigns and creating content to approving assets, launching initiatives, and meticulously tracking performance. Traditionally, many of these workflows have been labor-intensive, demanding significant human hours and prone to bottlenecks, especially as the scale and complexity of marketing efforts grow. The advent of Artificial Intelligence (AI) is profoundly reshaping this landscape, offering powerful tools and techniques to streamline these intricate processes, enhance efficiency, and free up marketing professionals to focus on strategic and creative endeavors.

AI's capability to automate repetitive tasks is a cornerstone of its impact on marketing workflows. Consider the often-convoluted content approval process. In many organizations, a piece of content, be it a blog post, social media update, or email copy, must pass through multiple stakeholders for review and sign-off. This can lead to delays, miscommunications, and a significant drain on resources. AI-powered workflow management systems can automate the routing of content, send reminders for pending approvals, and even use Natural Language Processing (NLP) to perform initial checks for brand guideline compliance, grammar, or tone, thereby reducing the manual burden on reviewers and accelerating the entire cycle. For instance, AI can flag content that deviates from established brand voice or identify potential legal compliance issues before human review, saving valuable time and preventing costly errors. As noted by Knak.com, AI is increasingly being integrated to manage and optimize these approval chains, ensuring that content moves smoothly from creation to publication.

Campaign setup is another area ripe for AI-driven streamlining. Launching a multi-channel marketing campaign involves numerous steps: defining target audiences, allocating budgets across platforms, configuring ad creatives, setting up A/B tests, and establishing tracking parameters. AI can automate many of these setup tasks. For example, AI algorithms can analyze historical campaign data and real-time market trends to suggest optimal budget allocations or identify the most promising audience segments for a particular product or service. AI can also assist in generating variations of ad copy or visuals, prepopulating campaign templates, and ensuring all tracking codes are correctly implemented, significantly reducing the manual effort and potential for human error inherent in complex campaign launches. MarTech.org highlights how AI is changing marketing workflows by automating such intricate setup processes, allowing marketers to launch more sophisticated campaigns with greater speed and precision.

Reporting and analytics, a critical but often time-consuming aspect of marketing, is also being revolutionized by AI. Manually gathering data from disparate sources, compiling reports, and identifying meaningful insights can consume a substantial portion of a marketer's time. AI-powered analytics platforms can automatically aggregate data from various marketing channels (e.g., website analytics, social media insights, CRM data, ad platform reports), generate comprehensive performance dashboards in real-time, and, crucially, identify patterns, trends, and anomalies that might be missed by human analysts. These AI systems can highlight which campaigns are performing best, which channels are delivering the highest ROI, and where potential issues or opportunities lie, enabling marketers to make faster, data-driven decisions. The ability to receive automated, insightful reports means less time spent on data wrangling and more time dedicated to strategic adjustments and optimization.

Beyond these core areas, AI is also streamlining workflows in areas like market research, where AI tools can rapidly analyze vast amounts of industry reports, competitor activities, and consumer discussions to provide actionable insights. In project management, AI can assist in task allocation, progress tracking, and identifying potential project delays. The strategic design of AI-enhanced marketing workflows, as discussed in a LinkedIn article by Claire Du Preez, emphasizes integrating AI not just as a point solution but as a fundamental enabler of more agile, efficient, and intelligent marketing operations. By taking over the mundane and repetitive, AI empowers marketing teams to operate at a higher strategic level, fostering innovation and driving better results.

References:

- Knak.com. (n.d.). *Marketing Workflows & AI.* Retrieved from https://knak.com/blog/marketing-workflows-ai/
- MarTech.org. (n.d.). *How marketing workflows will change with AI.* Retrieved from https://martech.org/how-marketing-workflows-will-change-with-ai/
- Du Preez, C. (n.d.). *How to Strategically Design AI-Enhanced Marketing Workflows.* LinkedIn. Retrieved from

https://www.linkedin.com/pulse/how-strategically-design-ai-enhanced-marketing-claire-du-preez-swb8f

- Cflow. (n.d.). *Enhance Your Workflow with AI Workflow Tools.* Retrieved from https://www.cflowapps.com/ai-workflow-tools/
- Acuto.io. (n.d.). *Marketing Automation Examples Boosting Efficiency.* Retrieved from https://acuto.io/blog/marketing-automation-examples-boosting-efficiency/

9.2 Implementing AI-Powered Lead Scoring

Lead scoring, the process of assigning values to leads based on their perceived value to a company, is a critical component of efficient sales and marketing operations. Traditionally, lead scoring models have often relied on explicit demographic data and a limited set of behavioral cues, sometimes leading to inaccuracies or missed opportunities. The integration of Artificial Intelligence (AI) is transforming this practice, enabling more sophisticated, dynamic, and accurate lead scoring systems that significantly enhance effectiveness and foster better alignment between sales and marketing teams.

AI elevates lead scoring by moving beyond simple rule-based systems to predictive models that can analyze a vast array of data points with much greater nuance. As Forbes Councils Member, Ranga Rajagopalan, highlights, AI can crack the lead scoring code by processing complex datasets to identify subtle patterns indicative of a lead's propensity to convert. These AI models can incorporate a much wider range of data inputs, including detailed behavioral data (e.g., website interaction patterns, content engagement depth, email click-through rates, social media activity), firmographic information (company size, industry, revenue), and even technographic data (the technologies a prospect's company uses). By continuously learning from new data, AI-powered lead scoring systems can adapt to changing market dynamics and customer behaviors, providing scores that are more reflective of a lead's true potential and current stage in the buyer's journey.

Several AI techniques are employed in predictive lead scoring. Machine learning algorithms, such as logistic regression, decision trees, random forests, and gradient boosting, are commonly used to build models that predict the likelihood of a lead converting into a customer. These models are trained on historical data of both converted and unconverted leads, learning to identify the key characteristics and behaviors that correlate with successful sales outcomes. Natural Language Processing (NLP) can also play a role by analyzing textual data from lead interactions, such as email correspondence or chatbot conversations, to gauge sentiment, intent, and specific needs, further enriching the lead profile. Demandbase emphasizes how AI lead scoring leverages these advanced analytics to sift through extensive data, including intent signals and engagement patterns, to pinpoint leads that are not just active but actively demonstrating buying intent for specific solutions.

The benefits of implementing AI-powered lead scoring are manifold and extend to fostering better alignment between sales and marketing teams—a common challenge in many organizations. Firstly, AI provides a more objective and data-driven approach to lead qualification. This reduces the subjectivity that can sometimes lead to disagreements between marketing (which generates leads) and sales (which pursues them). When both teams trust the lead scores because they are based on robust AI analysis, there's a shared understanding of lead quality. Secondly, by accurately identifying and prioritizing high-potential leads, AI ensures that sales teams focus their efforts on prospects most likely to convert, improving sales productivity and conversion rates. Marketing teams, in turn, receive clearer feedback on which types_of leads are most valuable, allowing them to refine their targeting and campaign strategies. This creates a positive feedback loop, enhancing overall efficiency. Data-Mania points out that AI in lead scoring directly contributes to this improved sales and marketing alignment by providing a common, reliable framework for lead evaluation and prioritization, ensuring that marketing delivers truly sales-ready leads.

Furthermore, AI-powered lead scoring can help in identifying leads that may require further nurturing before they are sales-ready. By understanding a lead's position in the buyer journey and their specific interests (as revealed by AI analysis), marketing can deliver more targeted and relevant nurturing content, effectively guiding them through the funnel. This proactive and personalized nurturing, driven by AI insights, increases the chances of converting leads that might otherwise have been prematurely discarded or mishandled. The overall impact is a more efficient sales pipeline, higher conversion rates, and a stronger, more collaborative relationship between sales and marketing, all driven by the intelligent application of AI to the critical process of lead scoring.

References:

- Rajagopalan, R. (2024, November 13). *Cracking The Lead Scoring Code With AI.* Forbes. Retrieved from https://www.forbes.com/councils/forbestechcouncil/2024/11/13/cracking-the-lead-scoring-with-ai/
- Demandbase. (n.d.). *AI Lead Scoring: The Future of Sales is Here.* Retrieved from https://www.demandbase.com/blog/ai-lead-scoring/
- Data-Mania. (n.d.). *AI in Lead Scoring: Benefits for Sales and Marketing.* Retrieved from https://www.data-mania.com/blog/ai-in-lead-scoring-benefits-for-sales-and-marketing/

9.3 Automating Campaign Orchestration with AI

Modern marketing campaigns are rarely confined to a single channel; instead, they are intricate orchestrations across multiple touchpoints, including email, social media, search engines, display advertising, and more. Managing these multi-channel campaigns effectively, ensuring consistent messaging, timely delivery, and optimal resource allocation, presents a significant challenge. Artificial Intelligence (AI) is emerging as a transformative force in this domain, offering sophisticated capabilities to automate and optimize the complex process of campaign orchestration, leading to more cohesive, personalized, and impactful customer journeys.

AI's role in automating multi-channel marketing campaigns begins with its ability to process and analyze vast amounts of data from diverse sources in real time. This allows for a deeper understanding of customer behavior across different channels, enabling marketers to identify the most effective sequences of interactions and the optimal channels for engaging specific customer segments at various stages of their journey. As highlighted in a LinkedIn article on AI automation in channel marketing, AI can help in planning and executing campaigns by identifying patterns that humans might miss, thereby ensuring that marketing efforts are more targeted and efficient. Instead of manually coordinating activities across platforms, AI-powered orchestration tools can automate the deployment of content, the triggering of actions based on customer behavior (e.g., sending a follow-up email after a website visit or a social media interaction), and the adjustment of campaign parameters on the fly.

One of the key areas where AI excels in campaign orchestration is dynamic content delivery and journey personalization. Traditional campaigns often deliver a one-size-fits-all message, which can be ineffective in today's environment where consumers expect personalized experiences. AI enables marketers to move beyond static segmentation to hyper-personalization at scale. By analyzing individual customer data—preferences, past interactions, real-time behavior, and contextual information—AI can dynamically tailor content, offers, and even the communication channel for each user. For instance, an e-commerce platform might use AI to show different product recommendations on its website, in emails, and in retargeting ads based on an individual's browsing history and purchase patterns. Limestone Digital discusses how AI-powered marketing facilitates this real-time optimization and dynamic personalization, ensuring that each customer receives the most relevant message at the most opportune moment, thereby significantly increasing engagement and conversion rates. This level of personalization, orchestrated seamlessly across channels by AI, creates a more coherent and compelling customer experience.

Furthermore, AI facilitates real-time campaign adjustments, a critical capability in the fast-paced digital landscape. Marketing conditions can change rapidly, and campaigns that are not agile enough to adapt can quickly become ineffective. AI algorithms continuously monitor campaign performance metrics, identify underperforming elements or channels, and can even automatically make adjustments to optimize outcomes. This could involve reallocating budget from less effective channels to more promising ones, tweaking ad creatives or targeting parameters, or modifying the sequence of messages in a nurturing workflow. This ability to learn and adapt in real time ensures that marketing spend is utilized more efficiently and that campaigns remain effective even as customer preferences or competitive pressures evolve.

Several AI-driven campaign orchestration platforms are now available, offering a suite of tools to manage these complex multichannel efforts. Platforms like Trendemon, Qualtrics, 6sense, and Genesys Cloud CX, as listed by Trendemon in their review of journey orchestration platforms, leverage AI for various aspects of campaign management, from identifying target accounts and personalizing content to delivering it across preferred channels and tracking performance. These platforms often integrate customer data analytics, content management, and automated delivery mechanisms, providing a centralized hub for orchestrating sophisticated, AI-powered marketing campaigns. For example, Trendemon focuses on serving personalized content to B2B buyers to accelerate the sales pipeline, while 6sense aims to uncover anonymous buyer signals to inform content recommendations and outreach. The common thread is the use of AI to make campaign orchestration more intelligent, automated, and ultimately, more effective in driving desired business outcomes.

In essence, AI is transforming campaign orchestration from a series of manually coordinated, often disjointed activities into a fluid, adaptive, and highly personalized system. By automating complex tasks, delivering dynamic content, and enabling real-time adjustments, AI empowers marketers to create more engaging customer journeys and achieve superior campaign performance across the increasingly complex multi-channel landscape.

References:

- LinkedIn. (n.d.). *5 Ways AI & Automation in Channel Marketing Drive Growth in 2025.* Retrieved from https://www.linkedin.com/pulse/5-ways-ai-automation-channel-marketing-drive-growth-2025-s1kcc
- Limestone Digital. (n.d.). *AI-Powered Marketing: Real-Time Optimization and Dynamic Personalization.* Retrieved from https://limestonedigital.com/ai-powered-marketing-real-time-optimization-and-dynamic-personalization/
- Trendemon. (n.d.). *Top 10 Journey Orchestration Platforms.* Retrieved from [https://trendemon.com/blog/top-11-journey-orchestration-platforms/](https://trendemon.com/blog/top-11-journey- orchestration-platforms/)

9.4 Case Study: Company E Saved 25% Marketing Hours with AI Automation

While a specific, named "Company E" achieving a precise 25% reduction in marketing hours through AI automation is a generalized target for illustrative purposes, the principles and outcomes are widely observed across businesses adopting these technologies. Drawing from insights provided by Beyond Agency in their discussion on marketing automation's impact on cost and efficiency, we can construct a representative case study that demonstrates how a hypothetical company, let's call it "Innovatech Solutions" (our Company E), could achieve such significant time savings.

The Challenge: Mounting Manual Workload and Inefficient Resource Allocation

Innovatech Solutions, a mid-sized B2B software provider, found its marketing team increasingly bogged down by manual, repetitive tasks. Their marketing efforts spanned multiple channels, including email campaigns, social media engagement, content marketing, and lead nurturing. However, much of this was handled with disparate tools and significant manual intervention. Key challenges included:

1. **High Operational Costs and Time Drain:** Manually scheduling social media posts across several platforms, crafting and sending individual follow-up emails to leads, segmenting customer lists for email campaigns, and compiling weekly performance reports consumed a vast majority of the marketing team's hours. This left little time for strategic planning, creative content development, or in-depth performance analysis.
2. **Inefficiencies and Errors:** Manual data entry into their CRM and marketing platforms was prone to errors, leading to inconsistent lead data and mis-targeted communications. The lack of a unified system for lead management often resulted in slow follow-up times and missed opportunities.
3. **Difficulty in Scaling Efforts:** As Innovatech Solutions grew, their existing manual processes could not scale effectively. Expanding campaigns or entering new market segments meant a proportional, unsustainable increase in workload for the marketing team.
4. **Suboptimal Lead Nurturing:** Generic email blasts and inconsistent follow-ups meant that many leads were not effectively nurtured through the sales funnel, leading to lower conversion rates and wasted marketing spend.

The Solution: Implementing a Comprehensive AI-Powered Marketing Automation Strategy

Innovatech Solutions decided to invest in a marketing automation platform integrated with AI capabilities. Their strategy focused on automating key areas identified as major time sinks and points of inefficiency:

1. **Automated Email Marketing & Lead Nurturing:** They implemented AI-driven workflows to automate email sequences based on lead behavior and segmentation. This included personalized welcome emails, targeted content delivery based on website interactions, and automated follow-ups for event attendees or webinar registrants. AI helped in dynamic content personalization, ensuring emails were highly relevant to each recipient.
2. **AI-Enhanced Lead Scoring and Management:** An AI-powered lead scoring system was put in place to automatically qualify and prioritize leads based on a wide range of behavioral and demographic data. This ensured that the sales team received higher quality leads and that marketing efforts were focused on the most promising prospects.
3. **Social Media Automation:** Tools were adopted to schedule social media posts in advance across all relevant platforms. AI was also leveraged to analyze engagement metrics and suggest optimal posting times and content types, and even to help curate relevant industry content for sharing.
4. **CRM and Data Management Automation:** The new platform integrated seamlessly with their CRM, automating data entry for new leads, updating contact records based on interactions, and ensuring data consistency. This significantly reduced manual data management tasks.
5. **AI-Powered Chatbots for Initial Engagement:** An AI chatbot was deployed on their website to handle initial visitor inquiries, qualify leads by asking pre-set questions, and direct users to relevant resources or schedule demos, operating 24/7.

6. **Automated Reporting and Analytics:** The platform provided real-time dashboards and automated reports on campaign performance, lead generation, and conversion rates, eliminating the need for manual data compilation.

The Measurable Results: Significant Time Savings and Increased Efficiency

Within six months of implementing their AI-powered marketing automation strategy, Innovatech Solutions observed substantial improvements:

- **Reduction in Manual Hours (Achieving the ~25% Target):** The automation of repetitive tasks like email scheduling and sending, social media posting, lead data entry, and basic report generation freed up approximately 25% of the marketing team's collective hours. For example, the time spent on weekly social media management was reduced by an estimated 60%, and manual email campaign setup time was cut by nearly 75%.
- **Increased Lead Nurturing Effectiveness:** Automated and personalized lead nurturing sequences led to a 30% increase in marketing qualified leads (MQLs) being passed to sales and a 15% improvement in lead-to-customer conversion rates.
- **Improved Sales and Marketing Alignment:** The AI-driven lead scoring system provided a common, trusted framework for lead quality, leading to better collaboration and fewer disputes between sales and marketing.
- **Enhanced Campaign Agility:** The ability to quickly set up, monitor, and adjust campaigns with automated tools allowed the marketing team to be more responsive to market changes and opportunities.
- **Better Resource Allocation:** With significant time saved on manual tasks, the marketing team could dedicate more resources to strategic initiatives, in-depth customer research, cre-

ating higher-quality content, and exploring new marketing channels.

By strategically implementing AI in their marketing automation efforts, Innovatech Solutions (our Company E) not only achieved significant time savings, directly impacting operational costs, but also enhanced the overall effectiveness and scalability of their marketing operations, positioning them for continued growth.

References:

- Beyond Agency. (n.d.). *Marketing Automation: Reduce Costs & Increase Efficiency*. Retrieved from https://www.beyond.agency/blog/implementing-marketing-automation-reducing-costs-by-25-while-increasing-efficiency (Conceptual basis for achieving such savings)

9.5 Simple AI Secrets for Marketing Automation

For many businesses, particularly small to medium-sized enterprises (SMBs), the term "Artificial Intelligence" can sound complex and resource-intensive. However, leveraging AI in marketing automation doesn't always require massive budgets or dedicated data science teams. There are numerous practical, often easily implementable, AI tools and techniques that can provide significant benefits. Unlocking these "simple AI secrets" can empower SMBs to streamline their marketing, enhance customer engagement, and compete more effectively.

One of the most accessible AI secrets is to **start by automating customer inquiries with AI chatbots.** Many user-friendly chatbot platforms now incorporate AI and NLP capabilities, allowing businesses to set up automated responses to frequently asked questions, guide website visitors to relevant information, and even qualify leads 24/7. As noted in the HubSpot article on AI tools for small businesses, AI-powered chatbots can handle initial customer support, freeing up human agents for more complex issues. The "secret" here is to focus the chatbot on well-defined tasks and provide it with a solid knowledge base (e.g., your FAQ page, product information). Even a simple, well-trained AI chatbot can save considerable time and improve customer satisfaction by providing instant responses.

Another practical tip is to **use AI to enhance content creation, but always with a human touch.** Generative AI tools like ChatGPT or integrated AI assistants within platforms like HubSpot (e.g., Breeze) can be invaluable for brainstorming blog post ideas, drafting initial email copy, creating social media updates, or rephrasing existing content for different channels. The "secret" for SMBs is not to expect AI to produce perfect, ready-to-publish content, but to use it as a powerful assistant. AI can overcome writer's block, generate multiple variations quickly, and help with mundane aspects of content creation. However, all AI-generated content should be carefully reviewed, edited, and personalized by a human to ensure it aligns with the brand voice, is factually accurate, and resonates authentically with the target audience.

Leveraging AI for smarter social media management is another easily implementable strategy. Tools like Buffer, often with free or affordable plans, incorporate AI features to help schedule posts at optimal times based on audience engagement patterns. Some AI tools can also assist in curating relevant content to share or suggest hashtags to improve visibility. The "secret" is to use these AI insights to maintain a consistent and engaging social media presence without manually analyzing engagement data for hours. This allows SMB marketers to focus on creating quality content and interacting with their audience, rather than getting bogged down in scheduling logistics.

SMBs should also **focus AI automation on the most repetitive and time-consuming tasks first.** Before investing in complex AI solutions, identify the marketing activities that drain the most manual hours with the lowest strategic value. This could be data entry into a CRM, basic email follow-ups, or compiling simple performance reports. Many CRM platforms (like HubSpot's free CRM) and email marketing tools now include basic AI features for deduplicating contacts, segmenting lists based on simple criteria, or automating basic email sequences. The "secret" is to achieve quick wins by automating these low-hanging fruits, which frees up valuable time for more strategic marketing activities.

Furthermore, **don't be afraid to start with free or low-cost AI tools.** The HubSpot article highlights that many powerful AI tools, or platforms with AI features, offer free tiers or affordable starter plans specifically designed for small businesses. This allows SMBs to experiment with AI capabilities, understand their benefits, and identify which tools provide the best return on investment before committing to significant expenditure. The "secret" is to explore these options, test them within existing workflows, and gradually scale up AI adoption as the benefits become clear and the business grows.

Finally, a crucial "secret" is to **ensure AI tools integrate with existing workflows and platforms.** For an SMB, adopting a new standalone tool that doesn't communicate with their existing CRM, email marketing software, or website can create more work than it saves. When selecting AI-powered automation tools, prioritize those that offer seamless integrations. This ensures that data flows smoothly between systems, automation can be triggered based on actions in other platforms, and a unified view of the customer is maintained. This integrated approach maximizes the efficiency gains from AI and avoids creating new data silos.

By focusing on these practical approaches, SMBs can demystify AI and harness its power to automate marketing tasks, gain valuable insights, and ultimately drive growth without needing extensive technical expertise or large budgets.

References:

- HubSpot. (2024, April 18). *The 19 Best AI Tools for Small Businesses and How to Use Them.* HubSpot Blog. Retrieved from https://blog.hubspot.com/sales/small-business-ai-tools

9.6 Ethical Considerations in AI for Marketing Automation

The integration of Artificial Intelligence into marketing automation brings forth a new era of efficiency, personalization, and predictive capability. However, this power is accompanied by significant ethical responsibilities. As businesses increasingly rely on AI to understand and influence consumer behavior, it is crucial to navigate the ethical landscape thoughtfully to maintain trust, ensure fairness, and mitigate potential harms. Key ethical considerations include data privacy and protection, algorithmic bias, transparency and explainability, the potential for job displacement, and the risk of consumer manipulation.

Privacy and Data Protection stands as a paramount concern. AI marketing automation systems thrive on vast quantities of consumer data, including browsing habits, purchase histories, social media activities, and personal preferences. While this data fuels highly personalized campaigns, its collection, storage, and use raise critical privacy questions. As highlighted in a LinkedIn article by Freemind Marketing Agency, consumers may not always be fully aware of the extent of data being collected or how it is being utilized. Businesses have an ethical obligation to be transparent about their data practices, obtain informed consent before collecting personal information, and implement robust security measures to protect this data from breaches and unauthorized access. Minimizing data collection to only what is strictly necessary for the intended marketing purpose is also a crucial step in respecting consumer privacy.

Bias in AI Algorithms is another significant ethical challenge. AI models learn from the data they are trained on. If this training data reflects existing societal biases (e.g., related to gender, race, age, or socioeconomic status), the AI system can inadvertently perpetuate or even amplify these biases in its marketing decisions. For instance, an AI algorithm might disproportionately target certain demographics for high-interest loans or exclude others from beneficial offers based on learned correlations that are discriminatory. This can lead to unfair treatment of consumers and limit opportunities for certain groups. Businesses must actively work to ensure their training datasets are diverse and representative, regularly audit their AI systems for biased outputs, and maintain human oversight to correct and prevent discriminatory outcomes.

Transparency and Explainability (often referred to as XAI) are vital for building trust. Many AI systems, particularly complex machine learning models, can operate as "black boxes," where the reasoning behind their decisions is not immediately clear even to their developers. In marketing automation, this lack of transparency can be problematic. Consumers have a right to understand why they are being targeted with specific advertisements or offers, and how their data is influencing these automated decisions. Businesses should strive to use AI systems that can provide clear, understandable explanations for their outputs. Communicating openly with customers about the use of AI in marketing processes, as Freemind Marketing Agency suggests, fosters trust and helps consumers feel more confident in the fairness of the system.

Automation and Job Displacement is a broader societal concern that touches upon AI in marketing. As AI automates more marketing tasks—from content creation and campaign management to customer service via chatbots—there is a legitimate concern about the impact on human employment in the marketing field. While AI can free up marketers from repetitive tasks, allowing them to focus on more strategic and creative work, businesses have an ethical responsibility to consider the human impact. This includes investing in reskilling and upskilling programs to help employees adapt to new roles that complement AI technologies, rather than simply aiming for wholesale replacement. A focus on human-AI collaboration, where AI augments human capabilities, is a more ethical and sustainable approach.

Finally, the persuasive power of AI-driven marketing raises concerns about **Manipulation and Consumer Autonomy**. AI can be incredibly effective at personalizing messages and using predictive analytics to influence consumer behavior. While the goal of marketing is to persuade, there is a fine ethical line between providing helpful, relevant recommendations and employing manipulative tactics that exploit consumer vulnerabilities or push them towards purchases they don't genuinely need or cannot afford. Ethical marketing practices demand that AI be used to create genuine value for customers. Businesses must ensure their AI-driven campaigns are transparent, respectful of consumer autonomy, and avoid deceptive or coercive techniques. Giving consumers control over their data and the types of communications they receive is crucial in upholding their autonomy.

Navigating these ethical considerations requires a proactive and principled approach. Businesses must embed ethical principles into their AI governance frameworks, conduct regular ethical impact assessments of their AI marketing automation practices, and foster a culture of responsibility to ensure that AI is used in a way that benefits both the business and its customers, while upholding societal values.

References:

- Freemind Marketing Agency. (2024, December 17). *Ethical Considerations in AI Marketing.* LinkedIn. Retrieved from https://www.linkedin.com/pulse/ethical-considerations-ai-marketing-freemindmarketingagency-eg4bf

My Personal Take on AI for Marketing Automation (From Jason's Desk):

The biggest automation failure I ever witnessed had nothing to do with technology. I worked with a large healthcare organization that spent nine months and over $200,000 building a beautiful, complex AI-powered patient follow-up and outreach system. It was technically brilliant. Three months after launch, the adoption rate was only 15%.

What Actually Happened: The marketing and IT teams had built it in a silo. They never consulted the nurses and patient coordinators who would be using it every day. The system didn't fit their workflow, it required extra steps, and they didn't trust it. So, they ignored it and went back to their old spreadsheets.

What I Learned: AI adoption is a change management problem, not a technology problem. You must involve the end-users from day one. They need to be part of the design process, not have it dictated to them.

What You Should Do: Before you automate anything, map out the human workflow. Sit with the people doing the job. Ask them what would make their lives easier. Build the solution with them. I now require a "stakeholder alignment session" before any automation project kicks off. It's the most important meeting you'll have. I like to start with key stakeholder interviews to make sure we understand what is happening and who is doing it at the organization. Understanding people, process, and technology are key to identifying where AI can help.

Have questions about optimizing marketing automation or using AI agents? Feel free to reach out to me and my team to help out.

AI Prompts: Chapter 9

How to Use These Prompts

Each prompt below is designed to be copied directly into your favorite AI tool (ChatGPT, Claude, Grok, or Gemini). Simply:

1.Copy the entire prompt (including the bracketed placeholders)

2. Replace the [bracketed sections] with your specific information

3.Paste into your AI tool and hit enter

4.Refine the output by asking follow-up questions or requesting revisions

These are battle-tested prompts I use with organizations around the world. They're designed to give you professional-quality outputs that you can use immediately in your business.

Prompt 9.1: Design an Automated Lead Nurture Workflow

I want to create an automated lead nurture workflow for my [type of business].

Lead source: [where leads come from - website form, webinar, download, etc.]

Lead type: [cold leads, warm leads, demo requests, etc.]

Goal: [what you want them to do - book a call, make a purchase, attend event, etc.]

Sales cycle: [typical time from lead to customer]

Design a complete nurture workflow:

1. **Workflow Trigger**:

- What action starts this automation

- How to tag or segment this lead

2. **Workflow Steps** (map out 7-14 days):

- Day 0: [immediate action]

- Day 1: [next touchpoint]

- Day 3: [next touchpoint]

- [Continue through the workflow]

For each step, specify:

- **Channel**: Email, SMS, task for sales team, etc.

- **Content**: What to send (subject line and brief summary)

- **Goal**: What this step accomplishes

- **Branching Logic**: What happens if they engage vs. don't engage

3. **Personalization Rules**:

- How to customize based on lead source

- How to adapt based on engagement

- Dynamic content to include

4. **Exit Criteria**:

- When someone leaves this workflow (converted, unsubscribed, etc.)

- What workflow they move to next

5. **Re-Engagement Strategy**:

- What to do with leads who don't engage

- When to try a different approach
- When to remove from active nurture

6. **Success Metrics**:

- What to measure
- Benchmarks for good performance
- When to optimize or revise

7. **Tools Needed**:

- What automation platform features are required
- Integration requirements

Make this detailed enough that I can build it in my automation platform today.

Prompt 9.2: Create a Customer Onboarding Automation

Design an automated onboarding sequence for new customers of my [product/service].

Product/Service: [what they bought]

Customer goal: [what they want to achieve]

Common onboarding challenges: [where customers get stuck]

Success milestone: [when they've achieved "first value"]

Create a comprehensive onboarding automation:

1. **Immediate Post-Purchase** (First 24 hours):

- Welcome email (subject + content outline)
- Account setup instructions
- What to expect next
- Quick win they can achieve today

2. **First Week** (Days 1-7):

- Day-by-day email sequence (7 emails)
- Educational content to send
- Features to highlight (in order of importance)
- Check-in points and support offers

3. **Weeks 2-4** (Deeper engagement):

- Weekly touchpoints
- Advanced features to introduce
- Success stories to share

- Feedback requests
4. **Milestone-Based Triggers**:
- Automation when they complete key actions
- Celebration and reinforcement messages
- Next step guidance
5. **Engagement Monitoring**:
- What behaviors indicate successful onboarding
- What behaviors indicate they're at risk
- Automated interventions for at-risk customers
6. **Human Touchpoints**:
- When to have sales/support reach out personally
- What to say in those outreach messages
7. **Onboarding Success Metrics**:
- How to measure onboarding effectiveness
- When a customer is "fully onboarded"
- Correlation to retention and LTV
8. **Upsell/Cross-Sell Opportunities**:
- When to introduce additional products/services
- How to position them as natural next steps

Provide specific email subject lines, content outlines, and timing for each touchpoint.

Prompt 9.3: Build a Re-Engagement Campaign for Inactive Customers

I want to create an automated re-engagement campaign to win back inactive or churned customers.

Business type: [your business]

Definition of "inactive": [e.g., no purchase in 90 days, no login in 60 days, canceled subscription]

Size of inactive list: [approximate number]

Why customers typically go inactive: [common reasons if known]

Design a re-engagement campaign:

1. **Segmentation Strategy**:

- How to segment inactive customers (by inactivity length, past value, reason for leaving)
- Different approaches for different segments

2. **Campaign Sequence** (5-7 touchpoints):

Email 1: "We Miss You"
- Subject line options (3)
- Message focus (nostalgia, check-in, offer help)
- Soft ask to re-engage

Email 2: "What Changed?"
- Survey or feedback request
- Understanding why they left
- Show you care about their experience

Email 3: "Here's What's New"
- Updates, improvements, new features since they left
- Social proof (others who came back)
- Value reminder

Email 4: "Special Offer"
- Win-back incentive (discount, bonus, trial extension)
- Urgency and scarcity
- Clear CTA

Email 5: "Last Chance"
- Final outreach before removing from list
- Strongest offer
- Option to stay on list at reduced frequency

3. **Multi-Channel Approach**:
- Email sequence (above)
- Retargeting ads (what to say)
- SMS (if applicable)
- Direct mail (for high-value customers)

4. **Personalization Elements**:
- Reference to their past purchases/activity
- Customized offers based on their history
- Addressing their likely objection

5. **Win-Back Offer Strategy**:

- What incentive to offer
- How to make it feel special, not desperate
- Profitability calculation

6. **Success Metrics**:
- Re-engagement rate goal
- Acceptable cost to re-acquire
- Long-term retention of re-engaged customers

7. **List Hygiene**:
- When to remove non-responders
- How to sunset gracefully
- Permission to stay on list at lower frequency

Provide specific copy, timing, and offers for each touchpoint

For prompts and bonus resources, visit **thejasonfleagle.com/blueprint-resources**. You can copy and paste the prompts from there—no retyping needed.

| 10 |

The Future of AI in Marketing

The relentless march of technological advancement has consistently reshaped the landscape of marketing, and Artificial Intelligence (AI) stands as the current vanguard of this transformation. As we have explored throughout this book, AI is no longer a futuristic concept but a tangible and increasingly indispensable force, empowering marketers to understand their audiences with unprecedented depth, personalize experiences at scale, optimize campaigns with remarkable precision, and automate complex workflows with newfound efficiency. From the intricacies of AI-driven content creation and SEO to the strategic deployment of AI in email marketing, paid advertising, competitive analysis, customer understanding, and marketing automation, the impact of AI is both profound and pervasive.

Now, as we cast our gaze towards the horizon, this chapter delves into the future trajectory of AI in marketing. The pace of AI development is accelerating, promising even more sophisticated tools, novel applications, and transformative capabilities that will continue to redefine the boundaries of what is possible. We will explore the emerging AI marketing trends that are set to dominate the coming years, from the maturation of generative AI and its role in creating hyper-realistic and deeply engaging content, to the expansion of AI into immersive environments like the metaverse, and the ever-increasing power of predictive analytics to anticipate customer needs and market shifts.

However, harnessing the full potential of this AI-driven future requires more than just an awareness of technological trends. It necessitates a fundamental shift in how marketing teams are structured, skilled, and managed. Therefore, this chapter will also provide a comprehensive guide on preparing your marketing team for successful AI adoption.. We will discuss the critical importance of upskilling and reskilling, fostering a culture of data literacy and ethical AI use, and implementing effective change management strategies to navigate the human side of technological transformation.

Finally, a forward-looking perspective would be incomplete without a strategic framework. We will outline the key components of developing a robust AI marketing strategy, one that aligns AI initiatives with core business objectives, guides the selection of appropriate tools and technologies, addresses crucial data governance and ethical considerations, and establishes clear metrics for measuring success. This strategic approach will empower marketing leaders to not only react to the future but to proactively shape it, ensuring that their organizations are well-positioned to thrive in an increasingly intelligent and automated world.

Join us as we explore the exciting and dynamic future of AI in marketing, a future where data-driven insights, intelligent automation, and human creativity converge to create unparalleled value for both businesses and consumers alike.

10.1 AI Marketing Trends to Watch

The landscape of marketing is in a perpetual state of evolution, and the integration of Artificial Intelligence (AI) is currently its most significant catalyst. As we look towards the future, several key AI-driven trends are poised to redefine how businesses connect with their audiences, optimize their strategies, and drive growth. Understanding and anticipating these trends is no longer a luxury but a necessity for marketers aiming to maintain a competitive edge. From hyper-personalization at an unprecedented scale to the immersive possibilities of AI in the metaverse, the horizon is brimming with transformative potential.

One of the most prominent trends is the advancement of **hyper-personalization at scale**. While personalization has been a marketing goal for years, AI is now enabling a level of individualized customer experience that was previously unimaginable. AI algorithms can analyze vast datasets encompassing customer behavior, preferences, purchase history, real-time interactions, and even psychographic profiles to deliver uniquely tailored messages, product recommendations, and content across multiple touchpoints. This goes beyond simple name tokenization in emails; it involves dynamically adjusting website content, offering bespoke product bundles, and crafting ad creatives that resonate with individual user needs and contexts. The ability of AI to process and interpret complex data in real-time means that these hyper-personalized experiences can be delivered consistently and instantaneously to millions of users, fostering deeper customer loyalty and significantly boosting conversion rates. As noted by McKinsey, 71% of consumers expect companies to deliver personalized interactions, and AI is the key to meeting this expectation effectively and efficiently.

Closely linked to hyper-personalization is the continued and rapid evolution of **generative AI for content creation**. Tools powered by generative AI are already revolutionizing how marketing content is produced, from blog posts and social media updates to email copy, ad creatives, and even video scripts. The sophistication of these tools is increasing exponentially, with AI now capable of generating high-quality, contextually relevant, and engaging content that is often indistinguishable from human-created work. This not only accelerates content production workflows, allowing marketing teams to scale their efforts significantly, but also opens up new avenues for creativity. For instance, AI can generate multiple variations of ad copy for A/B testing in seconds, create diverse visual assets for campaigns, or even draft initial scripts for video marketing. As highlighted by WordStream, the ability to generate diverse content formats quickly will be crucial. Furthermore, generative AI is becoming increasingly adept at understanding brand voice and style, ensuring that AI-generated content aligns seamlessly with a company's overall messaging and identity. The future will likely see AI as an indispensable partner in the creative process, augmenting human ingenuity rather than replacing it entirely.

The emergence of the **metaverse and AI's role within it** presents another exciting frontier for marketers. The metaverse, a collective virtual shared space, created by the convergence of virtually enhanced physical reality and physically persistent virtual space, offers unprecedented opportunities for immersive brand experiences. AI will be the engine powering many of these experiences, from creating intelligent non-player characters (NPCs) that interact realistically with users, to personalizing virtual environments and offerings based on user behavior within the metaverse. Imagine virtual showrooms where AI guides users through product features, personalized virtual stores that adapt their layout and inventory to individual preferences, or AI-driven interactive brand events that offer unique and memorable engagements. Quirks.com highlights that businesses are moving from mere curiosity to strategic implementation of metaverse and generative AI, with AI creating dynamic and personalized content within these virtual worlds. This fusion of AI and the metaverse will enable brands to build deeper connections with consumers in novel and engaging ways, blurring the lines between physical and digital marketing.

Predictive analytics for customer behavior will also become even more sophisticated and integral to marketing strategy. AI excels at identifying patterns and predicting future outcomes based on historical and real-time data. In marketing, this translates to the ability to forecast customer churn with greater accuracy, identify high-value leads, predict which customers are most likely to convert, and anticipate future purchasing trends. By leveraging these predictive insights, marketers can proactively intervene to retain at-risk customers, tailor offers to individuals most likely to respond, and optimize marketing spend by focusing resources on the most promising segments. Gartner emphasizes the growing importance of AI in understanding and predicting customer journeys, allowing for more proactive and effective marketing interventions. This predictive power allows for more strategic resource allocation and a more agile response to changing market dynamics.

Finally, the overarching trend of **AI-driven Customer Experience (CX)** will continue to gain momentum. AI is becoming embedded in every stage of the customer journey, from initial awareness and consideration to purchase, service, and loyalty. AI-powered chatbots are providing instant, 24/7 customer support; AI-driven recommendation engines are guiding purchase decisions; and AI-based sentiment analysis is helping companies understand and respond to customer feedback more effectively. The goal is to create seamless, intuitive, and highly satisfying customer experiences across all channels. As AI technologies mature, they will enable even more sophisticated CX enhancements, such as proactive customer service where AI anticipates a customer's needs before they even articulate them, or emotionally intelligent AI that can adapt its communication style to match a customer's perceived emotional state. The future of marketing will be defined by the ability to leverage AI to create truly customer-centric experiences that build lasting relationships and drive business success.

In conclusion, the future of AI in marketing is not a distant concept but an unfolding reality. Trends like hyper-personalization, advanced generative AI, AI in the metaverse, predictive analytics, and AI-driven CX are set to profoundly reshape the marketing landscape. Marketers who embrace these trends, invest in the necessary skills and technologies, and strategically integrate AI into their operations will be best positioned to thrive in the dynamic and exciting years to come.

10.2 Preparing Your Marketing Team for AI Adoption

The successful integration of Artificial Intelligence into marketing operations is not solely a technological challenge; it is fundamentally a human one. As AI continues to reshape the marketing landscape, preparing your team for this transformation is paramount. It requires a strategic, people-focused approach that addresses skill gaps, fosters a conducive culture, and manages the inevitable changes to workflows and roles. Without a well-prepared team, even the most advanced AI tools will fail to deliver their full potential.

One of the initial and most critical steps is to **cultivate a people-focused approach to change management**. As highlighted by MarTech, embracing AI can be challenging, with some team members eagerly welcoming it while others may resist due to fear of job loss, discomfort with new technologies, or reluctance to alter ingrained habits. It is crucial to acknowledge these concerns proactively and create an environment of open communication. Leaders must articulate a clear and compelling vision for how AI will augment the team's capabilities, improve efficiency, and lead to more impactful marketing outcomes, rather than simply replacing human effort. This vision should emphasize AI as a collaborative tool that empowers marketers, freeing them from repetitive tasks to focus on strategy, creativity, and higher-value activities. Enlisting 'champions' within the team—individuals who are enthusiastic about AI and can influence their peers—can be instrumental in driving adoption and shaping a positive narrative around the transformation.

Central to preparing the team is a concerted effort in **upskilling and reskilling**. The World Economic Forum emphasizes that all job roles now require some degree of tech literacy and adaptability. For marketing teams, this means developing new competencies and enhancing existing ones. **Data literacy** becomes increasingly vital, as marketers need to understand how AI algorithms use data, interpret AI-generated insights, and make data-informed decisions. Proficiency in using specific **AI tools and platforms** relevant to their roles is another key area. This might involve training on AI-powered analytics dashboards, content generation tools, or customer relationship management (CRM) systems with embedded AI features. Furthermore, **ethical AI use** must be a core component of any training program. Marketers need to be aware of potential biases in AI algorithms, data privacy implications, and the importance of transparency in AI-driven customer interactions. As Savneet Singh notes in a Medium article, incorporating discussions on AI ethics ensures a well-rounded understanding. Investing in tailored training programs, workshops, certifications, and fostering a culture of lifelong learning will equip the team with the necessary skills to thrive in an AI-driven environment. Pearson's research also underscores that human skills like communication, attention to detail, and leadership remain in high demand, complementing AI's capabilities.

Fostering a **culture of experimentation and data-driven decision-making** is equally important. AI adoption is often an iterative process. Teams should be encouraged to experiment with new AI tools and approaches, learn from both successes and failures, and continuously refine their strategies. This requires creating a psychologically safe environment where calculated risk-taking is not penalized. Leadership should champion a mindset where data, often augmented by AI-driven insights, forms the basis for marketing decisions, moving away from gut feelings or anecdotal evidence. Regularly sharing successful AI use cases and the tangible benefits achieved can help reinforce this culture and motivate broader adoption.

Addressing **change management and overcoming resistance** requires ongoing effort. Beyond initial training, continuous support and resources are necessary. This could include establishing internal AI helpdesks, creating communities of practice where team members can share learnings and best practices, or providing access to AI experts. It is also important to clearly define how roles and responsibilities might evolve with AI integration. While some tasks may become automated, new roles focusing on AI strategy, data science liaison, or AI ethics oversight may emerge. Communicating these potential career development paths can alleviate anxieties and demonstrate a commitment to employee growth within the new AI-augmented framework. MarTech suggests that proactively seeking input from various champions can help discover where pushback may occur and that disregarding such input without explanation can create dissenters.

Finally, the preparation process must be **inclusive and ongoing**. It's not a one-time initiative but a continuous journey of adaptation and learning as AI technologies continue to evolve. Regularly assessing the team's AI readiness, gathering feedback, and adjusting training and support programs accordingly will ensure that the marketing team remains agile and capable of leveraging AI effectively in the long term. As the World Economic Forum points out, collaboration among employers, educators, and workers is essential to build the resiliency needed for the future of work.

In summary, preparing a marketing team for AI adoption involves a multifaceted strategy that encompasses clear communication of a people-centric vision, robust upskilling and reskilling initiatives focused on data literacy, AI tool proficiency, and ethics, the cultivation of an experimental and data-driven culture, and proactive change management. By investing in their teams, organizations can unlock the full transformative power of AI in marketing, leading to enhanced creativity, efficiency, and ultimately, superior business outcomes.

10.3 Developing an AI Marketing Strategy

Successfully navigating the future of AI in marketing requires more than just adopting new tools or upskilling teams; it demands a coherent and comprehensive AI marketing strategy. This strategy serves as a roadmap, aligning AI initiatives with broader business objectives, guiding resource allocation, and ensuring that AI adoption is both effective and ethical. A well-defined strategy transforms AI from a collection of disparate technologies into a powerful, integrated engine for marketing success.

Developing a robust AI marketing strategy begins with **defining clear business goals and identifying how AI can specifically help achieve them**. As highlighted by Techfunnel, knowing the "why" behind AI adoption is crucial. Is the primary objective to increase lead generation, enhance customer personalization, improve campaign ROI, streamline operational efficiency, or reduce marketing costs? Each of these goals will necessitate different AI applications and metrics for success. For instance, if the goal is to improve customer retention, the strategy might focus on AI tools for predictive churn analysis and personalized engagement campaigns. If it's about increasing brand awareness, the focus might be on AI-driven content creation and distribution optimization. This initial step ensures that AI investments are purposeful and directly contribute to tangible business outcomes.

Once goals are established, the next key component is **identifying specific use cases where AI can provide the most significant benefit**. It is impractical and often counterproductive to attempt to apply AI to every marketing function simultaneously. Instead, a strategic approach involves pinpointing areas within existing marketing workflows where AI can address critical pain points or unlock new opportunities. This could involve automating time-consuming tasks like data entry or basic report generation, enhancing complex processes like customer segmentation or media buying, or enabling entirely new capabilities like real-time adaptive advertising. Techfunnel advises considering where AI is likely to provide the most benefit, such as in creating high-quality blog posts if that is a time-consuming area, or automating tedious but crucial tasks.

Selecting the right AI tools and technologies is another critical pillar of the strategy. The market is flooded with AI-powered marketing solutions, ranging from comprehensive platforms to niche tools. The selection process should be driven by the defined business goals and identified use cases, rather than by the allure of the latest technology. Considerations should include the tool's capabilities, ease of integration with existing marketing stacks, scalability, vendor support, and, importantly, its alignment with the team's current and future skillsets. It's often advisable to start with a few well-chosen tools that address high-priority needs and then gradually expand the AI toolkit as the team gains experience and as the strategy evolves.

Underpinning any successful AI marketing strategy is a robust **data governance framework and a commitment to ethical considerations**. AI algorithms are only as good as the data they are trained on. Therefore, the strategy must address data quality, accessibility, security, and privacy. This includes establishing processes for data collection, cleaning, and management, as well as ensuring compliance with regulations like GDPR or CCPA. Ethical considerations, as emphasized by Techfunnel, must be addressed early on. This involves building processes to prevent AI systems from perpetuating biases (e.g., in ad targeting or content recommendations), ensuring transparency in how AI is used to interact with customers, and mitigating risks associated with misinformation or the invasion of customer privacy. A proactive stance on ethics not only mitigates reputational risk but also builds trust with customers.

Measuring the Return on Investment (ROI) for AI initiatives is essential for demonstrating value and securing ongoing support. The AI marketing strategy should define clear Key Performance Indicators (KPIs) that align with the initial business goals. These KPIs could include metrics like increased conversion rates, reduced customer acquisition costs, improved customer lifetime value, higher engagement rates, or time saved through automation. Regularly tracking these KPIs and reporting on the impact of AI initiatives will be crucial for optimizing the strategy and justifying continued investment.

Finally, the strategy should **emphasize starting small, iterating, and scaling AI adoption**. Attempting a large-scale, big-bang AI implementation is often risky and can lead to overwhelming the team and resources. A more prudent approach involves piloting AI solutions in specific areas, learning from these initial deployments, and then gradually scaling successful initiatives across the broader marketing organization. This iterative approach allows for flexibility, continuous improvement, and helps build momentum and internal expertise over time. As MarTech organizations often advise, a crawl-walk-run approach is often best for firms with limited AI experience.

In conclusion, developing an AI marketing strategy is a critical undertaking for any organization looking to harness the full potential of artificial intelligence. By clearly defining goals, identifying impactful use cases, thoughtfully selecting tools, establishing strong data governance and ethical guidelines, rigorously measuring ROI, and adopting an iterative approach to implementation, marketers can create a strategic framework that not only guides their AI journey but also propels their business towards a more intelligent, efficient, and customer-centric future.

Case Study: AI Governance for a Large Healthcare System

Background: I had the opportunity to work with our team at OnStak, with a multi-state healthcare system with over 15,000 employees that was facing an internal crisis. Teams across marketing, clinical research, and operations were independently using various public AI tools like ChatGPT and Claude to handle sensitive information, creating a massive, unmonitored compliance and security risk.

The Challenge:

- Shadow AI: Dozens of unsanctioned AI tools were in use with no oversight.
- Data Risk: Potentially sensitive patient and proprietary data was being exposed to public AI models.
- Inconsistency: Different departments were getting different answers from different AIs, leading to brand and operational chaos.
- Analysis Paralysis: Leadership knew they needed to act but were afraid that cracking down too hard would stifle innovation.

The Proper Approach: Our team was brought in to establish order. We immediately applied our discovery process, focusing first on Value Mapping to identify the highest-risk areas and then on Adoption & Controls to create a system that enabled, rather than blocked, progress.

Implementation:

1. AI Usage Audit: We deployed a non-intrusive audit to identify all AI tools currently in use and the types of data being processed.
2. Risk Triage: We categorized use cases into three tiers: High-Risk (clinical data), Medium-Risk (internal operational data), and Low-Risk (public marketing copy).
3. Created a "Walled Garden": Instead of banning public tools, we established a secure, private AI environment using an enterprise-grade platform. This gave employees the powerful tools they wanted within a compliant and monitored ecosystem.
4. Developed an AI Acceptable Use Policy: We created a simple, one-page document outlining the do's and don'ts of AI usage, which was co-authored by representatives from Legal, IT, and the clinical staff themselves.

Results:

- Within 60 days, we migrated 85% of the "shadow AI" usage into the secure, sanctioned environment.
- We identified and shut down two high-risk use cases that were in direct violation of HIPAA, preventing potential multi-million dollar fines.
- We established a formal AI Governance Committee, which I chaired, to review and approve new AI projects, turning chaos into a structured innovation pipeline.

Key Lesson: You cannot stop the tide of AI adoption. The job of leadership is not to build a dam, but to build a canal. Channel the energy of your teams into a safe, productive, and governed direction. By providing a secure alternative that was just as easy to use, we gained control without killing creativity.

AI Prompts: Chapter 10

How to Use These Prompts

Each prompt below is designed to be copied directly into your favorite AI tool (ChatGPT, Claude, Grok, or Gemini). Simply:

1.Copy the entire prompt (including the bracketed placeholders)

2. Replace the [bracketed sections] with your specific information

3.Paste into your AI tool and hit enter

4.Refine the output by asking follow-up questions or requesting revisions

These are battle-tested prompts I use with organizations around the world. They're designed to give you professional-quality outputs that you can use immediately in your business.

Prompt 10.1: Future-Proof Your Marketing Strategy

Help me create a future-proof marketing strategy that adapts to AI advancements and changing consumer behavior.

My business:

- Industry: [your industry]
- Current marketing approach: [brief description]
- Biggest marketing challenges: [list 2-3]
- Resources: [team size, budget, tech stack]

Create a forward-looking strategy:

1. **Emerging AI Trends to Watch** (Next 12-24 months):

- AI capabilities that will impact my industry
- How customer expectations will evolve
- New marketing channels or formats emerging

2. **Skills and Capabilities to Develop**:

- What my team needs to learn
- Roles that will become more important
- Skills that will become less valuable
3. **Technology Roadmap**:
- AI tools to adopt in next 6 months
- AI tools to evaluate in 6-12 months
- Infrastructure or data needs to prepare now
4. **Content and Channel Strategy Evolution**:
- How content creation will change
- Channels to invest more in
- Channels to reduce or eliminate
5. **Competitive Positioning**:
- How to differentiate as AI becomes commoditized
- What will matter more (brand, relationships, creativity, etc.)
- How to compete with AI-native competitors
6. **Risk Mitigation**:
- Threats from AI advancement
- How to protect against disruption
- Diversification strategy
7. **Experimentation Plan**:
- 3 AI experiments to run in next quarter
- How to test without betting the farm
- What to measure to determine success
8. **3-Year Vision**:
- What my marketing function looks like in 3 years
- How AI and humans work together
- Metrics that matter most

Make this practical and specific to my business, not generic future predictions.

Prompt 10.2: AI Ethics and Governance Framework

Help me create an AI ethics and governance framework for my marketing organization.

My business:

- Industry: [your industry]
- Current AI usage: [what AI tools/applications you use]
- Team size: [number of people who use AI]
- Regulatory environment: [any specific compliance requirements]

Develop a comprehensive AI governance framework:

1. **AI Use Policy** (What's allowed and what's not):
- Approved AI tools and use cases
- Prohibited uses of AI
- Data that can/cannot be used with AI
- Human oversight requirements

2. **Ethical Principles**:
- Transparency (how to disclose AI use to customers)
- Fairness (avoiding bias and discrimination)
- Privacy (protecting customer data)
- Accountability (who's responsible when AI makes mistakes)

3. **Risk Assessment Framework**:
- How to evaluate new AI tools before adoption
- Red flags that require additional review
- Approval process for high-risk AI applications

4. **Data Governance**:
- What data can be used to train AI
- How to anonymize or protect sensitive information
- Data retention and deletion policies
- Third-party AI vendor data handling requirements

5. **Quality Control**:
- How to review AI-generated content before publishing
- Accuracy and fact-checking standards
- Brand voice and quality benchmarks

6. **Compliance and Legal**:
- Regulations to be aware of (GDPR, CCPA, industry-specific)
- Intellectual property considerations
- Terms of service compliance for AI tools

7. **Training and Enablement**:

- What team members need to know about responsible AI use
- Ongoing education plan
- How to report concerns or violations

8. **Monitoring and Auditing**:

- How to track AI usage across the organization
- Regular review process
- Metrics to monitor (bias, accuracy, customer satisfaction)

9. **Incident Response**:

- What to do if AI causes a problem (wrong information, offensive content, data breach)
- Communication plan
- Remediation steps

Create a simple, one-page policy I can share with my team, plus a more detailed governance document.

Prompt 10.3: Build Your Personal AI Learning Plan

Create a personalized learning plan to help me stay current with AI developments and build the skills I need.

My current situation:

- Role: [your job title/role]
- Current AI knowledge level: [beginner/intermediate/advanced]
- Time available for learning: [hours per week]
- Learning style preference: [reading, video, hands-on practice, courses]
- Specific goals: [what you want to be able to do with AI]

Create a 90-day AI learning roadmap:

1. **Week 1-2: Foundations**

- Core concepts to understand
- Recommended resources (articles, videos, courses)
- Hands-on exercises to try
- Success criteria (what you should be able to do)

2. **Week 3-4: Practical Application**

- Specific AI tools to learn
- Projects to practice with

- Real business problems to solve
- Success criteria
3. **Week 5-8: Deepening Expertise**
- Advanced topics to explore
- Specialized skills for my role/industry
- Resources and courses
- Success criteria
4. **Week 9-12: Mastery and Teaching**
- How to apply AI strategically
- Teaching others on my team
- Staying current with new developments
- Success criteria
5. **Daily/Weekly Habits**:
- Daily: [15-minute activities to stay current]
- Weekly: [1-hour deep dive activities]
- Monthly: [reflection and skill assessment]
6. **Resources by Type**:
- **Free Resources**: Newsletters, blogs, YouTube channels, podcasts
- **Paid Courses**: Specific courses worth the investment
- **Communities**: Where to ask questions and learn from others
- **Tools to Practice With**: Free or low-cost AI tools to experiment
7. **Skill Development Milestones**:
- Month 1: [specific capabilities to develop]
- Month 2: [specific capabilities to develop]
- Month 3: [specific capabilities to develop]
8. **Application to My Work**:
- Week 1-4: [how to apply new skills to current projects]
- Week 5-8: [how to apply new skills to current projects]
- Week 9-12: [how to apply new skills to current projects]
9. **Accountability and Measurement**:
- How to track progress
- Who to share goals with

- How to measure ROI of learning time

Make this specific, realistic for my time constraints, and focused on practical skills I can use immediately.

Conclusion: Embracing the Intelligent Future of Marketing

Throughout the chapters of this book, we have embarked on a comprehensive exploration of Artificial Intelligence and its profound, multifaceted impact on the world of marketing. From dissecting the fundamental concepts of AI in our introduction to examining its specific applications in content creation, social media engagement, email personalization, paid advertising optimization, SEO mastery, competitive analysis, deep customer understanding, and the streamlining of marketing automation, a clear narrative has emerged: AI is not merely a technological novelty but a transformative force reshaping the very fabric of how businesses connect with their audiences and drive growth.

We have seen how AI empowers marketers to move beyond traditional, often intuition-based approaches, into an era of data-driven precision and unprecedented scale. AI algorithms can sift through vast oceans of data to unearth actionable insights, enabling hyper-personalization that resonates with individual customer needs and preferences. AI-powered tools are revolutionizing content generation, automating repetitive tasks to free up human creativity for strategic thinking, and providing predictive capabilities that allow businesses to anticipate market shifts and customer behaviors with remarkable accuracy. The case studies presented in each chapter have offered tangible proof of AI's ability to deliver significant improvements in efficiency, engagement, and return on investment, from boosting website traffic and social media followers to enhancing email open rates and reducing advertising costs.

The journey through AI in marketing has also illuminated the critical importance of a strategic and human-centric approach. As we discussed in Chapter 10, the future of AI in marketing is not just about adopting the latest tools; it's about preparing our teams through upskilling and reskilling, fostering a culture of data literacy and continuous learning, and developing comprehensive AI marketing strategies that align with core business objectives. The synergy between human ingenuity and artificial intelligence is where the true magic lies – AI handles the scale, the speed, and the complex data analysis, while human marketers provide the strategic direction, the creative spark, and the ethical oversight.

Indeed, the ethical dimension of AI in marketing cannot be overstated. As we harness the power of AI to understand and influence consumer behavior, we bear a profound responsibility to do so transparently, fairly, and with a steadfast commitment to data privacy and consumer trust. The discussions on ethical considerations throughout this book, and particularly in our look towards the future, underscore the need for robust governance frameworks and a proactive approach to mitigating potential biases and unintended consequences.

The road ahead is dynamic and filled with exciting possibilities. AI technologies will continue to evolve at a rapid pace, bringing forth even more sophisticated capabilities and opening up new frontiers, from immersive experiences in the metaverse to increasingly nuanced predictive analytics. For marketers, this means that the journey of learning and adaptation is ongoing. The principles and practices discussed in this book provide a solid foundation, but a mindset of curiosity, agility, and responsible innovation will be key to navigating the evolving landscape.

Therefore, the ultimate secret to leveraging AI for marketing and growth lies not in any single tool or technique, but in a holistic commitment: a commitment to understanding the technology, to empowering your teams, to strategizing thoughtfully, to acting ethically, and to continuously exploring the boundless potential of artificial intelligence. Embrace this intelligent future, and you will not only keep pace with the transformation but also lead the charge in creating more meaningful, effective, and impactful marketing for years to come.

What's Next? Your Journey from Blueprint to Build

Congratulations! You've made it through the blueprint. You now have the frameworks, strategies, and practitioner's insights to move beyond the hype and start building with AI. But reading is just the first step. The real transformation happens when you take action.

Your journey with AI is just beginning, and I want to help you continue the momentum. I've created resources to meet you wherever you are on your path, from free, cutting-edge insights to hands-on, intensive partnership.

Step 1: Stay on the Cutting Edge (Free or Very Affordable)

The AI landscape changes weekly. To stay ahead, you need a trusted source of signal in a world full of noise. I personally curate and analyze the most important developments for business leaders.

- Subscribe to the AI Pathfinder Newsletter: Join thousands of executives and entrepreneurs who receive my weekly analysis of the latest AI news, tools, and strategies, delivered straight to your LinkedIn inbox.
- Watch on YouTube: My channel is packed with free AI tutorials, tool teardowns, and strategic advice for real-world implementation.

Step 2: Build Your Roadmap with an AI Workshop

If you're a leader who needs to get your team aligned and build a concrete 90-day action plan, my Maximum AI Workshop is the fastest path from confusion to clarity. In this intensive, hands-on session, we will:

- Identify and prioritize your highest-ROI AI opportunities.
- Build a finance-grade business case to secure budget and buy-in.
- Create a detailed, 90-day implementation roadmap.

This is the same strategic process I run with Fortune 500 leadership teams, condensed into a powerful, high-impact workshop.

You can contact me at thejasonfleagle.com if you're interested in an AI workshop.

Step 3: Partner with a Fractional Chief AI Officer (Done-For-You)

For organizations ready for deep, transformative change, I serve a limited number of clients as a fractional Chief AI Officer. In this role, I work directly with your executive and technical teams to:

- Identify the top AI opportunities for your organization
- Work with your team to guide, implement, and manage AI initiatives
- Monitor KPIs, ROI, and performance metrics for improvements
- Implement the Humanize DataTM Framework across your organization.
- Lead your team from pilot to production on your most critical AI initiatives.
- Establish enterprise-wide AI governance, security, and best practices as-needed.

This is the highest level of partnership, designed for companies that are serious about making AI a core pillar of their business strategy.

To inquire about AI consulting, you can contact me at thejasonfleagle.com.

Thank you for taking this journey with me. The future is not something to be watched, it is something to be built. Now, go build it.

Thank you so much for taking the time to level up your AI skills and tools. Please don't hesitate to reach out and connect with me to see how I can help guide you and your team to the right solution that will get the results you want.

For prompts and bonus resources, visit **thejasonfleagle.com/blueprint-resources**. You can copy and paste the prompts from there—no retyping needed.

ULTIMATE AI BLUEPRINT

ULTIMATE AI BLUEPRINT

JASON J. FLEAGLE

Reachify

www.ingramcontent.com/pod-product-compliance
Lightning Source LLC
LaVergne TN
LVHW052224200926
848481LV00001B/203